Business in the Information Age

Heading for New Processes

Springer
Berlin
Heidelberg
New York
Barcelona
Budapest
Hong Kong
London
Milan
Paris
Tokyo

Hubert Österle

Business in the Information Age

Heading for New Processes

With 198 Figures

 Springer

Prof. Dr. Hubert Österle
Institute for Information Management
University of St. Gallen
Dufourstraße 50
CH-9000 St. Gallen
Internet: OESTERLE @ SGCL1.UNISG.CH

Die Deutsche Bibliothek - CIP-Einheitsaufnahme

Österle, Hubert:
Business in the information age : heading for new processes /
Hubert Österle. - Berlin ; Heidelberg ; New York ; Barcelona ;
Budapest ; Hong Kong ; London ; Milan ; Paris ; Tokyo :
Springer, 1995
  ISBN 3-540-60023-X

ISBN 3-540-60023-X Springer-Verlag Berlin Heidelberg New York

SPIN 10506090   42/2202 - 5 4 3 2 1 0 – Printed on acid-free paper

Preface

The transition from an industrial to an information society requires new methods. Business Process Redesign, Business Engineering and similar concepts represent approaches to the fundamental restructuring of companies and the relationships between companies.

This book deals with principles of Business Engineering and techniques for developing business processes and information systems. It combines methods from strategic development, organization theory and information management.

Internet-Reactions "Business Engineering"

Business Engineering is a new area which is growing rapidly. We are setting up a platform on the Internet to register views on this topic and this book, with the following objectives:

- to discuss the foundations and techniques of Business Engineering

- to exchange experience with Business Engineering

- to report on practical cases

- to collect and "publish" feedback on this book

The Institute for Information Management at the University of St. Gallen will accept responsibility for maintaining the platform until further notice, i.e. it offers the opportunity to communicate reactions to the points listed above. These reactions will be collected and subsequently published via WWW. Anyone interested can contribute to the platform in two ways:

- On Internet via WWW on URL = http://www-iwi.unisg.ch/ (feedback form for reactions and publication of the results)

- Via E-Mail to the author:
  Internet: OESTERLE@SGCL1.UNISG.CH
  X.400:   s=oesterle ou=sgcl1 o=unisg p=switch a=arcom c=ch

The book provides managers and specialists from the user departments (Sales, Controlling, etc.) with an overview of the goals and methods of Business Engineering. It offers organization and information specialists a complete and practically applicable set of tools for innovation within business processes on the basis of information systems. Students of business management, and especially of information management, should gain insight into business procedures and information systems from the examples and methods presented, and obtain the skills necessary for structuring these procedures and systems.

The book is based on many years of work within the Institute for Information Management's research programme "IM HSG (Informationsmanagement Hochschule St. Gallen)" at the University of St. Gallen. The techniques have been applied and refined in many consultancy projects. Lectures at the University of St. Gallen and courses for practitioners have generated many didactic suggestions.

The design of business processes is based on the results of the competence centre "PRO (Prozeßentwicklung - Process Design)" headed by L. Brecht. The design of information systems is based on the results of the competence centre "RIM (Rechnergestütztes Informationsmanagement - computerized information management)" led by T. Gutzwiller.

Competence Centre "Process Design""

Company	Sector	Representative in working group
Bundesamt für Informatik	Public administration	C. Bavaud, R. Zimmermann
MIGROSBANK	Banking	M. Sollberger
PTT	Postal services	M. Herzig, A. Löhrer
Schweizerische Lebensversicherungs- und Rentenanstalt	Insurance	M. Fischer, M. Meyer, T. Morf
Schweizerische Bankgesellschaft	Banking	J. Ackermann, B. Gasser
Schweizerischer Bankverein	Banking	G. Bajardi, P. Cottier, J. Gabathuler, T. Gruber, A. Kiefer, M. Näscher
SECURA Versicherungen	Insurance	A. Meiler
Sulzer Informatik AG	Business services	S. Loretan, M. Rudolf, W. Schwab

Competence Centre "Computerized Information Management"

Company	Sector	Representative in working group
Bundesamt für Informatik	Public administration	P. Christensen, Dr. D. Keller
Bühler AG	Industry	R. Gamma, G. Härtel
Gebrüder Sulzer AG	Industry	B. Hösli
PTT	Postal services	H. U. Marti, G. Krähenbühl, J. Reichen
Schweizerische Bankgesellschaft	Banking	R. Ami, H. Färberböck, Ch. Henrici, S. Kasa
Schweizerischer Bankverein	Banking	S. Breinbauer, W. Wälti
Swissair	Airline	J. Drabek, Dr. Ch. Haenggi, Dr. U. Matter, P. Sturzenegger
Winterthur Versicherungen	Insurance	Th. Hobi, P. Petrinec, H.P. Schwarz, H. Weber
"Zürich" Versicherungs-Gesellschaft	Insurance	A. Meier, Dr. P. Morath, Dr. J. Remlinger

Many ideas were developed and tested in these groups. The following work by staff at the Institute for Information Management is also incorporated in the textbook.

Subject area	Publication
Business strategy	Brenner, C., Business Engineering, Dissertation (in preparation)
Data integration	Gaßner, Ch., Konzeptionelle Integration heterogener Transaktionssysteme, Dissertation (in preparation)
Data and function design	Gutzwiller, Th., Das CC RIM-Referenzmodell für den Entwurf von betrieblichen, transaktionsorientierten Informationssystemen, Habilitation 1993
Organization design	Hess, Th., Entwicklung einer Methode für den Prozeßentwurf, Dissertation (in preparation)
Principles of design methods	Heym, M., Methoden-Engineering, Dissertation 1993
Semantic and object-oriented data modelling	Lindtner, P., Domänenwissen in Methoden zur Analyse betrieblicher Informationssysteme, Dissertation 1992
Process management	Mende, M., Ein Führungssystem für Geschäftsprozesse, Dissertation 1994
Organizational monitoring	Saxer, R., Monitoring des Informationssystems - ein Instrument zur Organisationsanalyse, Dissertation 1994
IT assessment	Steinbock, H., Unternehmerische Potentiale der Informationstechnik in den neunziger Jahren, Dissertation 1993

C. Gaßner and T. Hess have given me great assistance in the task of writing. In addition, V. Bach, M. Mende and P. Vogler have undertaken preparatory work for some smaller sections. My thanks for your considerable dedication.

I would also like to thank the employees of the partner companies in both competence centres who have tested the techniques in practice, for their criticism and suggestions in the collaborative workshops.

Finally, my thanks also go to L. Brecht, C. Brenner, M. Derungs, E. Fleisch, T. Gutzwiller, J. Schmid, N. Schmider, and P. Vogler for their valuable comments on the drafts, to A. Glaus and M. Saupe for the orthographic, grammatical and stylistic quality control, and to S. Tummer and E. Österle for the graphic design. Again, I am specially thankful for the work of Irene Cameron who translated the book from German into English.

St. Gallen, June 1995   H. Österle

Table of Contents

List of Abbreviations

ANSI	American National Standards Institute
ANSI ASC X12	ANSI Accredited Standards Committee X12
ASDM	A Semantic Data Model
B-ISDN	Broadband ISDN
BLOB	Binary Large Object
BTX	Bildschirmtext
CAD	Computer Aided Design
CAM	Computer Aided Manufacturing
CASE	Computer Aided Software Engineering
CO	Computer
CS	Central Sales and Consultancy Management
CSF	Critical Success Factor
Datex-J	Data-Exchange-Dienst für Jedermann
DBMS	Data Base Management System
DDL	Data Definition Language
DIP	Document Image Processing
DML	Data Manipulation Language
EAN	European Article Number
EBS	Elektronische Börse Schweiz
EDI	Electronic Data Interchange
EDIFACT	Electronic Data Interchange for Administration, Commerce and Transport
ER	Entity-Relationship
ERA	Entity-Relationship-Attribute
FA	Financial Accounting
FDDI	Fiber Distributed Data Interface
GPS	Global Positioning System
GSM	Global System for Mobile Communication
Intersettle	Swiss Corporation for International Securities Settlement
IS	Information System
ISDN	Integrated Services Digital Network

IT	Information Technology
MD	Man-Day
MMS	Merchandise Management System
MY	Man-Year
O	Operator
OCR	Optical Character Recognition
ODA/ODIF	Open Document Architecture/Open Document Interchange Format
ODETTE	Organisation for Data Exchange through Teletransmission in Europe
OM	Order Management
OU	Organizational Unit
PDA	Personal Digital Assistant
PM	Product Management
RS	Regional Sales and Consultancy Management
SABRE	Semi-Automatic Business-Related Environment
SECOM	SEGA Communication System
SEDAS	Standardregelungen für einheitliche Datenaustauschsysteme
SEGA	Schweizerische Effekten-Giro AG
SIC	Swiss Interbank Clearing
SM	Sales Management
SOFFEX	Swiss Options and Financial Futures Exchange
SQL	Structured Query Language
SR	Sales Representative
SS	Sales Support
STEP	Standard for the Exchange of Product Model Data
SWIFT	Society for Worldwide Interbank Financial Telecommunication
TRADACOMS	Trading Data Communications Standards
WFMS	Workflow Management System

1. Introduction

Information technology transforms companies, economies and societies. New products, markets, forms of market access, processes, management tools, etc., constitute the great business challenge in the years ahead. Slogans like Business Process Redesign (Reengineering, Innovation, Improvement) or Business Engineering are expressions of this transformation, which centers around processes and information systems.

Section 1.1. of this Introduction first discusses some practical examples of this business transformation. Section 1.2. summarizes the changes that are to be expected from the business perspective, and the information techniques that make these changes possible. Section 1.3. describes Business Engineering as a means of mastering the challenge. Section 1.4. provides some information on the PROMET method. Finally, Section 1.5. gives the reader an overview of the structure of the book..

1.1. The Transformation of the Economy

The industrial society is undergoing transformation into an information society.

The information revolution is a fundamental transformation, just as the industrial revolution was 200 years ago. Companies are in the process of analyzing opportunities and dangers, and reformulating their business goals and methods. The term "Business Process Redesign" has been coined to refer to this.

The symptoms of the information revolution are manifold. Examples of minor changes are new products - like mobile telephones, interactive encyclopaedias, and financial derivatives - and new sales channels - such as telebanking - or the direct sale of insurance. Airline flight reservation systems have not only led to new flight booking procedures, they have also restructured the distribution of tasks between airlines, travel agents, car rental and credit card companies [see Copeland/McKenny 1988]. They are thus an example of the structural changes in business.

Further examples of change are the outsourcing of parts of companies to specialized companies (such as a bank's handling of securities), the creation of new business sectors (flight reservation, logistics, information services, etc.) and mergers between communication companies (telephone and cable network operators) and the media (the film industry, publishers, etc.). On a larger scale the information revolution enables global outsourcing (i.e. producing at the world's most favourable location) or necessitates larger economic territories, such as the European Union, in order to achieve the number of transactions required to amortize development costs or reach the critical mass for establishing standards (e.g. mobile telephones).

A few practical examples will provide a more detailed treatment of the information revolution and the restructuring of business processes (referred to briefly in the following work as processes) that it engenders:

Getzner Textile AG

Getzner Textile AG produces high quality, fashionable cotton material for shirts, dresses and bed linens. As a result of their textile skills, one hundred percent customer orientation, and efficient organization the company is successful in the textile industry, despite competition from low wage countries.

In 1988 Getzner Textile AG investigated the information technology potential for their company. They anticipated that the greatest benefits were to be achieved in simplifying order handling (from sales through production to delivery). They decided on across-the-board use of the R/2 package software from SAP AG, reorganized their process flows, and completed the introduction by the end of 1991.

Since the beginning of 1991 the entire administration has been operating on the basis of R/2, from sales through production planning and control to cost accounting. Despite rising order volume the level of administrative staffing was already reduced during the introduction phase from 233 to 208, and now stands at 177. Order processing time was also reduced from 8 to 6 weeks. Getzner is now in a position to offer flexible delivery dates on order confirmation and to guarantee them in production.

These effects are primarily attributable to data integration and the resulting process continuity. The following example elucidates this using a segment from the procurement process.

Fig 1.1./1 presents a segment from the procurement process prior to reorganization. This process was distributed over four organizational units (supplier, production, purchasing/inventory and accounting), each of which concentrated on its own area of responsibility and worked with separate programming systems which communicated with each other once a day via batch interfaces (symbolized by the shaded band in Fig. 1.1./1).

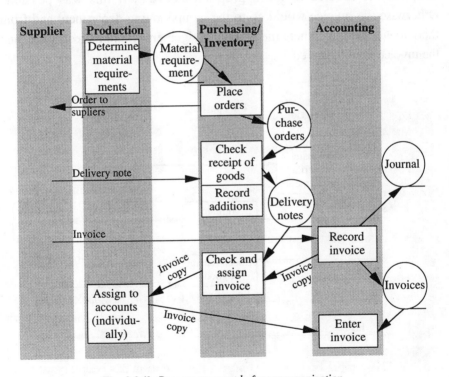

Fig. 1.1./1: Process segment before reorganization

Production Planning automatically derived the raw material requirements (cotton yarn, decorative yarns, etc.) from the orders. Purchasing then obtained daily summaries of the materials required. Once the Purchasing department had placed an order with a supplier it then recorded this in an "outstanding orders" file. On receipt of goods Purchasing would check the physical conformity of the delivery first against the delivery note, and then against the order list (a printout of the "outstanding orders" file). If the delivery was correct Purchasing would then assign the quantity of items to the appropriate inventory records. In the case of delays on the supplier side it was not possible to investigate which customer orders (requirement source) would be affected, so potential delivery delays to customers could not be identified early enough.

Once the invoice reached Accounting it would be entered into the journal, copied and filed. The copy of the invoice would go to Purchasing which then checked the conformity with the delivery and the delivery conditions and assigned the invoice to the appropriate account, if this was possible. Otherwise the invoice would go to the requisitioning department and from there to Accounting, where the account assignment would be rechecked, and the invoice finally entered.

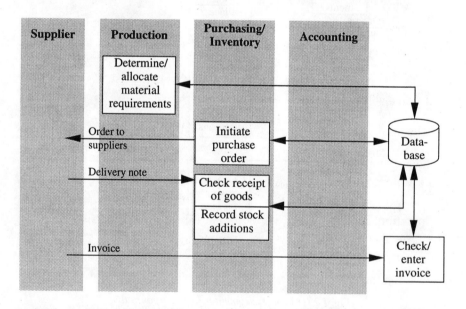

Fig. 1.1./2: Process segment after reorganization on the basis of data integration

Fig. 1.1./2 shows the functionally equivalent process after reorganization. Production Planning determines the primary requirements from the sales orders on the basis of the bill of materials breakdown, it charges the material requirement to the order that generated it, and releases it to the database (cylinder symbol) for purchasing, in accordance with the customer's desired delivery date. Purchasing then selects a supplier and initiates the purchase order.

Receiving checks the physical conformity of the delivery against the delivery note. The computer proposes purchase order items for the delivery note items, staff simply record quantity deviations from the order. The computer enters stock additions in both quantity and value terms (using Accounting's valuation rates). On entry, quantity information from the receipt of goods and price information from the purchase order are combined so that entry and invoice checking are undertaken in a single step. Only in the case of deviations detected by machine does purchasing need to be involved.

What are the most significant improvements from the company's perspective?

- Order-related purchasing eliminates the need for subsequent time-consuming journal entries.

- Checking the physical accuracy is separated from checking the computational accuracy (the four-eyes principle).

- Stock records are up-to-date in both quantity and value terms immediately after receipt.

- Scheduling can determine what impact delivery delays on the supplier side will have on their own delivery deadlines (with respect to customers).

The old approach had indeed been computerized, but it still reflected the manual process flows before the computerization of the 1970s, in which each organizational unit regarded its own area in isolation. It would have been easier for Getzner Textile AG to simply leave the old process flows and support them with new software, but the business advantage lies precisely in redesigning the process, and not in replacing old programmes with new ones.

The example of Getzner Textile AG illustrates the potential of internal innovation using information technology. It also indicates other approaches to redesign. EDI (electronic data interchange) could replace the written communication with suppliers, which would obviate the costs of record-keeping both for the suppliers and for Getzner Textile AG. One further step would in many cases eliminate purchasing altogether if the supplier had direct access to production planning and delivered "just-in-time" for production. In this case the need for in-house stock keeping also disappears.

Data integration eliminates the divisions that have arisen between departmental and company boundaries, and provides the basis for Business Process Redesign in this example. Data integration makes it possible or essential to organize process flows independent of departmental and company boundaries, to find new ways of combining, assigning and even eliminating tasks.

Data integration is the basis for processes extending beyond departmental or company boundaries.

A similar case, which has become a classic of Business Process Redesign, is that of the Ford Motor Company, which up until the start of the 1980s employed more than 500 staff in its accounts payable department [see Hammer 1990]. In 1989 Ford undertook a fundamental restructuring of this area on the basis of a new information system, thereby reducing the staff to 125. Given their market position they were also able to insist that they no longer receive invoices, but simply pay on the basis of delivery.

The reorganization of the procurement process at Getzner Textile AG was only a small component in the redesign of the entire administration and management. In addition to the improvements already mentioned, the use of CAD (Computer Aided Design) in patterning, the data capture system, and purely organizational measures also played their part.

Bayerische Landesbank

The Bayerische Landesbank is the holding company of the Bayerischen Sparkassen (Bavarian savings banks) and in this role takes on the handling of certain kinds of business for the savings banks. In addition it deals directly with business customers - primarily major accounts (its motto: the multi-branch bank for big customers).

In a redesign project in 1993 it analyzed its money market dealings, and identified four different processes for handling such trades - each supported by different applications and databases. The analysis of the four processes indicated a large number of identical or very similar activities. They succeeded in combining these four processes into one single process. The bank expected this to yield, among other things, a reduction in handling costs for their money market products of between 10 and 30%.

Lithonia Lighting

Lithonia Lighting is the US market leader in the production of lighting systems for commercial and industrial use. It sells its products - subdivided into technologically-categorised product lines - via sales representatives to wholesalers. Until the start of the 1980s Lithonia Lighting's sales representatives took orders from the wholesalers by telephone, filled out order forms - broken down by product line - and sent them by post to the Head Office, where they were again recorded manually. Then the company introduced an electronic ordering system, in which the wholesalers completed their order themselves and transmitted it electronically to Lithonia Lighting. The assignment of order items to product lines was taken over by the computer.

This information system (Agency Communication Environment) also offers the sales representative tools for configuring lighting systems, for preparing offers, for office functions (word processing, spreadsheet systems, etc.), information about the status of orders and business developments.

The Agency Communication Environment enabled the development of fundamentally new process flows within Sales, with shorter order processing times and lower sales costs. It strengthened the links between the wholesaler and the company. Sales management obtained a tool which allowed more detailed monitoring of processing times and costs.

In the 1980s Lithonia Lighting further consolidated its market share and attributed this primarily to a sales process more efficient than that of its competitors [see Berkley/Nohria 1991; Hofman/Rockart 1989]. It is an example of internal improvements (to the sales process), improvements to process flows between organizations (between Lithonia Lighting and the wholesalers), and new customer services in the form of configuration support.

Information systems facilitate new services and more efficient intra- and inter-organizational process flows .

SEGA / Intersettle

When a deal involving a financial security is made on the stock market this initiates a series of back-office tasks. In London the complete handling of a security deal can last several weeks. The Swiss banks are pursuing the aim of completing the handling within 24 hours of closure over all time zones. The securities should then pass from seller to purchaser at the time of payment [see SEGA 1994; SEGA o. J.].

In recent years the Swiss banks have created several joint companies to which they have transferred parts of their securities business. The EBS (Elektronische Börse Schweiz) and SOFFEX (Swiss Options and Financial Futures Exchange) have taken over electronic security dealing. SEGA (Schweizerische Effekten-Giro AG) handles the back-office completion of trading. In 1993 it started operating SECOM (SEGA Communication System) for the electronic handling of domestic securities. SIC (Swiss Interbank Clearing) handles the financial aspects (i.e. the payment of the price owed to the seller), while SEGA handles the delivery of the securities.

Intersettle (Swiss Corporation for International Securities Settlement), a sister company of SEGA, is currently creating a platform for handling international security transactions, with which SECOM will be involved. Intersettle's aim is to reduce the number of correspondence institutes world-wide, supported by the Swiss banks in handling the international security trade, from several hundred to 12 correspondence banks.

This clearing system will be extended into the most globally comprehensive securities clearing system. It is an excellent example of innovation in intra- and inter-organizational processes. Together with systems in other financial centres it revolutionizes an entire business sector. Lower costs per stock market transaction, speedier handling and the resulting reduction in credit and market risk for the parties involved, become cogent competitive arguments in favour of Switzerland as a financial centre.

Information technology permits the creation of fundamentally new business solutions which can revolutionize entire business sectors.

It is common to all these examples - whether intra- or inter-organizational - that information technology can bring about incremental or radical changes in the value creation process, but that this potential is only fully exploited through reorganization. The benefits result from the new business solution, not from the information technology.

Information technology creates potential, reorganization exploits it.

1.2. Business Transformation and its Roots

Business Transformation

The examples have highlighted some types of change; overall the following range of business opportunities are presenting themselves:

- *Optimizing internal processes*
  Data integration, automation, standardization, quality assurance, the restriction to core competences by outsourcing, and the attainment and maintenance of know-how are starting points for increasing the efficiency of processes.

- *Distributed structures and management*
  Management is still predominantly cost or sales oriented and hierarchically organized. The information revolution permits more detailed observation of processes, and allows direct performance indicators, such as speed, error rates, successful offer rates, to be established as success criteria, whose evaluation can increasingly be delegated to the individual or group. Comprehensive management information increases transparency within distributed organizations, thereby encouraging both autonomous handling of transactions on the customer front and central control.

- *New products and services*
  Information technology alters customer needs and the prerequisites for new products and services. The customer frequently expects one-stop, non-stop, at-any-point service which allows him to obtain outputs anywhere and at any time, completing his business in a single operation. Information technology opens up new ways of adapting products and services to individual customer needs (customizing). New combinations of services can provide a more comprehensive solution to customer problems.

- *Intra- and inter-organizational coordination*
  Even greater than the potential of internal processes, is that resulting from intra- and inter-organizational coordination. This has long been banished to a no-man's-land in terms of responsibility, has received poor technological support (communication networks and standards), and has frequently been impeded by government regulation. Business Process Redesign now concerns itself with processes that go beyond the company. The communication technology infrastructure is available at acceptable prices, and Western governments are tending to abolish efficiency-impeding regulations. Typical consequences are: inter-organizational logistic strategies in the transport of people and goods, the redistribution of tasks between providers of services (e.g. between banks and credit card suppliers), the elimination of intermediate steps (disintermediation) or the creation of new intermediate steps (virtual companies who combine the market output of diverse producers), and finally global outsourcing.

- *New markets and forms of market access*
  In addition to the market mechanisms just mentioned, customers are also changing. Digital technology, speech and data communication via ISDN, and the interactive use of television cable networks all ensure information technology's penetration of society. Games, simple interactive services, etc. generate a willingness in the vast majority of the population to conduct much business (banking, shopping, travel booking, news information) via electronic media.

All these developments are forerunners to the information society. They will be accompanied by many more changes that are not that obvious. In aggregate these imply radical changes in the business and economic world, with which they will be occupied for many years. How quickly companies exploit the opportunities will in many cases be decisive in determining their competitive position.

The information revolution transforms processes, management, products, company coordination and markets.

Fig. 1.2./1 summarizes some of the changes that are associated with the transition from the industrial to the information society [see also Picot 1993, p. 54].

For a more detailed analysis of the economic consequences of the information revolution see [Nefiodow 1990] and [Österle/Brecht 1994].

Aspect	Industrial society		Information society
Orientation	Inward looking: Corporate functions and products	→	Outward looking: Process output and customer
Focus	Strategy	→	Strategy and operative flows
Range	Company	→	Network of companies
Organizational structure	Strongly hierarchical	→	Flat, network of teams
Company size	Large, monolithic	→	Small, modular
Management	External control	→	Individual responsibility
Performance indicators	Financial indicators, esp. costs and turnover	→	Financial and process indicators, esp. time & quality
Process flows	Sequential	→	More parallelistic
Type of information	Standardized (coded)	→	Standardized and non-coded
Make or buy	In-house developments	→	Package software
Innovation impetus	Information technology	→	Business
Innovation	Perfecting	→	Redesigning
Organizational method	Intuitive	→	Engineering-based
Integration	Functional specialization	→	Optimization of inter-functional flows
Process	Complex	→	Simple
Personnel	Specialist	→	Holistic

Fig. 1.2./1: Change of paradigm in the organization

The Information Technology Roots of the Transformation

In certain respects our society could already be described as an information society. Compared with the information technology tools that will become available in the next ten years, however, the existing information technology (IT) base appears very modest.

- *European and world-wide communication infrastructure*
  By the end of this decade all economic participants will have access to networks for transmitting text, data, speech, graphics and videos at prices not unlike those of today's telephone charges. In the USA the National Information Infrastructure has even become a dominant political issue referred to as the "Information Super Highway". Standardization at the

technical level (network protocols, etc.) and at the applications level (e.g. EDIFACT for intra-organizational data, such as delivery notes) render the technical infrastructure useable at the company level.

- *Mobile computing*
  Computer miniaturization and global networks bring the prospect of the virtual office, in which an employee can undertake all important office tasks away from a fixed office workplace, at least partially into the realm of the possible.

- *Package software*
  With some exceptions, the days of the large in-house developments are over. Package software for all application areas from financial accounting, through security dealing, Computer Aided Design, to electronic product catalogues increases the speed with which technical possibilities can be converted into business solutions.

- *Workflow management*
  Workflow systems will control business activities (e.g. customer queries) from their origin through to their completion (activity control), and thus standardize organizational workflows. They will facilitate the cooperation between those involved in the process (workgroup computing)

- *Multimedia*
  Towards the end of the decade, document images, speech and video will be as natural a part of the man-machine interaction as text and formatted (coded) data.

- *Design and knowledge*
  Computer Aided Design will extend further beyond its original technical application area to include graphics, organization, creation of bank products, medicine and other areas. Design databases increasingly contain operational know-how in key areas. Access to external product databases, co-operative developments involving both customers and suppliers, simulation of designs in cyberspace (virtual reality), animation, etc. open up new ways of gaining knowledge, refining it, and making it available to third parties.

The impetus of technological innovation precedes market introduction.

To put the significance of information technology in context, it is only necessary to refer to the potential of gene technology, materials technology, or micromechanics. Furthermore, problems such as environmental protection, European traffic breakdown, political instability, migration and structural unemployment are also determinants of business solutions; information technology is not the sole cause of the radical structural change in economy, but it is a dominant one. Of course, the crucial element in mastering this transformation is the human factor.

1.3. Business Engineering

Information technology eliminates or alleviates fundamental restrictions on economic organization (space, time, use of resources). From the corporate management perspective this means a complete rethinking of all aspects of the business.

American exponents of management theory, and especially the large consultancy firms, have published their views on mastering this transformation using terms like Business Process Reengineering [see Hammer/Champy 1993], Business Process Improvement [see Harrington 1991] and Process Innovation [see Davenport 1993] and thereby initiated a widespread, if over-fashionable, movement in the Western business world. Since the processes represent only a partial view of the company, in the following treatment we follow [Davenport/Short 1990] in referring to the restructuring of the IT-based economy as *Business (Re-)Engineering*.

Business (Re-)Engineering transforms the industrial society into the information society. It is based on the information revolution in business and society.

How does a company find new strategies and implement them? Who is responsible for innovation? Who incorporates the IT possibilities in the business strategy? Who implements the strategy within the organization and the information system?

1.3.1.   From Business Strategy to Information System

Three years ago a chemical concern active throughout Europe, together with a management consultant (strategic advisor), began to reorganize the sale of its products to industrial customers. By centralizing Logistics the aim was to replace numerous local warehouses with a few nationally independent distribution centres. The basic idea - stimulated by examples from other sectors - was that simple process flows could reduce personnel costs, provide speedier and more reliable customer service, and reduce the level of total European stocks while improving delivery performance.

A team of five analyzed the existing sales system, designed their vision of a streamlined distribution logistics, planned future process flows in detail, and described the activities and organizational units of this new organization. Having produced an organizational plan of several hundred pages, and started to recruit management personnel for the new organization, the project team investigated package software for the sales logistics.

The company directors then engaged a further consultancy company (software consultants) to implement the organizational plan on the basis of the package software. The preliminary study soon made it clear that, while the elaborate organizational plan certainly contained good ideas for reorganization, it was not suitable for the implementation. It dealt in detail with many aspects, such as job descriptions of Sales personnel but paid inadequate attention to the real business requirements and the variety of package software solutions. In particular, it did not accurately represent business forms, which were sometimes contractually binding. For example, it ignored an important service - customer consignment stocks; these are stocks held by the customer but owned by the chemical company until the customer removes material, whereupon he is immediately invoiced.

Furthermore, the organizational plan did not address fundamental issues concerning the design of the information system. For example, it did not differentiate the legal form of the sales organizations and their balance sheet treatment, and did not consider questions of the transfer of ownership and customs-related issues. The solution of these problems led - quite independent of the software used - to fundamental modification of the organizational plan. This modification was ultimately so extensive that it was decided to rework the plan against the background of the information system.

Of course, the company was able to adopt many of the insights from the original organizational plan, but it finally cost about four million DEM in consultancy and internal project costs and - far more seriously - about a year in the implementation. This was caused by excessive separation of organization (business strategy and process design) and information system (customizing the package software and the subsequent detailed planning of process flows).

In contrast, the development of Getzner Textile AG's business strategy and information system were closely co-ordinated. In a preliminary step the company directors, middle management in the user departments and the IT department - supported by a consultant (for organization and software) -investigated the potential for IT in the company, decided on areas of emphasis in the use of IT, and incorporated the planned solutions in the business strategy. One result was the three year implementation plan, which controlled the sequencing and resourcing of the sub-projects and presented a cost-benefit analysis. In each sub-project representatives from the user departments and staff from the IT department collaborated on the design of the functional concepts, the process flows and the adjustments to the software used, and checked them using a prototype.

At no point was there any danger that the business strategy and the information system would diverge. The implementation was completed on schedule and - compared with similar projects in other companies - at low cost, surpassing the expected efficiency gains.

Business Engineering Levels

Business Engineering is associated with decisions at all levels in the structuring of a company:

- The business strategy covers corporate policy decisions concerning alliances, company structure or business segments, through to management instruments for a given business segment as well as the computer applications and databases needed (see. Fig. 1.3.1./1).

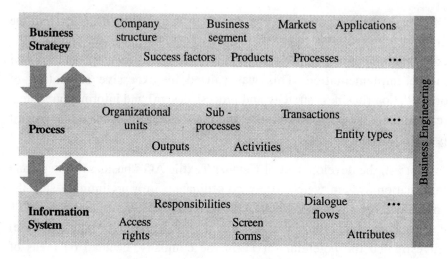

Fig. 1.3.1./1: Business Engineering levels

For example, a bank decides (see. Fig. 1.3.1./2) to divide its credit business into two segments in order to align service costs with the expected return or risk. This generates statements in the business strategy such as: In future the bank will differentiate two Business segments within the credit business, and design specific processes for each. It requires, among other things, a personal loan system application and will use the existing customer database.

- The process level determines the organizational units (customer handling, personal loan dept. etc.), the process outputs (e.g. homebanking) the sub-processes (e.g. mail offer procedures) and organizational activities (e.g. "offer credit") as well as the most important transactions (computer functions) and the entity types (e.g. account, customer) in the database. It thus specifies that the offer procedure uses a "record credit application" transaction, and the homebanking procedure needs a "customer authorization" transaction.

- The information system (IS) level then specifies the organization and the computerized information processing in detail. It determines signatory powers and responsibilities (e.g. credit approval authority), forms and computer screen masks (e.g. for credit applications), rights of access to transactions by different positions, events as process flow triggers (e.g. credit application); it specifies attributes (data records, e.g. a customer's credit limit) in the database, completes the transactions (functionality) within programs (e.g. cancel credit) and describes the dialogue flows (e.g. by means of the user interface menus).

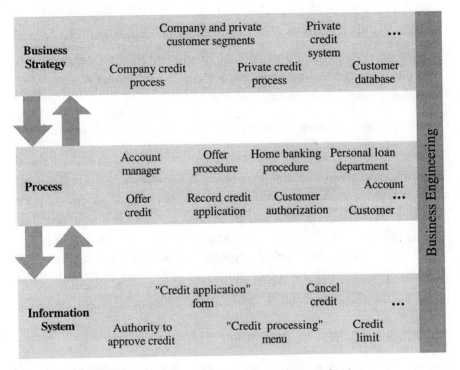

Fig. 1.3.1./2: Examples of decisions and dependencies

For instance, in the case of personal loans the process level will decide to create a Personal Credit department for the central processing of all personal loans, and to set up an offer procedure and home banking procedure as process variants. In this way the high personnel costs of processing personal loans at the branch level should be avoided.

Chapter 5 will describe the Business Engineering levels and their interactions in greater detail. The brief descriptions given here should suffice to highlight two basic Business Engineering principles:

Innovations affect the business strategy, process and information levels.
- Innovations can only be effective when they are implemented at all levels.
- The information system imposes restrictions on the higher levels.

Examples of restrictions arising from the information system are:

- The extension of the customer, customer handling and cost accounting database needed for a customer and customer handling performance analysis requires a lot of work and can be completed at the earliest in two years.

- Given the currently available communication and information technology, the customer authorization procedure within homebanking is so unwieldy that few customers are willing to use it.

- The package software available for handling personal loans does not include homebanking variants.

An experienced credit manager, together with his organizational and IT staff, would recognize such restrictions very quickly. In addition, there are many restrictions at a more detailed level that require considerable knowledge of the existing information system or of package software. The chemical concern referred to could have avoided the expensive diversion if it had planned the business, process and IS levels simultaneously, and brought together strategic, organizational and software consultants at an early stage.

The Process as Key to Innovation

Business Engineering makes the process the key to business reorganization. Fig. 1.3.1./3 summarizes the most important process characteristics using the example of business credit:

- The process is a sequence of activities (assess financial standing, offer credit, etc.).

- The activities can be distributed between several organizational units. In our example these are the customer himself, customer management and account management at the branch level, the credit department at Head Office and the reporting system.

- IT-applications support the performance of activities. For example, the customer management staff obtain customer documentation from the customer database for discussions with customers, and record the credit application in the credit system.

- A process produces and consumes outputs (thick arrows). The business credit process offers the customer advice, quotations, status information, etc. In return it obtains from the customer information on their financial status, wishes regarding the credit handling, the signed credit contract, etc.

- Process management sets goals (target values) for the process, measures the execution of the process using selected performance indicators, and compares the result (actual) with the target. Process management is the responsibility of a process manager and staff from the areas involved. Performance indicators in this example are the speed of execution between credit enquiry and offer of contract, the number of offers that are successful, and handling costs.

It is clear from Fig. 1.3.1./3 that from this perspective a process does indeed cover many aspects of a company, but by no means all of them.

The process is the key to Business Engineering.

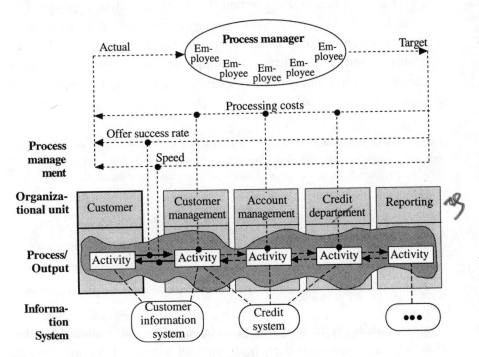

Fig. 1.3.1./3: Process

The Process as Link Between Strategic Development and Systems Development

Process development is a special form of flow organization. A process (e.g. personal loans) is a concrete manifestation of the business strategy, and links it with the information system. For the past thirty years the flow organization has been neglected both in theory and in practice. One reason for this might be that two separate disciplines have developed with different cultures:

- The management discipline develops the business strategy. It approaches the reorganization of operations from a holistic entrepreneurial standpoint. It usually has inadequate expertise in the IS development area, is consequently anxious about it, and as a result "delegates the details" to IT specialists (as in the example of the chemical concern). Their ideas do not significantly address the potential of IT, and often remain stuck at the strategy level, without being implemented.

- Information management and especially information science develop information systems using a technically-oriented, analytic approach. They often have too little business and management expertise, avoid problems that cannot be formalized, and tend to interpret the gulf between business managers and IT specialists as resulting from the incapacity for "analytic thought". As a result, in many cases they simply create IT support for the existing organization.

Process development brings about a renaissance in flow organization; it links strategy with (information) systems development (see. Fig. 1.3.1./4).

Fig. 1.3.1./4: Process development as the link between Strategic and IS-development

Since companies in the last thirty years have paid too little attention to their flow organization, it is precisely here - together with the IT possibilities - that enormous business potential is hidden. This currently gives rise to an over-emphasis, in which terms such as "Business Process Redesign" promote the total restructuring of business organizations through information technology; the process has become pars pro toto. In order to specify an appropriate role for process development we propose the following definition:

Business Engineering integrates strategic development and systems development via process development.

Process development (Business Process Redesign) is no substitute for strategic development, even if euphoric reports create this impression. A company still requires clear demarcation of Business segments, organizational structures and other strategic definitions. Process development is even less of a substitute for systems development; even the implementation of package software requires specific instruments.

More recent literature on strategic development, particularly relating to technology and innovation management [see Gerybadze 1995], links together the development of strategy and processes in the Business Engineering sense.

1.3.2. Business Engineering Procedures

Revolution or Evolution?

A project to restructure a bank's credit business or an industrial company's customer service brings a one-off thrust of innovation for the whole enterprise or large areas thereof. Undertaking the project allows fundamental analysis of the reorganization potential, comprehensive planning of new solutions, and the well-prepared introduction of change. Business Engineering in project form permits radical innovation.

Continuous improvement, in the sense of Japanese Kaizen, is a component of the routine management which analyzes the current operations, designs and gradually implements improvements. Continuous improvement rarely achieves fundamental innovation, but rather many small improvements derived directly from existing operations.

Many exponents of Business Engineering demand a radical, one-off change in the business, instead of this incrementalism [see Davenport 1993; Hammer/Champy 1993]. Others see the potential instead in a stepwise development by the staff in the organizational development sense [see Haist/Fromm 1991; Harrington 1991].

But is this really a question of "either" or "both"? Fundamental change can usually only be achieved at great expense in project form, but is not completed at the end of the project. The project must be followed by refinements which:

• improve the process on the basis of experience in routine operation,

• constantly steer the process towards the agreed goals (continuous improvement), and

• adjust the process to alterations in business conditions.

Getzner Textile AG provides an impressive example of this. The radical innovation was undertaken in a four year project. In the three years thereafter, continuous refinement yielded approximately the same improvement in costs, speed and quality.

Business Engineering first requires a project (revolution) and then refinement (evolution) by the process management (see Fig. 1.3.2./1).

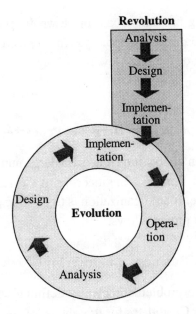

Fig. 1.3.2./1: Revolution and evolution

Managing a Business Engineering Project

The logic of the Business Engineering levels (see Fig. 1.3.1./1 and 2) suggests a top-down procedure: the business strategy is derived first, then the process and finally the supporting information system. The arrows in both directions already indicate that retrospective steps are needed. In the course of process and systems development opportunities and restrictions become apparent which cast doubt on previous assertions.

Operational reality brings additional complications: the existing business strategy is already obsolete in some sub-areas: corporate mergers have altered the structures; alterations in business turnover render planned process flows obsolete; a new software package opens up new possibilities etc.

In practice it should be accepted that a multitude of starting positions can initiate projects on any of the three levels. It should be ensured, however, that these projects do not lead to isolated strategic, process, or IS projects - as is so often observed - but involve all three Business Engineering levels.

Business Engineering basically runs top-down from the business strategy through the process to the information system. In practice, however, a project can be located at any of the three levels, as long as it incorporates the other two.

Focusing on Competitively Decisive Processes

Every company has an almost unmanageably large number of processes, but must restrict itself in Business Engineering to the few processes that are competitively decisive. If an organization is to be simple, it must concentrate on the most important process flows.

Responsibility for Business Engineering

Many companies have problems in clearly defining who is responsible for Business Engineering. Candidates for this are:

- *IT*
  The Computing or IT department regards its task as being restricted to the provision of applications in line with the requirements of the user departments. In many cases the user departments do not accept the IT department as competent collaborators in process development, precisely because they have in the past contributed so little in this area.

- *Organization*
  Because for a long time information technology has determined the organizational solutions, the Organization department has often simply abandoned the flow organization to the IT department, where it has at best been regarded from the technical perspective. Before the information revolution the flow organization was a central concern of the Organization department, and it is essential to restore it to this role. The number of staff in the Organization department, which in many companies had been shrinking for some time, is again growing - as a result of process development.

- *Controlling*
  The Controlling department is responsible for process management, and hence process evaluation. It thus occupies a key position in the continuous

improvement of processes, but its strengths are not typically in the information management and organizational areas.

- *External management consultants*
Many companies delegate reorganization that involves overcoming political barriers to external management consultants, in order to improve the chances of securing their acceptance without damaging the position of internal managers. However, external consultants only know the business from the outside, and cannot implement their concepts in day-to-day operation.

- *User department specialists and managers*
A further possibility lies within the user departments themselves. Specialists and line managers ultimately bear responsibility for the business strategies in their areas. They lack the methodical and technical knowledge and above all the time for the fundamental examination of their process, or perhaps the willingness to reserve such time. In addition, they represent a specific organizational unit, and consequently have difficulty designing strategies without reference to existing organizational structures.

The business expertise of the user departments will in future become even more of a critical success factor for Business Engineering. Managers in the user departments are increasingly recognizing and fulfilling their responsibility for their own processes. The relocation of development teams from the previously centralized IT department into the user departments is evidence of this.

Mixed teams are going to be needed to an even greater extent in the future. User specialists and managers must recognize and evaluate the business options. Since they lack the methods and the time to formulate these basic decisions as detailed solutions, they must delegate these tasks to employees who firstly understand enough about the business problem, but also understand enough about process and systems development. This might be the role of a business engineer or a modern organization specialist. The team then needs to be extended to include systems designers and perhaps other specialists (data management, security, etc.).

Numerous practical examples testify to the fact that purely additive team formation is inadequate. The knowledge of the team members in the areas of business strategy, process and information system must overlap significantly (see Fig. 1.3.2./2). Innovative solutions that recognize both the business and IT potential must ultimately be conceived, or at least evaluated, by a single mind.

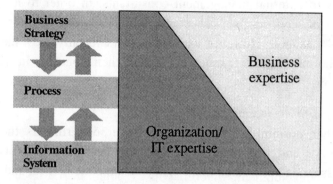

Fig. 1.3.2./2: Linking business, organizational and IT expertise

The responsibility for Business Engineering lies with user department management. Business Engineering requires on the one hand mixed teams, and on the other a holistic training and conceptual approach.

Clarity about the allocation of roles in Business Engineering, namely the responsibility and competence of employees with respect to business strategies, processes and information system, is the primary prerequisite for successful innovation.

1.3.3. The Business Engineering Discipline

Business Engineering seems to be developing into an independent scientific and practical discipline, which can be characterized as follows:

Business Engineering Sources

Many proven, and some new, management and systems development concepts have been incorporated in Business Engineering (see Fig. 1.3.3./1) [see also Osterloh/Frost 1994]:

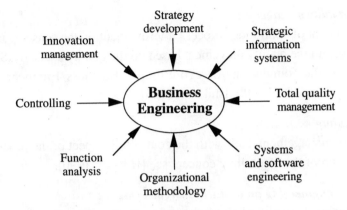

Fig. 1.3.3./1: Business Engineering Sources

- *Management theory*
  Strategy development, which has lost reputation as a result of lack of successful implementation, provides the basic structures and direction of the enterprise [see Bleicher 1992; Gomez 1993; Porter 1988; Pümpin 1986]. Innovation management provides greatest help in accomplishing the transformation within the company [see Bleicher 1992, p. 422-461; Gerybadze 1988].

- *Strategic information systems*
  In the 1980s the collection of so-called strategic information systems paved the way for Business Engineering [see Earl 1989; Mertens/Plattfaut 1986; Scott Morton 1991; Ward et al. 1990]. Examples of IT implementations that have had a dramatic influence on the company - usually in the form of case studies - were regarded as instructions in the search for IT-based innovations. Particular fame was achieved by American Airlines' flight reservation system (SABRE) [see Copeland/McKenny 1988] or Lithonia Lighting's light planning system [see Berkley/Nohria 1991]. Successful examples with potential for other sectors can also be a useful Business Engineering tool.

- *Organizational methodology*
  Organizational development and other proven organization techniques [see Gomez/Zimmermann 1993; Krüger 1993; Schmidt 1991] such as functional analysis or position description continue to provide a basis for process development.

- *Total quality management*
  The concept of continuous process improvement, in the sense of Japanese Kaizen, and the quality movement based on the quality standard ISO-9000 generate the foundation for evolutionary Business Engineering [see Deming 1982; DIN 1990; Ishikawa 1985].

- *Controlling*
  Process management deals with the controlling aspect of the process. For discussion of the controlling concept see [Horváth 1990].

- *Systems engineering and software engineering*
  The business administration systems approach as well as systems and software engineering are primarily responsible for the engineering aspects. The fundamental advances in understanding the development of information systems in the second half of the 1980s continue to provide a methodical framework for structuring strategies and processes [see Gutzwiller 1994].

Business Engineering combines management theory, organizational methodology, total quality management, controlling, systems and software engineering within a single approach.

Business Engineering Dimensions

Every business strategy has many dimensions. Taking the example of the credit business introduced in Section 1.3.1. let us consider the decision to set up a personal loan process, and within that to differentiate the offer procedure and homebanking variants. Several dimensions need to be taken into account here:

- *Organization*
  Setting up a personal loans department, assigning authority for establishing credit conditions, credit investigation procedures, etc.

- *Functions*
  Access to a public data network (e.g. Videotext), purchasing a homebanking program package, transactions (computer functions) for the personal loans department (e.g. for downgrading credit standing) etc.

- *Data*
  Abiding by the SWIFT standards for data exchange, extending the customer data to include authorization data for checking access rights, transferring customer data from the branches to the central Personal Loan department, etc.

- *Personnel*
  Training of employees in the Personal Loan department, setting up a customer hotline, specifying staff performance goals, etc.

- *Marketing*
  Advertizing campaign for the introduction of the new service, operating instructions for customers using the homebanking procedure, selection of pilot customers, etc.

- *Legal*
  Legal status of an electronic order, customer data protection, etc.

- ...

Every management and systems development concept must concentrate on certain levels and dimensions (see Fig. 1.3.3./2). At the business strategy level strategic development considers Business segments, strategic controlling, management tools, etc. Systems development, especially Computer Aided Software Engineering (CASE) concentrates on the information system level and the data and function dimensions [see Gutzwiller 1994].

Business Engineering structures the organization, data and function dimensions at the business strategy, process and information system levels.

	Organization e.g.	Data e.g.	Functions e.g.	Personnel e.g.	...
Business Strategy	Business segment	Data-bases	Applica-tions	Career plans	
Process	Activities	Entity types	Trans-actions	Team formation	
Information System	Responsi-bilities	Attributes	Dialogue flows	Employee evaluations	

Fig. 1.3.3./2: Dimensions of Business Engineering

This book restricts itself to process and IS development. It presumes the techniques of strategic development. Process development deals with the organization, data, and function dimensions at the process level, while IS development deals with them at the information system level. Chapter 5 considers the Business Engineering dimensions and their interactions in greater detail.

Business Engineering does not thereby deny the other dimensions, but delegates them to other disciplines. Foremost among these is innovation management, which pays particular attention to the personal and political dimensions to ensure that the transformation is actually successful. The opinions of employees can promote innovation or, in extreme cases prevent it. Business Engineering provides the instruments for the operational dimensions of innovation.

Business Engineering Characteristics

Business Engineering is a management discipline which exploits the potential of information technology, thus contributing to the transformation of the industrial society into the information society. Its characteristics are:

• Information technology as innovation enabler

• Linking of strategy, process, and information system

• The process as the key to change

- The process as the key to change

- Focusing on competitively decisive processes

- Directing processes towards customer benefits

- Responsibility of departmental management for their own processes

- Operational process management

- Networked organization of independent units

- Revolution and evolution

- Project management based on an engineering approach

1.4.   The PROMET Method

PROMET is a comprehensive method for process development (PROMET BPR) and the process-oriented introduction of package software (PROMET SSW) [see IMG 1994a, 1994b]. References to PROMET in the following discussion always relate to PROMET BPR.

PROMET assists in recognizing, planning and implementing operational innovations using information technology. It consists of a procedural model (activities and sequences), a documentation model (results), a role model (organization) and Business Engineering techniques. PROMET is based on a comprehensive meta-model of process and systems development which adopts the principles of Method Engineering [see Heym 1995]. This meta-model helps firstly with the design and understanding of techniques; it also describes the interfaces between strategy, process and information system, and in this way ensures the continuity of the strategy through the process to the information system.

PROMET is a process development method, consisting of techniques, a procedural model, a documentation model and a role model.

This book provides an introduction to selected PROMET techniques, extending them to include systems development techniques. For practical work in Business Engineering projects, the PROMET handbooks provide the additional method components mentioned above, as well as operative tools such as forms.

1.5.   Reader's Guide

Structure of the Book

This book deals with the techniques of organization and systems design in Chapters 2, 3 and 4, and presents some of their foundations in Chapter 1. Finally, Chapter 5 provides an introduction to the basics of the Business Engineering methods, which link the organization, data and function dimensions at the strategy, process and information system levels (see Fig. 1.5./1). Since small, artificial examples are not well suited to illustrate the essentials of organization and information system design, throughout this book a relatively realistic example will be used consistently, even if in many places it must be simplified further for reasons of size and complexity. This example describes UNTEL Switzerland AG (referred to simply as UNTEL) the marketing subsidiary of a multinational consumer electronics and computing group. It arose originally from a real case, and was adjusted for didactic purposes.

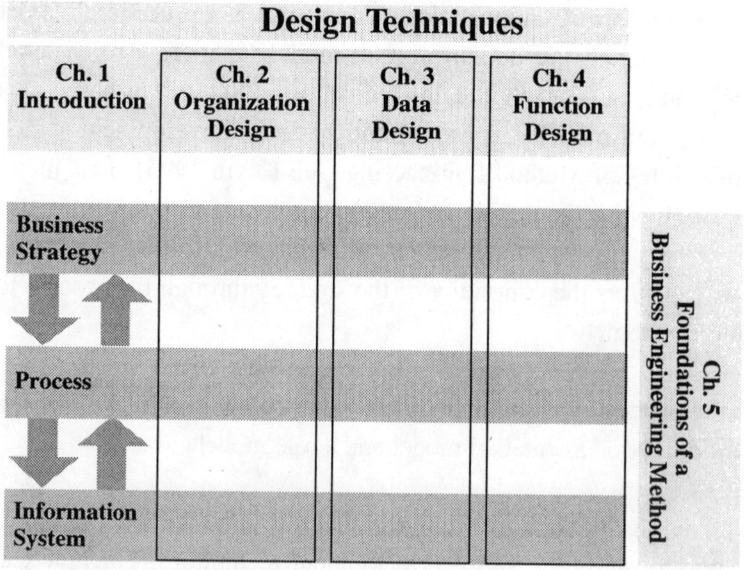

Fig. 1.5./1: Structure of the book

Textbook Character

The book is a textbook which gives practical applicability and didactic form precedence over theory. In many places it dispenses with formal exactitude where this is considered unnecessary for the practical work and the audience. The aim is not to give a detailed scientific treatment of individual areas such as data modelling, but to present a comprehensive guide to process and systems development. The explanations are based on examples, which are then generalized. This should allow intuitive insight, without sacrificing generality. At the end of Chapters 2, 3 and 4 a table presents literature references for further reading.

Restriction to Process and Systems Development

This book does not deal with Business Engineering in its entirety, but concentrates on the development of business processes and information systems. It builds upon the business strategy and establishes standards for software development (or the use of package software). Proven methods exist for strategic development [see Hamel/Prahalad 1994; Hax/Majluf 1984; Porter 1985; Rowe 1989]. For software development the reader can refer to Gutzwiller's reference model [Gutzwiller 1994], which has served here as the basis for several IS development techniques.

The Audience

This book addresses the following audience:

- *Managers and specialists from the business segment.* Employees in the Business segments tend to think in terms of concrete solutions rather than design techniques. The consistent use of a case study should facilitate their understanding of the associated techniques.

- *Staff in the organization and IT departments*
  Organizational and IT specialists usually have abundant training and experience in the planning and implementation of computerized processes. The techniques used should be of primary interest to them. The examples should provide this audience with additional insights.

- *Students of business administration and especially information management*
  The business world expects graduates of business and management studies to be able to analyze, assess and reformulate the processes and information processing in their specialist area. The techniques in this book provide a basic framework for this task. Since students typically have not yet acquired a great deal of practical experience, the case study should help them understand the techniques.

2. Organization Design

Organization design is concerned with the organizational dimension of a business solution (see Fig. 2./1).

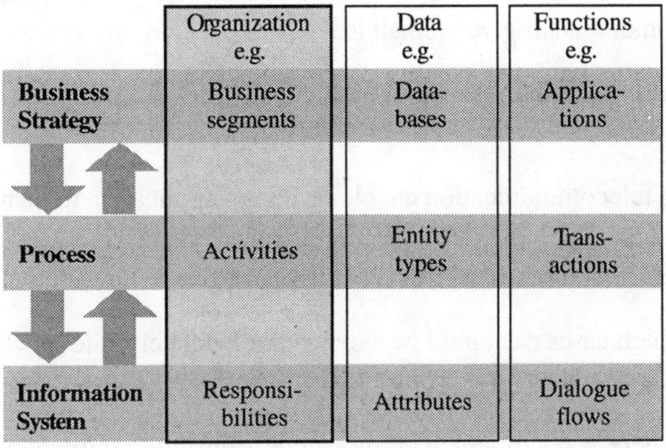

	Organization e.g.	Data e.g.	Functions e.g.
Business Strategy	Business segments	Data-bases	Applica-tions
Process	Activities	Entity types	Trans-actions
Information System	Responsi-bilities	Attributes	Dialogue flows

Fig. 2./1: Organization design as part of Business Engineering

At the strategy level organization design consists of establishing the market/product combinations (business segments), the processes, the organizational structure, etc. In our credit example this would include customer segmentation, and the business credit and personal credit processes (see Fig. 1.3.1./2). *(handwritten: kundengruppe (?))*

At the process level organization design covers the organizational units (e.g. account management), activities (e.g. offer credit), process outputs (e.g. homebanking), etc. *(handwritten: Aufgaben (?))*

Finally, at the IS-level organization design specifies details such as competence and responsibility, forms, etc.

Organization design determines what outputs (effectiveness) are to be generated in what way (efficiency).

2.1. The Goals of Organization Design

This book restricts itself to the process and information system levels. Consequently, the organization design proceeds from an existing strategy, and asks - in the personal credit example - questions such as:

1. Can the company dispense with credit checks for long-standing customers seeking very small loans?

2. Would the customer database allow the separation of problem customers?

3. Does telecommunication enable the credit application to be made at the time and place in which the credit requirement arises, e.g. from the travel agency when the trip is being booked?

4. In which cases can credit be extended immediately, and in which within 24 hours?

5. Are there ways in which credit can be adjusted to individual customer needs, e.g. with regard to repayment schemes, without incurring additional personnel costs?

6. Would it be cheaper to delegate the handling of problem loans to specialist companies?

7. Which activities are performed by Head Office, and which at branch level?

8. How is the performance of the Personal Loan department to be measured?

The impact of information technology is no longer restricted to the computerized support of existing process flows, but enables radical transformation of the organization. This means that the organization design must distance itself from the existing situation, investigate all aspects of the business strategy, and search for fundamentally new approaches. It should exhaust all the potential arising on the one hand from outdated process flows, and on the other from information technology.

Information technology cannot eliminate all restrictions, however; the organization is still subject to limitations, as the following examples show:

- The existing computer application for credit handling is not very well suited to the personal loan process. Adjusting it would require considerable investment and would not come on stream for two years.

- A software package is indeed available on the market, but involves considerable interface problems.

- The market penetration of Teletext is inadequate.

- Employees have insufficient expertise.

2.2. Process Model

The process, as a special organizational concept, is the key to Business Engineering (see Section 1.3.1.). Before considering some organization design techniques, let us examine more closely what constitutes a process, and what potential lies in process reorganization.

To understand Business Engineering it is helpful to proceed on the basis of a realistic example. To this end we have developed a comprehensive case study relating to UNTEL Switzerland AG (referred to briefly as UNTEL). It is the regional marketing company of a multinational electronics concern. It sells consumer electronics equipment to retailers and wholesalers, buying this equipment primarily from the parent company UNTEL International.

Using the example of UNTEL's sales process, Section 2.2.1. first shows what can be achieved from a process orientation, and provides an intuitive understanding of processes. Section 2.2.2. then summarizes the essential process components in a process model. Since here in the context of organization design we are only dealing with the organization of processes, for the moment we can equate organization design with process design (see Chapter 5 on the distinction between the two concepts).

2.2.1. An Example of Process Design

Against the background of UNTEL's business strategy, the following discussion contrasts the actual and target state of the sales process.

2.2.1.1. The Sales Process at the Macro-Level

Actual State

In the past UNTEL has been a distribution organization responsible also for technical customer service, rather than taking an active market role as a sales organization. The actual state of the sales process reflects this (see Fig. 2.2.1.1./1).

The main participants in the sales process are the customer, UNTEL's sales representatives, and UNTEL's order recording and marketing. The process therefore involves four organizational units (including the customer), which are represented in the figure by grey boxes. Process design examines *process flows without regard to organizational boundaries*, whether within or between organizations.

From the perspective of UNTEL's sales process, the customer undertakes the following activities:

- Agree framework contract: Within the framework contract he would agree territorial protection, turnover-related discount rates, cash discounts, etc. with his main suppliers.

- Develop sales strategy: He determines his product range, his discount policy, his strategy towards presenting goods in the store, he classifies his customers, and selects his main suppliers.

- Inventory control: The storage of goods delivered, recording of stock removals, stocktaking, stock evaluation, etc. are all components of the inventory control activity.

- Determine requirements: Up to now the customer has determined the type and quantity of goods he wishes to procure on the basis of manually recorded sales statistics and physical stocktaking.

- Select suppliers: Despite the framework contract, with many products the customer still has the opportunity to decide in favour of the range offered by alternative suppliers. For example, in the case of televisions he decides which supplier he will purchase from after completion of the requirement determination process.

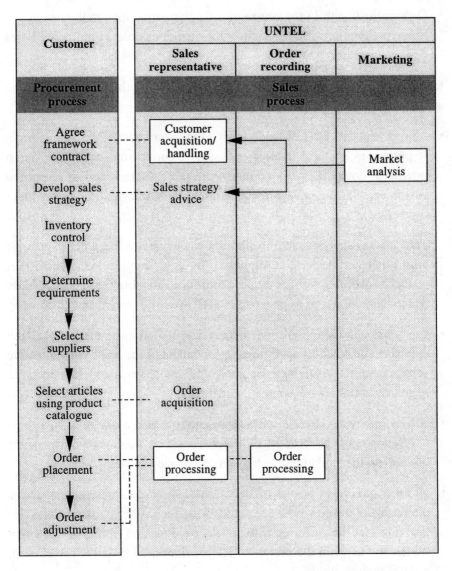

Fig. 2.2.1.1./1: Activity chain for the actual sales process

- Select articles using product catalogue: Using the suppliers' product catalogues he selects the model variants (colour, design options, etc.) and determines the article number and delivery conditions.

- Place order: He then fills out an order form, or has the sales representative do it on his behalf.

- Order adjustment: In the course of the order period the retailer can assess his actual requirements, and adjust the quantities ordered in line with this new information.

Up to now UNTEL's sales department has supported the customer in these activities in the following ways:

- Market analysis: UNTEL undertakes a modest amount of market research. It purchases sectoral studies and sales figures from market research institutes, compares its own sales with these figures, and provides the customer, via the sales representatives, with information about these figures.

  The "market analysis" activity appears in a white box, because, in contrast with other activities, it is supported by computer. In fact, the market research institute provides a query tool for evaluating the sales database, which marketing uses to generate UNTEL-specific reports and graphics.

- Customer acquisition/account management: Using the market research database and a sector-specific address database, the sales representative selects potential customers. He approaches these firms and, if successful, negotiates a framework contract with them.

- Sales strategy advice: The sales representative advises the retailer on how to develop his sales strategy. He bases this not only on his own experience but also on the market research results mentioned above.

- Order acquisition: In one or two visits a year the sales representative obtains from the customer a standing order for easily forecast articles. He also provides the customer with assistance in making further orders either by telephone or on the premises. He provides advice on the selection of articles and quantities.

- Order processing: Finally, the sales representative obtains the order forms and either adds further details or fills them out himself on the basis of customer information. He then faxes them to order recording, which enters them into the order handling system

The graphical representation of this process in Fig. 2.2.1.1./1 (activity chain diagram) gives a broad overview of the entire sales process. We refer to this as the macro-level. The diagram shows the activities (nodes), some of them with computer support, and the sequence in which they are carried out. An arrow (unbroken, directional edge) signifies that the following activity can begin immediately after completion of the preceding one. Broken lines (non-directional edges) indicate that two activities should be undertaken simultaneously. In this rough representation, however, these sequential relationships should only be regarded as tentative. Activities that are not linked by an edge are concurrent, i.e. they are undertaken without any mutual temporal dependency.

Potential

Market saturation in consumer electronics has given rise to massive predatory competition. If UNTEL wants to at least maintain its market share it must fundamentally rethink its Sales. What contribution could information technology make here? What options are open to UNTEL?

- *Differentiation by customer segment*
  A software producer offers a customer performance analysis for wholesalers. On the basis of detailed recording and evaluation of sales costs and returns, it could help to concentrate sales resources on profitable customers.

- *Differentiation by product segment*
  A product performance analysis offers similar possibilities with respect to the product range.

- *Outsourcing sales*
  A radical solution would be to dissolve UNTEL's own sales organization and transfer Sales to a wholesaler. UNTEL would then be left with Logistics and Customer Service (repairs). A prerequisite for this solution would be a clean interface between Sales and Logistics, common planning

and control tools based on a detailed sales database run by the wholesaler, close electronic communication with Logistics, and flexible sales control based on an article- and customer-specific provisioning system.

Process orientation increases the tendency to evaluate operational sub-processes in terms of their costs and benefits, and to check out alternatives within and beyond the company (in- and outsourcing).

- *Include external product ranges*
  Instead of outsourcing Sales, UNTEL could also include complementary, or even competing product ranges within their own Sales, thus becoming a wholesaler itself. Information technology would permit cheap, speedy solutions. The external suppliers would continue to be responsible for delivery to the retailer, so additional transport and storage would not be required; they would make their product ranges available in the same format as UNTEL, so that the costs of catalogue production, order recording, provisioning, etc. would remain low.

- *Direct sales to the consumer*
  Teleshopping and other forms of approaching the customer directly could permit UNTEL to establish direct sales to the consumer alongside the sales channel via retailers, so that in some circumstances the intermediate trading level could be avoided (disintermediation).

- *Pan-European logisitics concept*
  UNTEL Europe plans to consolidate its logistics at three locations (north, south, east), as part of its pan-European strategy.

- *Improving customer benefits*
  UNTEL could employ information technology to increase the customer benefits within Sales (value added services), and bind the customer more closely. Using the sales figures from the retailer's point of sale scanners, UNTEL could take over the retailer's inventory control; differentiated market research and sales figures could be used to prepare restocking proposals and if necessary provide suggestions about the sales situation via the sales representative if unusual inventory situations are observed. Instead of the usual paper catalogue they could offer the customer an electronic catalogue with greater functionality. The new product catalogue mounted on a personal computer could simplify the search for articles,

permit checks on the consistency and completeness of configurations, and allow direct (online) order placement.

- *Reducing sales costs*
  UNTEL's costs, disregarding the costs of inventories, constitute about 20% of turnover. A sector comparison has indicated that other companies have reduced the cost component to 15% as a result of wide-ranging use of information technology. Since the predatory competition also manifests itself in price terms, the costs argument is paramount.

- *Performance-oriented management*
  An extensive sales information system would allow differentiated, performance-oriented management of sales staff - see the discussion of differentiation above.

As the above examples of reorganization indicate, information technology opens up large areas within the business management environment. It is the "enabler" for many business solutions which up to now have been impeded by costs (e.g. of data recording), availability of data (e.g. the sales data from point-of-sale scanners), speed (e.g. of the information flow in the role of marketing middleman for external suppliers), and other restrictions.

As well as the potential of information technology, this kind of reorganization naturally requires that all other business options be examined. These extend from training, through marketing to the exchange of staff.

Target State

UNTEL designs a reorganization of its sales in line with Fig. 2.2.1.1./2.

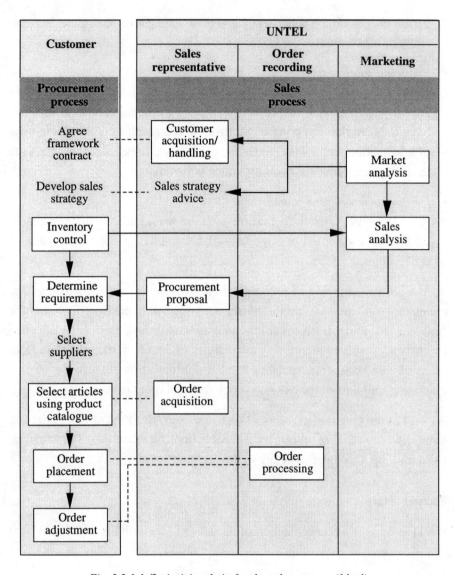

Fig. 2.2.1.1./2: Activity chain for the sales process (Ideal)

UNTEL retains its own independent sales organization and pursues the following actions:

- Extending market research and its provision to customer

- A new service - a merchandise management system

- Procurement proposals based on the data from the merchandise management system and market research

- Electronic product catalogue with online order placement

- Differentiated performance-oriented sales management

- The inclusion of external product ranges in the wholesale sense

- Cost reduction by lowering personnel costs

- Outsourcing of Logistics

Fig. 2.2.1.1./2 shows that these actions significantly increase customer binding.

UNTEL analyzes the temporal and financial costs of these actions and the prerequisites at the customer level and decides to achieve this vision of the sales process in the long term (5 years), but also to pursue as stage 1 a quickly implementable partial solution, as described in Section 2.5.

2.2.1.2.   The Sales Process at the Micro-Level

The macro-level gives an overview of the process. It documents the fundamental process design decisions. The macro process design is generally broken down into sub-processes, and finalized in detailed activity chains. Process innovations with considerable effects are also often conceived at the micro-level.

The micro-level of a process is achieved when the activities are so detailed that the employees can implement them as working instructions in their daily business. A manager can control the operational flows at the micro-level using the activity chain.

The most detailed form of the micro-process is the so-called workflow. In this case the computer, rather than the manager, takes over the flow control. Fig. 2.2.1.2./1 illustrates the micro-process (workflow) "accept EDIFACT order".

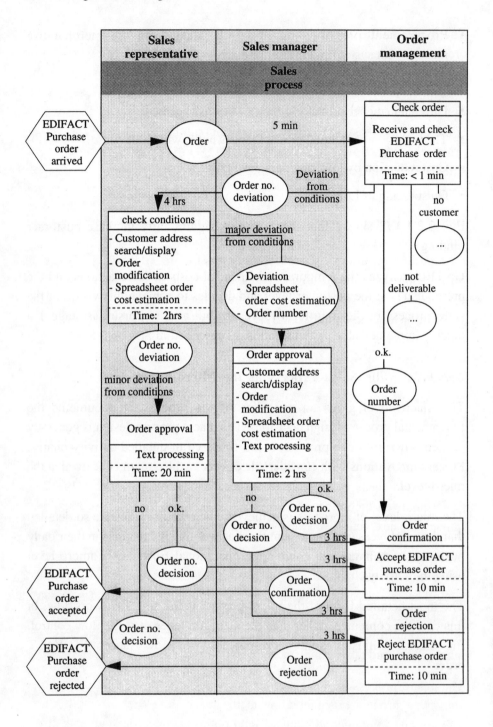

Fig. 2.2.1.2./1: Micro-process (workflow) "accept EDIFACT order"

The event "EDIFACT purchase order arrives" initiates the workflow. An order, which the customer sends to UNTEL as an EDIFACT (Electronic Data Interchange for Administration, Commerce and Transport) message, is the data flow. At UNTEL the computer receives and checks the message about 5 minutes later (the "receive and check EDIFACT purchase order " transaction) If the customer has modified the standard conditions (e.g. payment date or price), the Workflow Management System (WFMS) places the order in the sales representative's incoming mail and displays the modification to conditions.

Half a day later, on average, the sales representative undertakes the activity "check conditions", which typically takes two hours. Using the transaction (computer function) "search/display customer address" he obtains information about the customer details, conducts telephone discussions with the customer, and, with the help of a spreadsheet analysis, he determines the value of the altered conditions. If he agrees to the conditions that he has the power to approve, he records them using the "order modification" transaction and releases the order. The computer then produces an electronic order confirmation for the customer. If the deviation in conditions exceeds his authorization power, he passes the order on electronically to the regional sales manager, who decides about the order on average half a day later. In doing this he uses the sales representative's spreadsheet analysis.

The WFMS controls the process flow. It checks the result of the transaction "receive and check EDIFACT purchase order", places the order in the sales representative's incoming mail, monitors the time needed for processing and initiates the next activity on the basis of the feedback.

In the case of automated activity control the micro-process is described in much more detail than in case of manual control. Automated operational control has the advantage that the WFMS monitors the operation (in this case an EDIFACT order) through to completion, and passes on the necessary information from one activity to the next. This means that process flows are quicker (reduced down time) and safer (no forgetting).

The macro-process for sales and the micro-process for the EDIFACT order show that process reorganization at the macro-level permits both wide-ranging and fundamental changes, and optimizes specific segments at the micro-level.

2.2.1.3. Summary of the Process Design for UNTEL's Sales

The example of UNTEL's sales process indicates the thrust of process design:

- Process design emphasizes the operative view of the company, particularly the flow organization. Every potential discussed in the example generates clearly defined actions with verifiable results.

- Information technology generates a large part of the potential for reorganization. It overcomes boundaries such as organizational units by computerized management tools, physical distances by telecommunication, temporal delays by eliminating transport times, limits arising from personnel costs by automation, etc.

- The information revolution is no longer restricted to the computerization of existing process flows, but transforms the very goals and methods of business activity.

- Process design examines administrative processes in the same way that engineering examines the production process. It breaks them down into steps, decides between in-house production and external procurement, optimizes the production facilities (computer use), and documents the administrative process in the same way as a technical process (see especially the next section). This partly justifies the fact that process design is also referred to as reengineering.

- Process design seeks out both radical innovations and incremental improvements. At the macro-level the fundamental transformations are at the forefront, while at the micro-level it is the smaller steps that dominate.

2.2.2. Process Model

The example was intended simply to give an intuitive understanding of the process and process design. The concepts were not clearly defined, and important aspects - such as process management - were referred to only implicitly or tangentially. Below we formulate a general process model which explains the components of processes and provides a framework for designing specific processes. Fig. 2.2.2./1 summarizes the five most important components:

- *Activity chain* (2 workflow)

  Activity chain diagrams describe the core of the process, the activities and their flows.

- *Information system*

  The information system supports the activities with applications and databases.

- *Outputs*

  Processes consume and produce outputs which they exchange with other processes.

- *Process management*

  Process management ensures the quality of the process. It determines performance indicators, sets standards, and checks them using measuring points within the process. It derives operating requirements, decides on actions for further improvements and monitors their execution.

- *Process development*

  Process development implements the actions for process reorganization from the project-based process design and the continuous process management.

2.2.2.1. Activity Chains

The *activity chain* shows the most important activities within a process and their sequence.

The *macro-level* gives an overview of the entire process. It is broken down into sub-processes, which are described in detailed activity chains.

At the *micro-level* the activities are described in such detail that they represent clear working instructions for the employee. The micro-level proceeds from a business event and describes all the activities that are initiated by it.

The *workflow* is an activity chain and serves as a blueprint for a WFMS. It must be specified in greater detail than the guidelines for manual execution.

In practice it is important to distinguish between the macro-level and the micro-level. Too much detail too soon obstructs the view of potential solutions; too little detail typically hinders implementation; detailed specification is a prerequisite of a Workflow Management System.

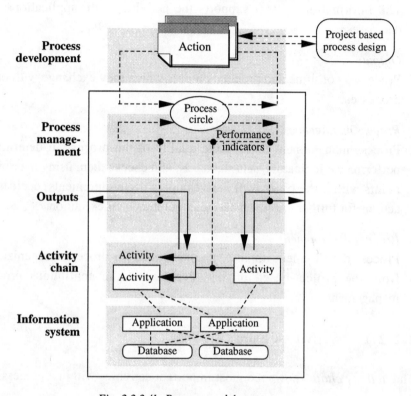

Fig. 2.2.2./1: Process model components

Activity

An *activity* is an operational function with a specifiable result. It is undertaken by man or machine or both.

The activity chain diagrams in the previous section contained examples of important activities such as "develop sales strategy", but also of minor activities, such as "order recording". Part of the activities is computerized.

Event

An *event* is the initiator or result of a process flow.

Sequence

The *sequence* describes whether an activity is undertaken after another activity (sequential), at the same time (parallel) or independently (concurrent).

In its least detailed form the sequence represents a fundamental directional flow. In refining the activity chain the sequence is then specified in concrete terms down to the flow of records, which does not typically consist of physical records, but of references to electronic documents (see Fig. 2.2.1.2./1).

Organizational Unit

An *organizational unit* is the combination of one or more positions into an independent part of the organizational structure. It can be located either within or outside the company.

Fig. 2.2.2.2./1 distinguishes five organizational units - the customer, the sales representative, Sales Support, Marketing and Logistics - distributed over three processes. Thus external partners also count as organizational units. When they are not part of the process being examined, we often equate the process with the organizational unit (customer, Logistics). Individual positions (e.g. sales representative) are organizational units every bit as much as aggregates (e.g. Sales Support). However, we do consider only the position, and not the employee who fills it.

The activities in a process can be distributed over several organizational units, regardless of the existing organizational structure, i.e. a process includes several organizational units. Conversely, an organizational unit can be involved in several processes. Partner companies (e.g. customers) are treated as organizational units.

One special case of the organizational unit is the computer. If an activity is undertaken without human influence, it is assigned to the "organizational unit": computer (white background). Fig. 2.2.1.2./1 gives an example with the organizational unit order management.

2.2.2.2.   Outputs

Outputs are the results of a process, which go to internal or external customers. The recipient of an output is another process either within or outside the company. An output can be material or immaterial.

UNTEL's most important output to its customers are consumer electronics equipment. However, UNTEL's output is not the production of this equipment, but making it available to the customer. This consists firstly of the logistics outputs (procurement, storage and customer-specific delivery) and secondly the sales outputs (see Fig. 2.2.2.2./1). Procurement proposal, framework contract, and sales strategy are outputs that the sales process provides to the customer. The customer's (reciprocal) output is the order. The dispatch advice is an output for the logistics process, which in return sends a dispatch confirmation as reciprocal output to the sales process.

The output is the result of a process's value creation. Its value to the process customer (need, quality, etc.) determines the prices of the reciprocal output. The outputs constitute the starting point of process development.

From a process-oriented perspective outputs flow between processes, not between organizational units, since output measurement also relates to the process.

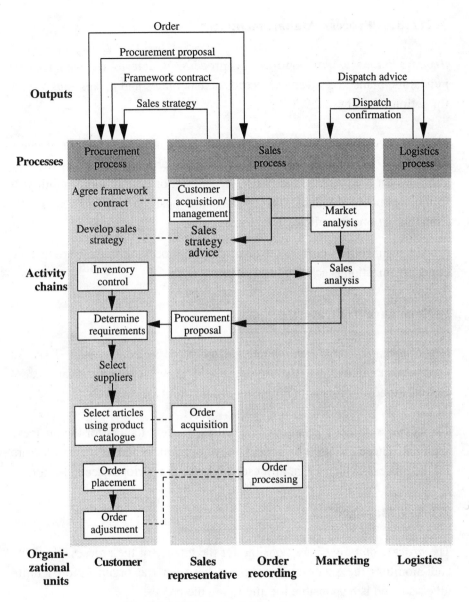

Fig. 2.2.2.2./1: Outputs of the sales process

Where customer orientation is emphasized the process customers play an important role in process development. Process customers are the processes that receive the outputs. In the case of the company's customers, it is usual to regard the process customer as being the customer himself, rather than his individual processes.

2.2.2.3. Process Management

Process management controls the process. It determines performance indicators, plans target values, records actual values and makes suggestions for action (see Fig. 2.2.2.3./1).

Process development requires criteria for evaluating the position reached. This is the job of process management. It plans and monitors the key variables for the process, such as service speed, or customer profitability. It formulates planned values, records the actual position reached, and derives from this actions for refining the process.

Process management ensures the quality of the process. It makes sure that the target organization is achieved and refined.

Performance Indicators

Performance indicators are operationalized process characteristics. They are used to plan and evaluate the process quality in the sense of critical success factors, especially time, quality, costs and flexibility.

The business strategy lays down the critical success factors for the business segment. These are used by process development to derive success factors for the process, which are in turn used to derive the performance indicators.

Process Manager

The *process manager* is responsible for the quality of the process. He plans and monitors the process, coordinates between the organizational units involved, and is responsible for improving the process.

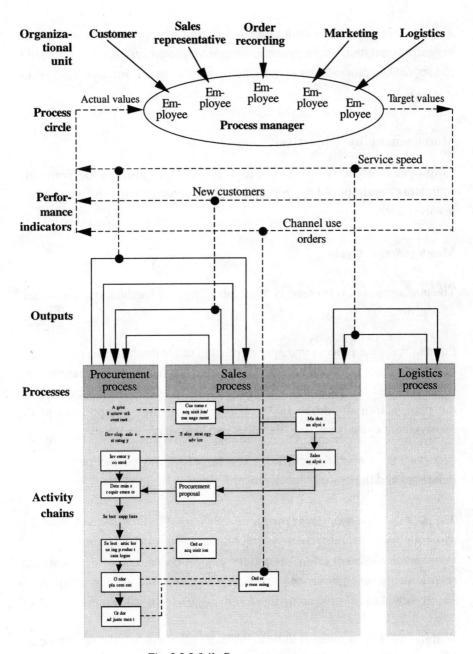

Fig. 2.2.2.3./1: Process management

Process Circle

The *process circle* is a committee consisting of representatives of all the organizational units in the process, headed by the process manager. Its job is to support the process manager in the management and improvement of the process.

Management by Objectives

Employees' objectives should incorporate the process performance indicators, and should be planned and monitored with the employees' involvement.

Management Cycle

The *management cycle* consists of the planning, implementation, and control of decisions.

For example, the process manager or process circle establishes a target value of 50 new customers per year. Every quarter he checks the increase in new customers and compares this with the plan. If the actual values deviate from the plan, action should be taken. If one of the three components of the management cycle is missing, the other two are usually ineffective.

Process management decides on the target values of the performance indicators and the process development actions.

2.2.2.4.   Process Development

Process development refers both to the project-based, one-off, fundamental restructuring of the process (process design) and to the continuous improvement of the process by those actively involved in the process.

Within UNTEL a project is to be undertaken to restructure the sales process. Ms. Schulz from short-term planning is the head of the sales project. Together with Ms. Meier from the Organization department, Mr. Müller from

Sales and Mr. Nolte from the IT department she forms the project team and is responsible for transforming the process as the project result.

On completion of the project Mr. Schwätzer (head of Sales and Advice) takes over responsibility for the process. Together with process participants from all the departments involved (Ms. Flockig from Marketing, Mr. Gütig from Sales Support and Mr. Umschläger from Logistics) he works on improving the process. He continuously analyzes the strengths and weaknesses of the process and formulates action to be taken.

Process development as part of Business Engineering (see Section 1.3.2.) thus consists on the one hand of project-based process design (revolution) and on the other of continuous process improvement (evolution) within the process management framework.

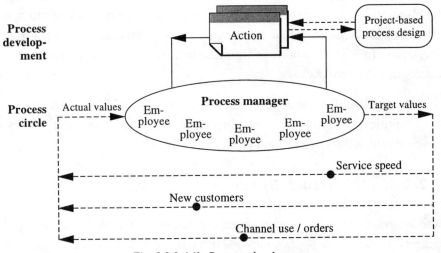

Fig. 2.2.2.4./1: Process development

Permanent process development is not the responsibility of a business consultant, an internal controller, organization or business information specialist, or a line manager. Process development (see Fig. 2.2.2.4./1) is primarily the responsibility of all process participants under the leadership of a process manager, and supported by the controller, organization or information specialist. At periodic meetings of the process circle (e.g. quarterly) the process participants analyze the process, discuss the actual position and improvement possibilities, and plan actions. The starting point for such discussions is the deviation of actual values from target values of the performance indicators.

Actions *Maßnahmen*

> *Actions* refer to all kinds of undertakings aimed at process transformation. It is important to specify the result, the person responsible, and the deadline for any action.

For example, an employee could be given the task of drawing up a list of customers who, for low turnover, are especially costly in handling terms. Further examples of actions within the sales process are the classification of an article as an inventory article, intensification of customer visits by a specific sales representative, a reassignment of customers to sales representatives, an improvement to the order management application, a special multi-media campaign, a relocation of the "sales analysis" output from Marketing to Sales Support, or the introduction of an "electronic product catalogue" software package.

Actions can therefore be either short activities by individual employees, or larger projects. The process employees have to undertake the process development actions as well as their routine activities.

2.2.2.5.   Information System

> The *information system* refers to (computerized) information processing in its entirety. It consists of applications and databases which support the execution of activities (see Fig. 2.2.2.5/1).

Applications

Within his procurement process the retailer uses UNTEL's order management application to place orders with UNTEL. He uses the "online order recording by the customer" transaction (computer function) within the order management system to specify the articles, quantities, delivery conditions, etc.

On UNTEL's side the "receive and check EDIFACT purchase order" transaction (see Fig. 2.2.1.2./1) from the order management application is initiated automatically as soon as an EDIFACT purchase order is received.

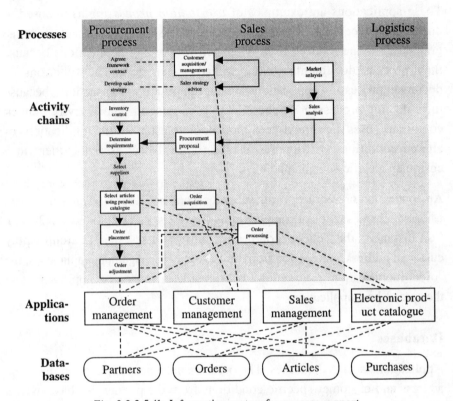

Fig. 2.2.2.5./1: Information system for process support

Transactions are sub-functions of an application for altering or querying a database. They are equivalent to machine jobs (e.g. milling) in the production of physical goods. They are tasks that arise on the computer repeatedly in similar form, which an employee can initiate (call up) when performing an activity, or which run automatically when initiated by the computer. Provisionally we adopt the following definitions (see Sections 4.2. and. 4.5. for more exact definitions):

A *transaction* is a computerized procedure performed on a database. An *application* is a combination of all transactions in a given area of work.

A customer performance analysis for the wholesaler, a planning and control system based on a sales database, and an order handling system are all examples of applications within the sales process.

These applications are examples of *transaction processing* as opposed to document processing. Tools for word processing, spreadsheet systems, graphics, etc. are referred to as *document processing* applications because they process documents (texts, spreadsheets, etc.). The functions of document processing applications are not referred to as transactions, because they do not process a database, but a document. The activity "check conditions" uses the spreadsheet application to establish the implications of altered conditions. It files the resulting spreadsheet as a document in a customer-specific documentation.

An application or transaction can support several activities, and an activity can use several transactions or applications (see Figs. 2.2.1.2./1 and 2.2.2.5./1). For instance, the "check conditions' activity uses the "search/display customer address" transaction from the customer management application, the "order modification" transaction from the order management application and the spreadsheet application.

Databases

Applications access databases. The order management application reads the address and customer-specific conditions from the partner database, writes new orders to the order database, reads article descriptions and quantities available from the article database, etc. A transaction-oriented application can access several databases, and several applications can access a given database.

A *database* is a collection of data relating to a given work object.

We use the term database to refer only to coded information (see Section 3.2.). Roughly speaking, this refers to data records whose contents have a strict format and possess a defined meaning independent of an application. Document processing applications, in contrast, generate collections of documents, that you could refer to as documentbases. The format of the document is not fixed and the significance of the contents (non-coded information) is subject to the interpretation of the processor. In Fig. 2.2.2.5./1 the term "database" is used to refer to both "data- and documentbases".

All the applications and databases of a company or area together constitute the *(computerized) information system* (frequently referred to in the sections below simply as the *system*

2.2.2.6.   Process Architecture

Fig 2.2.2.6./1 describes UNTEL's process architecture as part of the business strategy. It shows the sales, customer service, logistics and management processes, together with the most important corresponding processes on the customer side (procurement and service) and on the supplier side (sales).

UNTEL regards the processes listed as competitively decisive, and therefore explicitly makes them the subject of its process organization in accordance with the process model. This means that it presents their process flows as activity chains, establishes the computer support and sets up process management. All other processes within the company - such as personnel recruiting - are not the subject of a standardized process organization.

A company's processes are largely autonomous entities. Just as in an inter-organizational market, the processes coordinate their value creation process via the level of output, internal orders, transfer prices, etc. In the extreme case the sales process will obtain an offer from a logistics company to compete with the services provided by their own Logistics department.

The *process architecture* concentrates on a few competitively decisive processes within the company and their coordination via the exchange of outputs.

The process architecture helps to establish and communicate the important processes within the company, to delimit processes that can be managed well, and to coordinate with other aspects of the business strategy, such as business segments or the organizational structure.

The process architecture is not valid for the company from a particular point in time. Rather it is a vision of the company's process organization, which it aims to achieve gradually through a series of projects. It changes over time in response to market developments and new organizational insights.

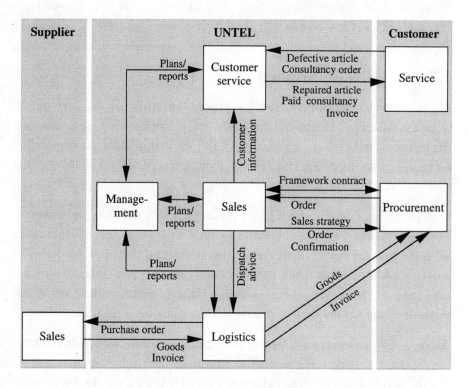

Fig. 2.2.2.6./1: UNTEL's process architecture

2.2.2.7. Summary

A *process* is a set of activities, which are to be undertaken in a specified sequence and which are supported by information technology applications. Its value creation consists of the outputs to process customers. The process has its own management, which steers and designs the process in line with the business strategy using performance indicators derived from it (see Fig. 2.2.2.7./1). A company concentrates on those few processes that determine its competitiveness.

2.3. Process Vision

The goal of process design is to identify new business concepts (innovations), which improve customer benefits (effectiveness) and reduce costs (improve efficiency). The process vision technique helps to identify fundamentally new concepts and provide the outline of the new process.

The example of UNTEL's sales process in Section 2.2.1. shows what potential lies hidden within the process. This extends from process differentiation by customer segment, through electronic sales assistance (product catalogue) to outsourcing of the process. But how do we uncover this potential? Is there a systematic approach?

Process vision pursues the following sub-goals:

*   *Radical innovation*
    Process vision is a technique of organization design, which aims at radical innovation. It subjects the cornerstones of the process to evaluation.

*   *Linking strategy and process*
    Starting from the business strategy, the process vision derives standards for the process, gives substance to and checks the strategic assertions, and brings new perspectives on the strategic development (see Section 1.3.1.).

*   *Long-term perspective*
    The process vision relates to a three to five year timescale, or even longer.

*   *Exploiting IT potential*
    The process vision investigates the implications of information technology for the process environment and the process potential.

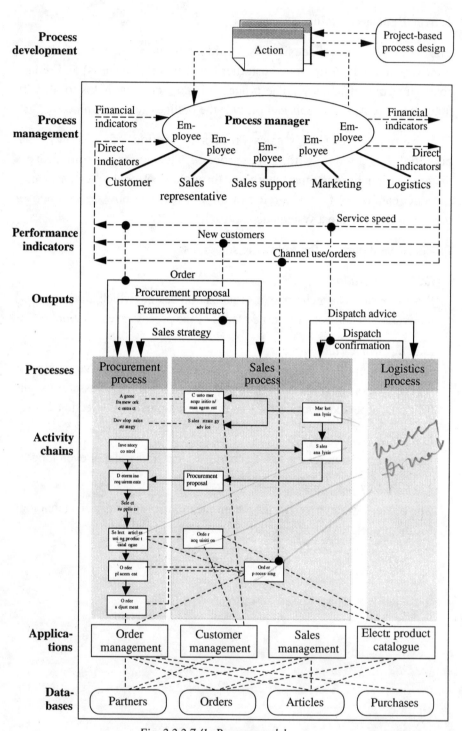

Fig. 2.2.2.7./1: Process model

- *Holistic view*
  The process vision aims at a holistic examination of all aspects of the process. It leaves the detailing to other organization design techniques (see Section 2.4. ff.).

This vision of the sales process helps UNTEL to discuss new sales formats, to think through the consequences of electronic business transactions, and to develop a picture of future sales in the minds of the decision makers.

The process vision is no substitute for the business strategy. This includes not only the process vision, but also aspects of marketing, human resources, financing, etc. and has its own proven techniques from business segment analysis through to the experience curve.

2.3.1. Sources of Process Innovation

How do innovations arise in a company?

- *Employees' expertise*
  The first and most important source is the expertise of employees in the business. They know the requirements and the problems, they have observed various approaches to finding solutions both in their own company and among competitors and in doing so have developed their own ideas.

- *Case Studies*
  Examples of innovative ideas from their own or other business sectors often provide the starting point for process ideas. In the Business Engineering literature, Strategic Information Systems has emerged as an independent area to deal with this.

- *Systematic search*
  Certain techniques offer tools to assist in the systematic search for innovations.

The use of techniques is only effective in combination with the first two sources. Creativity techniques in the broadest sense can develop and organize half-formed ideas; they can point out influencing factors and structuring possibilities and expose interdependences.

2.3.2. Analysis of the Business Network

All too often a process is only examined in its familiar context. For example, UNTEL's sales staff tend to look for solutions to their own daily problems in the process design. Examples might be personnel problems in order handling, a high level of bad debts, or conflicts arising from the commission procedure.

They have far less immediate concern with the fact that the retailers are having problems with merchandise management, that consumer electronics and communication technology are merging, that home shopping could become a serious sales channel for UNTEL products, and that transport firms could handle logistics more efficiently than UNTEL.

The business network sets the process in the larger context of the economic sector. It thus draws attention to all the relevant market participants, their value creation and interdependences within the sector. For the sake of clarity it considers only the interactions of the market participants, regarding each participant as a process. For particularly relevant market participants (e.g. consumers) it shows the most important activities in their process. Fig. 2.3.2./1 presents a business network from UNTEL's (sales process) perspective.

The User

The business network proceeds from the user of the company's market outputs (not the process outputs). In UNTEL's case this is the consumer. Ultimately it is the consumer who decides on the value of a product, irrespective of how many stages it passes through before it reaches him. This applies to investment goods as well as consumer goods, to physical goods and to services.

The Value Creation Process

From the user we move backwards as many steps as are relevant to the company's market output. In UNTEL's case these are the steps back to the production of the equipment (consumer electronics, computing and communications technology) and of the media (films, music, publications, programs, games, etc.). For reasons of space Fig. 2.3.2./1 contains only three branches.

Support Processes

The value creation process makes use of many support processes. These range from transport services to the distribution of entertainment media products by television companies, the installation of equipment in the household, and bank credit.

Market services that bring together information about the supply of products and services on one side, and the demand on the other constitute a special kind of support process. This is one of the most important commercial tasks. It is given particular emphasis here because these kinds of market services are increasingly being provided via electronic media, especially networks.

For example, the firm TeleCD offers an online ordering service via Datex-J (formerly BTX) for 130,000 CD titles. For about 100 of these titles the customer can even listen to 15-second excerpts via a voice mailbox [see Brenner/Kolbe 1994, p. 373].

Activities

For the user and other important market participants we formulate the most important activities. The consumer of the electrical entertainment products informs himself about the range of equipment, music, etc. available, purchases and installs the products, uses them, and finally disposes of them. This generates the requirements imposed on the suppliers' processes.

The *business network* shows the significant market participants, the relationships between them, and their most important activities relating to the process outputs.

The customer relationship analysis in Section 2.10. extends the examination of the customer's activities and links them to the activities of the process being investigated.

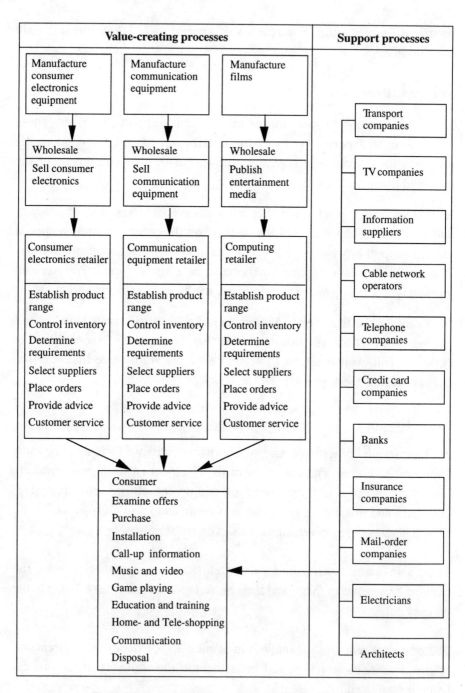

Fig. 2.3.2./1: Business network for UNTEL's sales process

Questions

Against the background of the business network we pose the following questions:

- *Which outputs does the user need?*
  The consumer's activities give rise to his needs. What can UNTEL, and particularly the sales process, contribute to meeting these needs? Examples might be an electronic product catalogue on the public network, support in configuring household electronics and in organizing films, music and photographs.

- *What outputs are exchanged at intermediate stages?*
  What outputs could the process transfer to, or obtain from, other intermediate stages of output creation? The most important market participants from UNTEL's perspective are the retailers. Fig. 2.3.2./2 summarizes some ideas for new or improved trading outputs. Outputs to the manufacturer are also perfectly conceivable. UNTEL could allow suppliers to include their own product information in the electronic product catalogue made available to UNTEL retailers or consumers.

- *What outputs are exchanged with the support processes?*
  The support processes are closely linked with the output creation processes. It is quite natural to offer some outputs oneself, to delegate the provision of other outputs to third parties, or to provide outputs jointly (see the output "direct supply to consumers", for example, in Fig. 2.3.2./2).

- *What outputs do our suppliers, partners and competitors offer?*
  Which of these outputs could we replace with outputs of our own? If the firm TeleCD is successful with its sales via Datex-J, it would be possible to extend its product range to include our products at little technical cost.

Idea Description of the solution	Activities
Periodic market research reports for retailers	Market analysis Sales analysis Sales strategy advice
Using panel data from a market research institute as well as UNTEL customers' sales data a "sales analysis" activity determines sales statistics broken down by manufacturer, type of business, region and product category. In the activity "sales strategy advice" the sales representative discusses these quarterly reports with the customers.	
Merchandise management for retailers	Inventory control (retailer)
Against payment UNTEL offers the retailer a merchandise management system, which determines the target inventory levels using sales as recorded by the point of sale scanners and deliveries from UNTEL. It also handles the usual inventory management functions (e.g. stocktaking) and prepares requirement forecasts on the basis of the retailer's own sales.	
Procurement proposals for retailers	Market analysis Sales analysis Procurement proposal
UNTEL forecasts the retailer's sales and derives a procurement proposal on the basis of sales figures from all UNTEL retailers, market research data, and UNTEL International's sales prognoses, together with the individual retailer's sales figures .	
Electronic product catalogue for retailers	Select article (retailer) Place order (retailer) Order acquisition
The electronic product catalogue replaces the traditional paper catalogue and offers additional functionality, such as extensive detail description, a variety of search possibilities and help in configuring systems.	
Performance-oriented sales management	Sales process management
Performance-oriented sales management is a performance analysis (financial performance indicators) broken down by product, customer and sales representative, and also a process evaluation tool (speed errors, etc.).	
External product ranges	Product range management Search for suppliers Catalogue maintenance
UNTEL's product range is extended to include non-UNTEL products. In particular, these are articles not manufactured by UNTEL.	
Sales costs	Order acquisition
The elimination of avoidable activities within the sales process, and automating sales management as far as possible (e.g. customers' order recording) should lower costs and make competitive pricing possible.	
Product catalogue for consumers	Product range management Catalogue maintenance
UNTEL offers a consumer electronics catalogue directly to the consumer, which contains not only equipment and accessories, but also videos, CDs, etc. Given its worldwide presence the costs to UNTEL of maintaining the product database are low.	

Fig. 2.3.2./2: Directory of ideas (extract)

Idea	**Activity**
Description of the solution	
Direct delivery to consumers	Logistics (UNTEL)
	Customer service (Händler)
	Transport
The retailer configures an order on the basis of the electronic product catalogue. He no longer holds the merchandise in his own stores and transports them to the customer, but instead transmits the order to UNTEL, which then delivers the complete order within 24 hours by direct transport to the customer. If necessary, an electrical engineer can be requested to undertake the installation.	
Electronic product catalogue for suppliers (manufacturers)	Product catalogue management
By means of the product catalogue, UNTEL offers manufacturers a cheap and direct sales channel to the individual retailer and later even to the consumer. The costs to UNTEL consist of those incurred in providing the software for adding new product ranges and for forwarding orders. The UNTEL network must compete, however, with a retailers' business network.	
Shared sales organization	Sales
UNTEL could cooperate with other marketing companies with similar organizational framework conditions in using a shared sales process, and thus exploiting synergies.	
...	

Fig. 2.3.2./2: Directory of ideas (extract, continuation)

- *What outputs can our company offer?*
  Where do our areas of core competence lie? Core competence is that know-how that raises our market output above that of our competitors. What additional outputs could the process offer on the market by exploiting this core competence? UNTEL's core competence currently lies in its knowledge of the regional market and UNTEL products, and as such is fairly narrow. If UNTEL extended its core competence it could potentially convince the retailers of its role as a wholesaler of a wide range of manufacturers, and provide them with support in structuring their product range, finding suppliers and in their merchandise management.

- *How could the outputs be produced?*
  The business network can also yield ideas for potential value creation opportunities. For example, UNTEL could combine with other marketing companies, increasing the number of transactions and thus lowering the fixed cost factor (e.g. per order). Or they could collaborate with electrical engineers in achieving the prerequisites for low-cost household IT systems.

Analysis of the business network proceeds from the needs of the user, translated into demand for market outputs, examines the outputs and their producers, checks the relationships between the market participants, and queries the methods used in output creation.

Result

The business network is a process-oriented extension of Porter's value system [see Porter 1988]. The business network concentrates on outputs and their users, rather than on the kind of output creation process. It makes it easier to recognize a process's potential independent of its actual condition and taking IT possibilities into account.

The result of the sector analysis is a directory of ideas (see Fig. 2.3.2./2).

2.3.3.   The Ideal Process

A second approach to the development of a process vision is in terms of the characteristics of an ideal process. The literature, and practical process design case studies in particular, frequently specify similar process characteristics as the result of a successful redesign. Examples are the avoidance of down time, standardization of process flows, or small, autonomous organizational units.

Section 1.2. summarized business transformations arising from the information revolution and the reorientation of the organization (see Fig. 1.2./1) and thus offers ideas for reassessing processes.

[Davenport 1993, p. 50] subdivided the potential of the information revolution into nine categories. They are also characteristics of an ideal process and hence provide starting points for process assessment:

- *Automational*
  Replacing human effort with computers

- *Informational*
  Management by process indicators

- *Sequential*
  Altering the sequence of process flows or parallelizing tasks

- *Tracking*
  Tracking of business transactions by machine

- *Analytical*
  Improving decision making

- *Geographical*
  Coordinating spatially-distant processes

- *Integrational*
  Coordination between activities and processes

- *Intellectual*
  Collection, communication and preparation of operational knowledge

- *Disintermediating*
  Eliminating intermediate stages in processes

All attempts to describe the ideal characteristics of a process in generally valid terms result in very abstract formulations, which can contribute in only a limited way to the process vision. Attempts to give these characteristics more substance run the risk of requiring a large number of business concepts to be presented repeatedly.

2.3.4. Information Technology

Section 2.9. describes the IT developments, and the derivation of a process-specific IT map. This summarizes the information techniques that are suitable for supporting the process.

By information technology we are referring here less to the IT components (chips, operating systems, network techniques, etc.) than to the application-specific solutions (e.g. package software for electronic product catalogues). In this sense information technology incorporates business concepts and can contribute substantially to the process vision.

2.3.5. Reconciliation of Business Strategy and Process Vision

Reconciliation of the process vision and the business strategy aims to implement the business strategy in the process, and to incorporate the insights of the process vision in the strategy.

UNTEL's business strategy indicates that UNTEL delivers only to the retailer and not directly to the customer. In the vision of the sales process, options for a direct relationship between UNTEL and the consumer arise repeatedly. These options certainly deserve examination, but at the strategy level it is necessary to decide whether UNTEL wants to alter its sales policy so dramatically, especially since direct sales can scarcely be regarded as an extension, but rather as an alternative, to sales via the retailer.

A further example is the three logistical classes of UNTEL's product range. UNTEL aims to deliver A-articles within 24 hours. The sales process must record orders and pass them on to the logistics process in a way that does not endanger this objective. Order recording becomes critical, for example, if the customer faxes his order to his sales representative, who records his orders directly in the order management application every evening.

If a company has specified its current strategy in written terms at all, it can exist in many forms; the content of a business strategy is not standardized. Fig. 2.3.5./1 shows the contents of a strategy to which the process development relates. We restrict ourselves here to the strategy of a strategic business unit. A strategic business unit is a homogenous area of a company's activities, which relates to specific products and/or markets.

Reconciliation of the business strategy and the process vision pursues several goals:

- *Incorporating the strategic targets*
  The targets specified in the business strategy are incorporated in the process vision. The breakdown of the strategy in Fig. 2.3.5./1 helps to check the completeness of the targets.

Mission
Strategic direction
Market
    Sector
        Factors of influence
        Opportunities and dangers
        Competition
        Strengths and weaknesses
    Business partners
        Suppliers
        Customers
        Alliances
    Sales channels
    Market outputs
        Products
        Services
        Pricing policy
    Segmentation
Action plans
    Marketing
    Organization (migration plan)
    Management
    ...

Organization
    Characteristics
    Organizational structure
        Primary org. structure
        Organization of business
segments
        Process organization
        Accounting units
    Locations
    IS-architecture
        Data architecture
        Applications architecture
    IT architecture
Management system
    Success factors
    Performance indicators
        Direct performance indicators
        Financial perform. indicators
    Business objectives
    Management process
Resources
    Finance
    Personnel
    ...

Fig. 2.3.5./1: Contents of a strategy from the process development perspective

- *Considering the dimensions of a process*
  Those aspects that need to be considered within strategic development are also typically relevant to the process. Process development potential can be found in all areas of the strategy and its implementation.

- *Suggestions for strategic development*
  The process vision checks all the decisions in the business strategy from the perspective of the process, and supplements them with additional ideas. These suggestions then flow back into the strategic development.

- *Prioritizing ideas from the development of the vision*
  Reconciliation of the strategy and the vision generate the cornerstones of the process (see Fig. 2.3.5./2), which the detailed design has to accommodate. UNTEL has assigned priority levels (1 to 3) to the principles that are associated with project activities.

Strategic point Principles	Prior- ities
Segmentation	
Differentiation by product and customer segment: The sales process does not differentiate either product or customer segments. The logistic classes are handled identically by sales.	-
Primary organizational structure	
Outsourcing of sales: Sales will not be moved out of UNTEL.	-
Outsourcing of logistics: At the moment there are two competing ideas. The first envisages an UNTEL-specific, pan-European logistics, concentrated in three centres. The second is examining the combining of logistics in Switzerland with two allied companies. The decision remains open.	?
Cost in man-days per year: Reducing the cost of "order acquisition" from 3,000 to 2,000.	1
Sales channels	
Product catalogue for consumers: see directory of ideas. Not currently implementable in the market.	3
Products	
External product ranges: The UNTEL-product range is to be extended to include non-UNTEL products, as soon as the electronic management of the product catalogue is feasible to handle order recording through to transmission of orders to the suppliers and the associated cost allocation. This will ensure that handling costs within UNTEL are low.	2
Services	
Merchandise management: see directory of ideas.	1
Procurement proposals for retailers: see directory of ideas.	2
Electronic product catalogue for retailers: Planned and timetabled.	1
Periodic market research reports: Postponed.	3
Direct delivery to consumers: see directory of ideas. Preliminary study authorized.	2
Financial performance indicators	
Sales process performance analysis by customer, product and sales representative.	1
Direct performance indicators	
Direct performance indicators as specified in the business strategy.	1
...	...

Fig. 2.3.5./2: Principles of the sales process (extract)

2.3.6. General Techniques

The development of a vision is a creative, situation-specific process, for which there are no generally valid techniques. Of course, many of the tried and tested techniques used in strategic development are applicable. Examples are feedback analysis for recognizing factors of influence, developments and interactive effects, and stakeholder analysis for checking the political viability of new organizational forms, etc.

The significance of 'soft' factors must also be emphasized here. Process innovation places stringent demands on the corporate culture, since it aims at transformation across organizational boundaries and involves continuous improvement. We provide references to the relevant literature at the end of the chapter, and restrict ourselves here to techniques for developing the formalized parts of the process.

2.3.7. Summary

The process vision technique aims at radical innovations and the reconciliation of business strategy and process. It uses four components:

- Analysis of the business network

- Characteristics of an ideal process

- Evaluation of information technology

- Checklists for the strategic contents from the process perspective.

Depending on the situation it can be extended to include other techniques, especially those from strategic development.

The results of the process vision are

- a business network,

- a directory of ideas, and

- process principles reconciled with the business strategy.

2.4.   Output Analysis

The output analysis should provide a realistic estimate of process outputs with respect to process customers and in relation to the competition.

UNTEL delivers consumer electronics equipment, such as video recorders, to its customers, the retailers. The retailers sell the video recorders to the consumers. The delivery of video recorders to the retailers is thus an UNTEL output. From this output the retailer obtains the advantage that he is able to make sales to the customer. The price that the retailer is prepared to pay UNTEL for the video recorders depends on the benefit he himself expects from them.

If MITECH, a competitor of UNTEL, offered equivalent video recorders at a lower price, while having a similar market image, the retailer would obtain his video recorders from MITECH. The retailer is prepared to buy video recorders from UNTEL despite the higher price if UNTEL, unlike their competitors, provides a three year guarantee for the equipment, thus offering an additional output that the customer feels is worth the higher price. Another reason for buying from UNTEL might be that UNTEL delivers its video recorders within 24 hours of order receipt. With longer waiting times the retailer runs the risk of losing customers to his competitors.

A company's success depends on what benefits it can offer its customers in comparison with its competitors (value creation - see [Porter 1988]). The same applies to a process, which we can regard as a kind of company within a company (entrepreneurship). Process design must proceed from the customer benefits, and analyze the outputs that a process either obtains (inputs) or delivers (outputs).

UNTEL must establish which outputs it might offer the customer, and how the quality of these outputs compares with that of its competitors. The following treatment is restricted to the sales process and its outputs. The distribution of the merchandise is the responsibility of the logistics process. The sales process must therefore offer its customers other benefits. What is the nature of these benefits?

2.4.1. Context Diagram

A context diagram provides a preliminary overview of a process's inputs and outputs (see Fig. 2.4.1./1 for the sales process).

The *context diagram* shows the flow of outputs between processes. The nodes represent the process under examination and the processes that communicate with it, the arrows represent the outputs that are exchanged between the processes. For clarity's sake the context diagram only contains the important outputs.

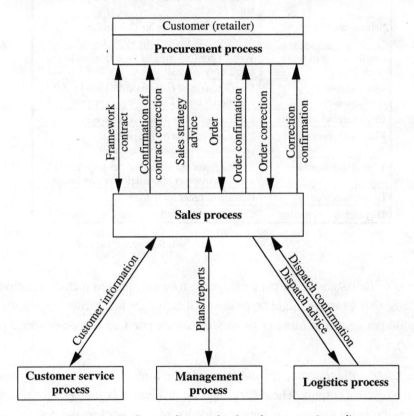

Fig. 2.4.1./1: Context diagram for the sales process (actual)

2.4.2.   Output Catalogue

The *output catalogue* supplements the context diagram with a verbal description of the outputs (see Fig 2.4.2./1).

Output	Description
Order	Single order from retailer Variant A: via sales representative Variant B: via telephone / fax / letter
Order confirmation	Order confirmation by telephone / letter / fax
Order amendment	Retailer's order amendment by telephone / letter / fax
Sales strategy advice	Unpaid advice to the handler on the development of his own sales strategy
Confirmation of order modification	Written confirmation of modification to the framework contract
Modification confirmation	Confirmation of order modification by telephone/ letter / fax
Customer information	Current customer data in a database
Plans and reports	Plans and reports on the process's performance indicators (database)
Framework contract	Basic agreement in writing between UNTEL and the customer about delivery conditions
Dispatch advice	Release of order for delivery (database)
Dispatch confirmation	Confirmation of order delivery (database)

Fig. 2.4.2./1: Output catalogue for sales process (actual)

For specific issues the output catalogue can be extended to include additional details. One example might be process indicators for measuring the quality of the output (e.g. the number of modifications per framework contract per year).

The context diagram and the output catalogue force the explicit specification of the process outputs. The difficulties that this typically involves for process development within companies is evidence of how unclear the notions of a process's outputs often are. As a result it is also unclear what value the process offers its customers, and whether the costs are in line with the benefits.

If UNTEL were to query the quality of its outputs, it might make the following statements:

- Many customers feel that important details are missing from the order confirmation, for example, delivery dates for each item ordered.

- Many customers are dissatisfied with the advise provided by UNTEL in developing their own sales strategy.

- Many customers regard confirmation of modifications to the framework contract as unnecessary.

The context diagram and/or the output catalogue give rise to a broad analysis of outputs, in which questions such as the following are posed:

- Are outputs unimportant to the customer, and hence superfluous?
- Do the outputs fulfil the requirements and expectations of the process customers?
- Are some outputs missing?
- Is the existing number of output types and variants appropriate?

2.4.3. Quality Profile

The quality profile is a tool for the detailed analysis of individual outputs.

For example, if UNTEL discovers that many retailers are dissatisfied with the support they are given in developing their sales strategy it must identify the causes and ways of making improvements. Would it be appropriate to double the number of customer visits? Or does the customer expect to be provided with more detailed market analyses?

A quality profile is based on four steps:

- Identification of output components and output characteristics

- Selection of customer sample

- Surveying the process customers

- Evaluation

We will discuss these four steps using the example of the output "sales strategy advice".

Identification of Output Components and Output Characteristics

Under the heading "sales strategy advice" retailers currently receive the following output components from their suppliers:

- The provision of market analyses

- Help in positioning their merchandise within the shop

- Help in composing their product range

- Electronic product and service catalogue

UNTEL does not currrently provide help in composing their product range or an electronic product catalogue. On this basis alone their output "sales strategy advice" is regarded by the customers as meagre.

The first criterion for evaluating an output is in terms of the *components* that an output incorporates.

UNTEL's customers are also dissatisfied with the two output components that UNTEL does offer. The advice is perceived as not sufficiently competent, too infrequent and too brief. Competence, frequency of visits and consultancy time are characteristics that relate to the individual output components, or the entire output.

The second criterion for the quality of an output is that of the *characteristics* of individual output components or the output as a whole.

Output characteristics are a particular kind of performance indicator and, like them, can be derived from the success factors (see Section 2.7.).

Output components and characteristics together constitute the criteria for evaluating an output (see Fig. 2.4.3./1).

Output components	Significance	Present ⬅————➡ Absent				
Preparation of market analysis	⬤				●⎯⎯○	
Placement of goods	⬤		○	●		
Composition of product range	⬤		○			●
Electronic product catalogue	⬤					●○

Output attributes	Significance	Completely fulfilled ⬅————➡ Not fulfilled				
Competence of sales representatives	⬤	○			●	
Frequency of visits	⬤			○	●	
Consultation time	⬤				●○	

Legend:
——— Own company (UNTEL)
- - - - Strongest competitor (MITECH)

Fig. 2.4.3./1: Quality profile for the output "sales strategy advice""

Selection of Customer Sample

The output "sales strategy advice" applies to the 690 specialist and discount stores (97 % of UNTEL customers with 75 % of the turnover), whereas the department stores and mail order firms develop their strategy independently. The survey can therefore be restricted to this customer segment.

Since a complete survey of all the 690 retailers would be unjustifiably expensive, the project team selects a total of 50 customers, who are approximately evenly distributed over the regions.

The sample to be surveyed for the quality profile must clearly delineate the customer segment, and pay attention to the most important influences within that segment. Such influences might be regional peculiarities (e.g. purchasing power), customer details (e.g. retailer size) etc.

Surveying the Process Customers

The interviewer records the following evaluations from the customer (see Fig. 2.4.3./1):

- The importance of the components and their characteristics to him (unimportant, important, very important)

- The quality of the components and their characteristics with respect to UNTEL

- The quality of the components and their characteristics with respect to UNTEL's most significant competitor.

Evaluation

The assessments recorded in the survey generate the quality profile (see Fig. 2.4.3./1):

What can UNTEL deduce from the quality profile? Where are the opportunities for offering the customer a significant benefit advantage as compared with competitors?

- The customers are less satisfied with the UNTEL's sales representatives' competence and frequency of visits than with MITECH's. In both cases the gap between UNTEL and the strongest competitor is considerable.

- A good opportunity exists to differentiate UNTEL from MITECH in the case of the two components: "provision of market analyses" and "electronic product catalogue". In both components the customers see considerable room for improvement.

Quality is not to be achieved at any price. The necessary quality level is a consequence of the customer benefits and the comparison with competitors. For example, it would make no sense in cost terms to double the outlay on market analyses, when this would not generate any additional benefits to the customer for which he would be prepared to pay a higher price, and when the competition has no advantage in this area.

The *quality profile* of outputs shows

- the components and characteristics of the process outputs,
- their significance for the process customers, and
- the process customers' evaluation of one's own outputs and those of the most significant competitor.

It helps in assessing the customer benefits, establishing the company's own position in relation to competitors, and deriving actions (aimed at components and characteristics) .

2.4.4. Summary

Process design must proceed from the benefits that the process can offer its customers as compared with the competition. Once the process vision has focused attention on the outputs, it is the task of output analysis to record, evaluate and document the outputs in detail. Since the customer is in the best position to assess his requirements and the benefits of outputs offered, he should be included in the design.

2.5. Flow Planning

The purpose of flow planning is to determine a process's activities and their sequence, and assign them to the organizational units. Applying flow planning to UNTEL's sales process yields (see Fig. 2.5.1./1) the activities "order acquisition" and "order processing". Executed in this order these activities produce the outputs "order confirmation" and "dispatch advice". "Order acquisition" is the activity of a sales representative, "order processing" is carried out by Sales Support. An application supports both activities.

Output analysis determines the content of a process, that is its effectiveness, in that it establishes the outputs to the process customers.
Flow planning is concerned with the method of the process, that is its efficiency. It establishes which activities carried out in which order produce the predefined outputs.

2.5.1. Deriving the Process Flows

Which activities does UNTEL's sales process require? We use the following approaches to identify the activities:

Derivation from the Outputs

In Section 2.4. we identified the outputs of UNTEL's sales process for this process's customers (customers' procurement and service, management and logistics in UNTEL). The most important were: sales strategy, framework contract, order confirmation, correction confirmation, customer information, plans and reports, and dispatch advice. The activities of the sales process must generate these outputs.

For the sales strategy output, for example, we could derive the following:

• Advise the customer on procurement

• Prepare consultative discussion

• Customer acquisition and account management

• Market analysis

Starting from the output we proceed backwards to the activities, including supporting preparatory activities, that collectively generate the output.

The process typology from the architecture planning can help to check the completeness of the activities (see Fig. 2.8.1./2). It describes activities that arise in one form or another in the production of any given market output - irrespective of the sector.

Derivation from Business Objects

The outputs listed above are based on the following *business objects*: market analysis, framework contract, article, order and customer. An output is the result of processing an object. For example, the "framework contract" output is the result of several activities for adjusting a standard contract to a specific customer.

What activities arise in connection with the object "framework contract"?

- Preparation of a framework contract
- Preparation of a consultative discussion (the consultative discussion deals with conditions)
- Create contract offer (adjustment to the specific customer)
- Negotiate and agree framework contract
- Check framework contract (for conformity with sales guidelines)
- Adjust framework contract
- Terminate framework contract

A *business object* is a real or conceptual object of output creation Business partner, assets, materials, orders, contracts, etc. are typical examples.

For any business object, a process must carry out a sequence of activities from its creation to its termination.

The derivation of activities from business objects within organization design corresponds to the derivation of transactions from the "Entity Life History" in functional design (see Section 4.4.2.).

Derivation of Activities from Process Customers

UNTEL subdivides a retailer's procurement process into its most important components. In describing the customer's procurement process all those activities associated with the procurement of merchandise, from agreeing on a framework contract through to processing an order, are taken into account (see Section 2.10.).

Following the customer's procurement process, the sequence of activities in their own sales process is defined, and at the same time the links between the two corresponding processes are indicated.

The benefits of an output can be identified most easily by examining the needs of the output customer. This requires analysis of the process customer's activities.

Derivation From the Actual State

The activity chain diagram and the activity catalogue describe the existing state of the activities that Sales currently undertakes. For example, they indicate that the customer places an order with the sales representative, that he receives the order, which is then centrally recorded and confirmed.

Derivation from the activities in the actual state carries with it the danger that the new process cannot disassociate itself from the existing situation; it impedes the search for fundamentally new approaches. However, the activities in the existing process are an important checklist for assessing the completeness of a target state that has been derived from the outputs.

The actual state serves to check the completeness of a target state.

Selecting the Important Activities

If we exhaust all four sources from which activities can be derived we obtain a considerable number of activities for the sales process. But our preliminary aim is to obtain an overview, and develop a preliminary outline of the process flow. So we summarize the activities and disregard unimportant aspects.

But what is important? The answer lies basically in the intuition of the designer. The following criteria can provide some direction:

- An activity should constitute about 10% of the total process effort.
- An activity should be standardizable. Standardization means that the activity should proceed identically, irrespective of the employee undertaking it, or the place and time of processing, and should produce the same results.
- An activity either creates or uses an important result (e.g. a decision).

Similarly, we concentrate on the most important dependencies between the activities and the most important task bearers.

Flow planning for the sales process has produced the activity chain diagram in Fig. 2.5.1./1. Each activity fulfils one or more of the above criteria:

- "Order acquisition" and "customer acquisition and account management" constitute a large proportion of the cost of the sales process. At present a sales representative makes 250 visits to potential customers, and advises existing customers 750 times. At the same time sales representatives and order recording currently record 15,000 orders and 4,500 order amendments per year.

- The activities "order acquisition" and "order processing" are highly standardized. The remaining activities leave the employee considerable freedom, and require situation-specific handling. We can regard these as standardized to the extent that they should always generate the same results.

- The activities "develop sales strategy", "market analysis" and "order processing" do not (any longer) involve great expense in the target state, but they do generate important results.

UNTEL has decided to aim at a medium term implementation of the merchandise management system and other options mentioned in Section 2.2. At the moment it is restricting itself to the core of the sales process, as shown in the activity chain diagram in Fig. 2.5.1./1.

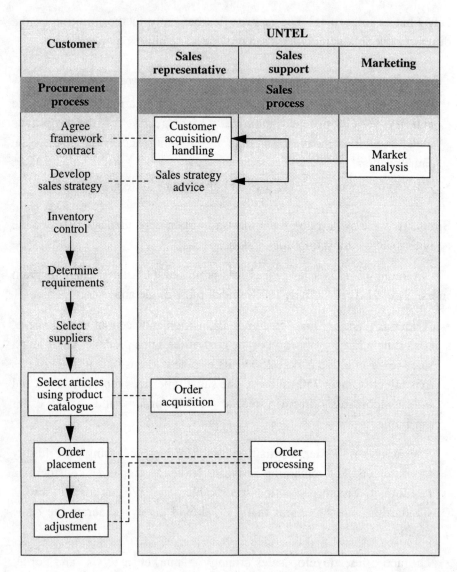

Fig. 2.5.1./1: Breakdown of UNTEL's (target) sales process

2.5.2.   Detailing the Flow

Fig. 2.5.1./1 provides an introduction to the sales process. It gives an overview and helps to elucidate fundamental issues (e.g. outputs to customers) at the macro-level.

The highest level of flow description is referred to as the *macro-level*. It gives an overview of the entire process.

Many possibilities for improving processes are to be found in the detailed flows. If UNTEL's sales process circle is looking for the source of errors in order recording, or considering the possibilities for early recognition of sales trends, i.e. improvements in sales planning, it must investigate the activities in greater detail. Similarly, a systems designer must examine every single order recording step for an order management application.

For example, UNTEL refines the sales process into the sub-process "order acquisition" (see Fig. 2.5.2./1). It breaks down the activities "order acquisition" and "order processing" into the sub-tasks "accept order via sales representative", "record EDIFACT purchase order", "check extraordinary cases", "order recording" and "order confirmation" and determines the sequence of activities. In addition it differentiates the customer's activities by sales channel.

Since the activity "record EDIFACT purchase order" is undertaken by the computer (order management application) without staff intervention, it is located in the order management column. The order management column has a white background to indicate that the process is performed by computer and not manually.

This increased level of detail makes it possible to recognize transport times (e.g. postal order placement), multiple tasks, problematic sub-activities (e.g. receive order via sales representative), etc. We therefore break down individual activities at the macro-level into their sub-activities, specify their sequence and assign them to the processors. The rules for deriving and selecting activities in Section 2.5.1. apply similarly here.

Extent of the Breakdown

The detailing of a process can extend through several levels. But how far should the activities be broken down? A sub-process should be broken down until the flow is clear to the design team, the process circle and the process employees.

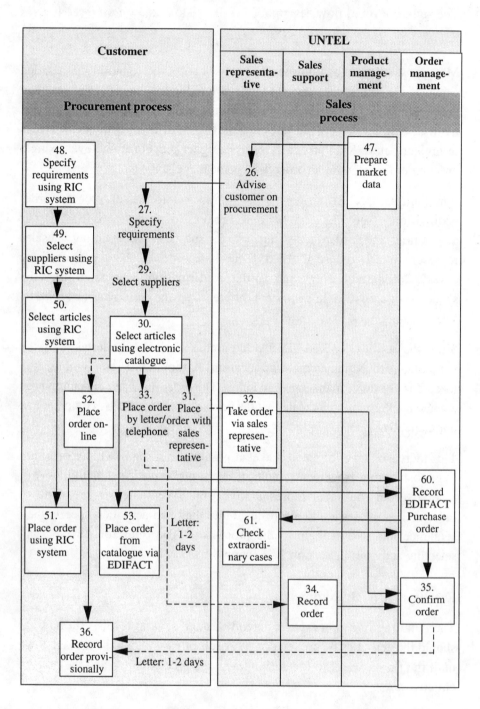

Fig. 2.5.2./1: Activity chain for the "order acquisition" sub-process (target)

A sub-process is excessively broken down,

- if no significant improvements result from the breakdown, or

- if the process employees reject the working instructions because they regulate the obvious.

Fig. 2.5.2./1, for example, could also describe what should happen in the case of errors in order receipts by sales representatives. The employees concerned would regard this as bureaucratic over-regimentation, since the cost of formalizing outweighs the benefits to be expected from it.

The *micro-level* describes activities, their sequence and their assignment to processors in sufficient detail that their contents are clear to the employees responsible.

To execute the process and develop supporting computer applications it is necessary that the process flow is clear to all employees involved.

Criteria for Defining a Sub-Process

A process can be broken down in many different ways. Are there criteria for a "good" breakdown? Why did we derive the sub-process "order acquisition" in the sales process example?

It is difficult to specify generally valid rules. Basically the criteria for deriving activities (see Section 2.5.1.) and the criteria for deriving processes (see Section 2.8.) may be similarly applied to the derivation of sub-processes:

- *Outputs to the process customers*
  The sub-process combines all the activities involved in producing an output or set of outputs.

- *Business objects*
  The sub-process combines all those activities needed throughout the existence of a business object.

- *Customer processors*
  The sub-process corresponds to a customer's process.

- *Process types*
  The sub-process covers one or more operational functions from a process typology (e.g. Fig. 2.8.1./2).

- *Segmentation*
  The sub-process deals with one process variant for a specific segments of customers, products, regions, technologies, or certain sales channels, etc. (see Section 2.8.1. on segmentation).

Often the different breakdown criteria give rise to the same results. The breakdown criterion generating the most efficient flow can be determined by comparing the results of the alternative methods.

Modelling the Actual State

To what extent must or can we model the actual state?

Considering only the actual state prevents the design process from adequately disassociating itself from the existing situation and involves high recording costs. These problems can be mitigated by the benefits from insights into the target state:

- *Checking completeness*
  The completeness of the target state could be checked against the actual state (see "Derivation from the Activities of the Actual State" above).

- *Explaining the Change*
  Explaining a reorganization proposal (particularly its efficiency) often requires a comparison of the target and the actual states.

The actual state is required to check the completeness of the target state and to explain reorganization proposals.

2.5.3.   Documenting the Flow

The result of flow planning is a *flow specification*, which first serves the process employees as a blueprint for their practical work, but also forms the basis for the IS development (or software selection and introduction). The

flow specification consists of the activity chain diagram, the activity catalogue
and the job documentation.

Activity Chain Diagram

The activity chain diagram documents the flow of a process or sub-process. It
is the central document in the conception, and above all, the communication
of processes.

Nodes

In an activity chain diagram a node represents an activity. Completely or
partially computerized activities have a light background. At the micro-level
(see Fig. 2.5.2./1) each activity receives an activity number, which creates an
unambiguous reference to the activity in the activity catalogue (see below).

Edges

Edges (lines) describe temporal dependencies between activities:

- A broken, horizontal line indicates that both activities are undertaken
  simultaneously.
- A solid arrow (directional edge) indicates that the next activity can only
  begin on completion of the preceding one.
- A broken arrow indicates that the next activity can begin only after some
  delay.
- If two activities are linked neither directly nor indirectly, they are
  concurrent, i.e. they can be undertaken sequentially or simultaneously.

Columns

Columns (vertical boxes) represent processors. Processors are either
organizational units (grey background) or applications (white background).
Activities in the columns are assigned to organizational units or applications.

The activity chain diagram for a process also generally describes the activities
of the cooperating process.

The activity chain diagram in the style of Fig. 2.5.1./1 contains little detail
about a process; in the case of specific questions it needs to be supplemented
with details such as:

- Transport, down times and processing times

- Frequency of flows (e.g. order channels)

- Control constructs (rules for selecting alternative process flows)

- A set of symbols for types of activities (e.g. data recording, corrections, queries).

Thus information is used depending on the context (see time details in Fig. 2.5.2./1.). Organization design typically employs design tools which determine the use of such data in the activity chain diagram.

Activity Catalogue

The activity chain diagram presented covers only the core of the organization design. It does not help UNTEL deduce which activities contribute to the high sales costs, or how many employees are needed for each sales region?

The activity chain diagram presents an overview; to handle specific issues it is supplemented by the activity catalogue (see Fig. 2.5.3./1). For each activity this contains an unambiguous activity number, the name of the activity, the organizational unit undertaking it, the application or transaction supporting the activity, and details of the orders of magnitude.

Much information arises during organization design. For instance, details of the applications or transactions are initially vague, but by the end of the organization design the transactions or applications like text processing must be specified precisely.

The *activity catalogue* supplements the activity chain diagram with additional details relating to the individual activities.

No	Activity	OU	Application/ Transaction	Frequency		
					Time needed	
						Cost
47	Prepare market data	PM	Nielson information system	6	16	96
26	Advise customer on procurement	SR		3'000	4	12'000
32	Receive order via sales representative	SR	OM/central online order recording	3'000	1	3'000
34	Order recording	SA	OM/central online order recording	3'000	0.25	750
60	Record EDIFACT purchase order	CM	OM/receive and check EDIFACT purchase order	6'000	-	-
61	Clarify special cases	SR	OR/order modification CM/search and display customer address Text processing Spreadsheet analysis	1'000	0.5	500
35	Order confirmation	CO	OM/print order / modification confirmation OM/accept EDIFACT purchase order OM/Reject EDIFACT purchase order	12'000	-	-

Fig. 2.5.3./1: Activity catalogue for the sub-process "order acquisition" (see List of Abbreviations for abbreviations used)

High administrative costs per order are one of UNTEL's central problems. Using process cost estimation UNTEL determines the costs per activity and extends the "standard activity catalogue" with an additional column for the costs per activity. Typical additions to the activity catalogue are costs, error rates, locations, equipment, authority and execution prescriptions.

Position Documents

In addition to the activity chain diagram and the activity catalogue, a position assessment is also needed in the design of a process. The position documents summarize activities by position (smallest organizational unit) and determine the required number of positions on the basis of a capacity plan. In addition, it describes the competence and responsibility of every position, the qualification requirements, rules of deputization, etc.

The structure of positions and capacity planning, as well as the documents they generate (typically function diagram, position description and organizational chart) receive detailed treatment in the organization literature [e.g. Schmidt 1991, pp. 263-272] and can be applied to a process-oriented organization without any difficulty. Consequently, we do not discuss them further here.

2.5.4. Summary

Beginning with the outputs, flow planning specifies the process method, that is the activities, their sequence, and their assignment to the organizational units. Activities can be derived from the process outputs, the business objects, and the process customers' activities, and can be checked for completeness against the actual state.

Flow planning breaks down the macro-level, through a number of steps, to the micro-level. The macro-level gives an overview of the entire process; the micro-level provides directions for executing the process.

The core of the flow specification consists of the activity chain diagram, the activity catalogue, supplemented by position documents (function diagram, position description, etc.)

2.6. Workflow Planning

The result of the flow planning (Section 2.5.) is the flow specification. It consists of the activity chain diagram, the activity catalogue and the position documents. The flow specification is so detailed that those involved in the process can work from it (see the micro-process "order acquisition" in Fig. 2.5.2./1). The process employees attempt to undertake the tasks (e.g. orders) according to the specification. Adherence to the specification and the details of the flow are left to the employees.

2.6.1. Manual Flow Control

How does manual flow control operate in the case of the "order acquisition" micro-process? Let us restrict ourselves to the acceptance of an EDIFACT order (see Section 2.2.1.2.). A customer places an order with UNTEL via

EDIFACT, but modifies the conditions agreed in the framework contract. This initiates the following activities within UNTEL:

- The order management application checks the EDIFACT order, establishes the deviation in conditions, and notifies the sales representative responsible.

- The sales representative decides whether the modified conditions can simply be accepted, or whether a discussion with the customer is needed to clarify the conditions. If the deviation is only minor (e.g. extending the payment period by two weeks), the sales representative can exercise his own judgement. In doing so he uses the customer management application to examine the customer's payment behaviour and his contribution margin. Using a spreadsheet he determines what the deviation in conditions will cost, and compares these costs with the contribution margin for the order.

- For a payment period of more than 30 days the sales representative's instructions are that he must make credit inquiries before accepting the order.

- In the case of major deviation from the conditions he must inform the sales manager. The sales manager receives the spreadsheet, the relevant extracts from the customer documentation, and a proposed decision from the sales representative. On the basis of this information the sales manager decides whether to accept or reject the order.

- The sales representative or sales manager use text processing to prepare a personalized message to the customer, which is passed on to the order management application, together with the acceptance or rejection decision. From here the personalized text is sent to the customer with the order confirmation or rejection.

Manual flow control can give rise to problems such as the following:

- A sales representative exceeds his authority in accepting orders, because adherence to the authorization regulations is not monitored, or because new sales representatives are not informed of the existing rules. If the case involves an important customer and a short term delivery deadline the sales representative may by-pass the sales manager to avoid losing the order or the customer.

- For reasons of time the sales representatives tend to obtain credit information after accepting the order.

- If the customer attempts to find out whether his order has been accepted, there are problems identifying its current location, since the sales representative and the sales manager are both difficult to contact. An important customer may apply pressure, leading to an over-hasty acceptance.

- Since several positions are involved and at busy times such tasks are easily deferred, several days may pass before the order is confirmed - a delay which the customer perceives as poor service.

Summarizing, we can conclude that:

In *manual flow control* the employees are responsible for controlling the flow. The employee is given considerable freedom to interpret the specification of the flow; adherence to instructions is difficult to monitor; passing on documentation in paper form costs much time; and it is difficult to establish the degree of progress in processing the task.

2.6.2. Flow Control Using a Workflow Management System

Using a Workflow Management System (WFMS) to control the process flows helps mitigate the problem above. The WFMS initiates activities, provides the necessary data, checks the results of the activity, monitors deadlines, etc.

A *Workflow Management System* controls the workflow between the positions involved and in accordance with the flow specification.

Let us examine the same flow as above, as it would be controlled by a Workflow Management System (WFMS) (see Fig. 2.6.2./1). The event "EDIFACT purchase order arrives" initiates a procedure (workflow). If the "receive and check EDIFACT purchase order" transaction in the order management application establishes that the customer has specified conditions that do not accord with those agreed, the WFMS assigns the sales representative the task of checking the conditions. It also informs him of the order number and the deviation in conditions that has been identified. The WFMS stores the order passed to the employee as an outstanding item.

The sales representative receives the message that a new task has arrived. The task is removed from his electronic mailbox, which contains all the tasks awaiting processing. As the sales representative selects a task from his mailbox the WFMS calls up the necessary transaction. In the case of checking the order conditions the WFMS starts up the "search/display customer address" and "order modification" transactions and loads a spreadsheet program. In a formatted spreadsheet (template) the sales representative can calculate various alternatives for presentation to the customer.

If the deviation in conditions exceeds the sales representatives authority, the WFMS passes on the order (electronically), after it is processed by the sales representative, to the sales manager. If the deviation is only minor the sales representative can authorize the order himself ("order modification" transaction).

The WFMS provides the sales representative with a text processing program, with which he can either select prepared pieces of text or enter his own individual text. This text, which presents a statement regarding the deviation in conditions, is incorporated in a "purchase order response message" to the customer.

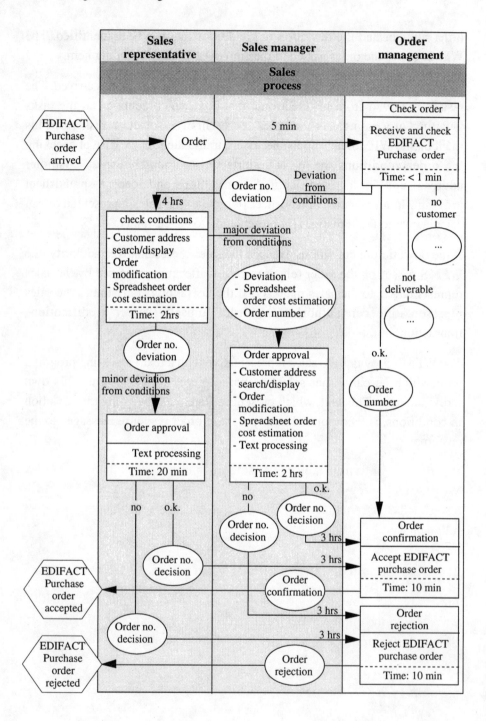

Fig. 2.6.2./1: Sub-process (workflow) "accept EDIFACT order"

If the flow specification requires a credit investigation to be made, the WFMS can ensure that the credit information must be in the system (e.g. as a document read in via a scanner) before the sales representative can accept the order. The "order modification" transaction can check this.

If the WFMS passes on an order with major deviation in conditions to the sales manager it not only transfers the order number and the deviation to the sales manager, but also the spreadsheet with the sales representative's proposal.

The WFMS ensures that the flow specification is followed. It controls the progress of a task from its initiation to its conclusion (event) and supports its execution by providing information, transactions and applications. It provides information about the processing status, about employees' work loads, about the number of repeated operations, etc. It takes on, within administration, a similar function to that of the manufacturing control centre in a factory. A brief introduction to the functionality of a WFMS is given in Section 4.11. "Workflow Design".

Flow control by machine requires a high level of flow standardization. It is only economically feasible for flows in which many operations have to be undertaken in accordance with clear rules.

WFMSs are only in use in a few experimental pilot installations. Neither WFMS technology nor workflow planning techniques are yet well-developed. Consequently, this discussion of workflow planning is rather rudimentary.

2.6.3. Extended Activity Chain Diagram

In Section 2.5, flow planning broke down a flow to the micro-level until it was clear to the employees involved. If a WFMS is to control the flow, the flow specification needs to be refined and supplemented by the following points.

- *Event*
  One or more (start) events (in our example "receive EDIFACT purchase order) initiate an operation. One or more (end) events (e.g. "order rejected" or "order accepted") conclude the operation.

- *Applications and transactions*
  For the WFMS to provide the necessary computer support for undertaking activities, the office applications (text processing including forms, spreadsheet analysis including templates, etc.) and the transactions ("receive and check EDIFACT purchase order" etc.) must be specified.

- *Data flow*
  The data flow describes the data exchanged between the activities. It consists of "coded" data, such as an order number, and "non-coded" documents, such as spreadsheets.

- *Conditions*
  Conditions contain the prerequisites for initiation of an activity by the WFMS. An example might be the conditions for determining minor or major deviations from framework contract conditions. The condition for a minor deviation might be framed as follows:

  Minor deviation from conditions
  IF   credit required <= 120 % of credit limit
  AND   order discount <= maximum order discount
  AND   article price >= purchase price + 2 * contribution margin 1

To handle these additional details the activity chain diagram from Section 2.5. needs to be extended:

- *Activity nodes (rectangle)*
  In addition to order number and description, the transactions and applications used, as well as the average processing time are specified.

- *Data nodes (oval)*
  Data and documents that flow between the activities are represented within ovals.

- *Event-nodes (hexagon)*
  Events are states arising as a result of an activity or time. Examples are "EDIFACT purchase order arrives" or "6:00 pm".

- *Edge inscriptions*

- Condition
  An edge can be inscribed at its starting point with a condition for selecting this route.

- Time delay
  Down times and transport times are indicated at the end of an edge.

A *workflow* is a special kind of flow at the micro-level, for which a Workflow Management System, and not the process employee, coordinates activities. The WFMS requires additional details to facilitate flow control by machine.

2.6.4. Summary

A Workflow Management System controls the execution of a flow. Flow control by machine requires a much more highly detailed specification than manual flow control. The cost of this flow formalization is justified only if the flow is executed very frequently.

2.7. Process Management

The aim of *process management* is the continuous improvement of the effectiveness and efficiency of a process.

Process management plans, structures, and observes the process (see Fig. 2.7./1). It determines the performance indicators for evaluating the process, sets objectives, compares targets with achievements, derives actions for improving the process and monitors process implementation.

At UNTEL, sales have been managed primarily via turnover, broken down by customer, article and sales representative. UNTEL has two contribution margins: contribution margin 1 (turnover - cost price - representatives commission) and contribution margin 2 (contribution margin 1 - logistics costs - administrative costs).

These figures provide only limited assistance in managing the sales process, because there is no direct link to the employees' activities. The sales representatives do not know the profitability of the individual orders, since the contribution margins are only summaries and are not calculated on an order-specific basis. In addition the sales manager cannot discover the source of his costs, whether they are from smaller order quantities, frequent reworking of orders, or cumbersome procedures. He also has no idea whether the quality of advice is improving. Those involved in the process do not receive the right information to allow them to evaluate the process.

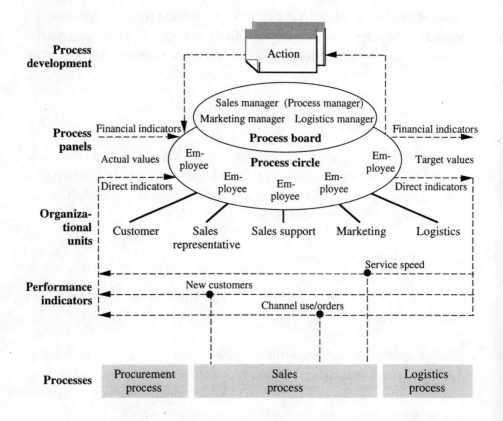

Fig. 2.7./1: Process management in the process model

Financial indicators such as the contribution margin per sales representative are derived variables. They are condensed, monetarized, and frequently available only much later. They document the result of a process, but do not explain it. An employee would have difficulty in deriving measures to improve his operative activities or in recognizing fundamental problems with the process.

In the existing organization UNTEL also has no systematic approach to process improvement. The sales staff take the flows as given and do not take the initiative themselves. Ideas and actions arise by chance and are badly implemented. Sales representatives and sales support each maintain their isolated perspective and blame each other for any shortcomings. Nobody is responsible for the process as a whole.

How can a company develop effective process management? Fig. 2.7./2 presents three steps: First, the company must identify those factors that are decisive to the success of the process concerned. Second, it must identify variables for measuring these success factors (performance indicators) which can be used to assess its progress. Third, it must agree on the competence and responsibility for the effectiveness and efficiency of the process.

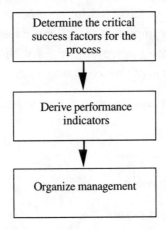

Fig. 2.7./2: Procedure for establishing process management

2.7.1. Determining a Process's Critical Success Factors

UNTEL's success depends primarily on its competence, its brand image, speed and costs. Of course, other factors also influence its success e.g. cash management or customer relations. But management means concentrating on what is important (reducing complexity). UNTEL's corporate management therefore aim their actions primarily at these four factors, the critical success factors (CSFs).

The *concept of critical success factors* states that a few factors are decisive to the success of a company or a process. The critical success factors help process management to concentrate on what matters.

For overall success, above-average outputs are required from each of the success factors; the success factors must always be examined in their entirety. UNTEL will not be successful if it carries excessive inventories in order to fulfil immediately every customer requirement, but ignores the costs of such inventories.

How does UNTEL identify the critical success factors? The sales representatives, sales manager and corporate management respectively consider close customer ties, administrative efficiency and the company image as especially important. Although determining the critical success factors by a team of those involved in the process presents difficulties in practice, it is particularly important that all those responsible for the process (process board, see below) agree objectives with each other and pursue common aims in the course of process management.

Three starting points can provide orientation for deriving the critical success factors:

- The corporate critical success factors

- Generally applicable process success factors

- Process-specific success factors

Corporate Critical Success Factors

UNTEL's business strategy specifies competence, image, speed and costs as the critical success factors for the entire company. From these, success factors for the sales process can be derived (see Fig. 2.7.1./1).

UNTEL success factor	Derived success factors for UNTEL's sales process	Critical success factor?
Competence	Quality of sales representatives advice	yes
Image	Error-free handling of customer contacts	yes
Speed	Speed	yes
Costs	Sales costs	yes

Fig 2.7.1./1: Deriving the process CSFs from the corporate CSFs

Generally Applicable Process Success Factors

Satisfying customer needs is the basis for the success of every process. The customer wants the output at a specific time for a specific price and with specific characteristics. Furthermore, different customers have different and changing requirements. This gives rise to generally applicable process success factors:

- *Time*
  Process outputs are created quickly; agreed deadlines are met.

- *Quality*
  The output fulfils customer requirements when compared with competitors.

- *Costs*
  The output is produced efficiently, and hence at a competitive price.

- *Flexibility*
  The outputs meet the varying customer needs.

Fig. 2.7.1./2 illustrates these four factors together with the process characteristics that contribute to these success factors.

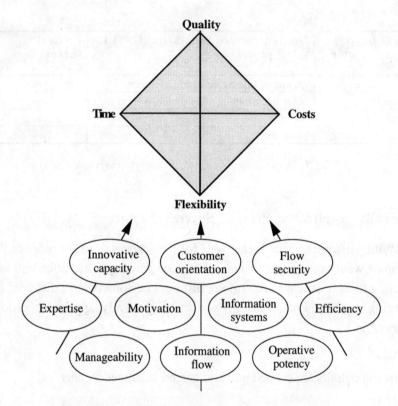

Fig. 2.7.1./2: Generally applicable process success factors

From these UNTEL has derived the success factors in Fig. 2.7.1./3.

General process success factors	Success factors for UNTEL's sales process	Critical success factor?
Time	Processing speed (offers, orders, etc..)	yes
Costs	Sales costs	yes
Quality	Account management quality (error-free handling, range of management outputs, etc.)	yes
Flexibility	Ability to handle special requirements (e.g. delivery of configured systems)	no
Know-how	Sales representatives' know-how	yes

Fig. 2.7.1./3: Generally applicable process success factors for the sales example

The selection of these five success factors does not imply that other factors such as motivation or innovative capacity are of no importance, but that UNTEL regards the factors selected as critical.

Process-Specific Success Factors

In addition to success factors that apply to the whole company or to processes generally, each process has its own specific situation. Two approaches to identifying process-specific success factors are:

- *Feedback diagram*
  A simple feedback diagram describes the interplay of influential factors. A network diagram helps to recognize factors that have been ignored thus far.

- *Stakeholder analysis*
  Stakeholder analysis identifies the group of people who influence the process and apply different measures of success. Typical influence groups are:

  - Employees
    Worker representatives, process participants, management staff, etc.

  - Market participants
    Customers, suppliers, competitors, cooperating partners, etc.

  - Providers of capital
    Shareholders, lenders etc.

  - The public
    Consumer protection groups, environmental protection groups, traffic, etc.

Analysis of technical development (especially in public data networks) and market participants demonstrate to UNTEL that close electronic customer links will have a decisive effect on costs and customer ties within a few years.

Combining all this, UNTEL identifies the following critical success factors for its sales:

- Processing speed
- Sales representatives' know-how
- Sales costs
- Quality of account management
- Utilization of electronic customer links

Not more than five success factors should be defined as critical for any single process.

Fig. 2.7.1./4 gives an overview of the procedure for establishing a process's critical success factors. Deriving, weighting and achieving consensus on the process CSFs is the responsibility of the line managers in the organizational units involved in the process. Process management can only be successful if its tools are understood and accepted. If it can also involve process customers in the consensus reached this is an important step towards meaningful customer orientation.

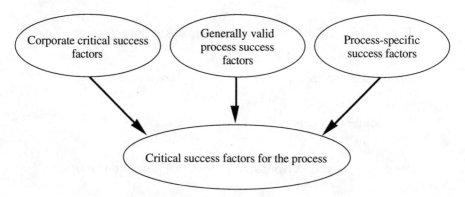

Fig. 2.7.1./4: Identifying a process's critical success factors

2.7.2.   Deriving the Performance Indicators

Success factors can only become effective if they influence the operative management. Performance indicators link the process with its success factors. They indicate the status a process has achieved with respect to its critical success factors. In other words, they indicate a process's effectiveness and efficiency.

Performance indicators are variables for measuring the critical success factors. We differentiate financial and direct indicators.

Financial indicators within process management are variables from financial accounting.

Examples of financial indicators are process costs or customer profitability. Financial indicators are derived variables that the employee (process participant) can only associate indirectly with his operative activities. The number of new customers in the last three months gives an UNTEL sales representative more insight into possible courses of action as the sales volume, for example.

Direct performance indicators describe directly observable features of process components.

Examples of direct process indicators might be service speed, the number of new customers or use of order distribution channels. Direct performance indicators relate directly to sales objects and activities such as customers, orders, etc. The process participant can immediately see the relationship to his own activities and derive actions. The computerization of administration has created the prerequisites for this: financial, and especially direct, performance indicators, which prior to computerization were difficult or impossible to record, are now measurable at negligible extra cost.

Once UNTEL has identified its sales process CSFs, it must derive performance indicators from them. For the success factor "processing speed" this is simple. Potential variables might be average order processing time, or the proportion of orders taking more than 10 days to be processed. For the success factor "sales representatives' know-how" the operationalization is not so straightforward.

On the basis of the general success factors a list of generally utilizable performance indicators can be created, whose measurement and application is appropriate for any process (see left side of Fig. 2.7.2./1). For a specific process, such as sales, this list can provide a starting point. From it UNTEL derives the performance indicators in 2.7.2./1.

General performance indicators	Performance indicators for UNTEL's sales process
Average processing time for an operation	Average processing time for an order in sales, i.e. up to Sales' release of dispatch note to Logistics
Rate of meeting deadlines	Proportion of delivery deadlines fulfilled
Error rate	Proportion of wrongly composed deliveries resulting from errors in sales Proportion of false order confirmations Number of order corrections
Rate of complaints	Proportion of complaints arising from errors in sales
Quality cost types as a percentage of total costs	Costs of redeliveries arising from errors in sales
Cost types as a percentage of total costs	Sales personnel costs as a percentage of total costs
Cost types per operation	Sales personnel costs per order
Staff productivity	Contribution margin per sales representative Number of order per sales support employee
Process volumes	Number of orders Number of new customers Number of sales strategies
Product range structure	Number of orders via the various ordering channels Number of orders over 50,000 CHF

Fig. 2.7.2./1: General and specific process performance indicators

The variables in this list would not normally be sufficient for process management. But they constitute a starting point for further considerations of how to operationalize the success factors, in which examples from other companies can be particularly helpful.

By adjusting the generally applicable variables and examples from other companies (see Fig. 2.7.2./2) many performance indicators can be derived, but here too it is necessary to concentrate on the important aspects. The result of the derivation should be a few meaningful variables for each success factor.

Fig. 2.7.2./3 presents the performance indicators for UNTEL's sales process together with brief definitions.

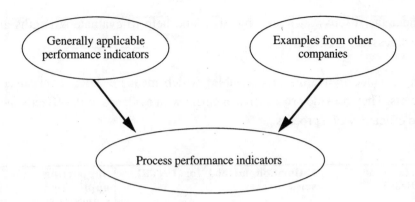

Fig. 2.7.2./2: Derivation of performance indicators

Finally, it is necessary to check the extent to which the performance indicators selected represent the success factors (see Fig. 2.7.2./4). It is especially important to ensure that the performance indicators do not give rise to systematic management distortions. For instance, many companies control sales by heavy emphasis on turnover. This concentration on turnover can first push the wrong products and customers in the interests of financial success, and second favours short-term turnover above long-term customer care.

The operationalized performance indicators alone do not suffice for sound process evaluation. Success factors such as sales representatives' know-how are difficult to evaluate on the basis of quantitative variables alone. In such cases process management must be based on qualitative statements. But even here they can attempt to operationalize them using questionnaires, for example.

Process management must evaluate the success factors using quantitative and qualitative measures.

The performance indicators also do not provide any recommendations for action. A high proportion of delayed orders or a large number of complaints indicate problems, but they do not explain their causes. Process management must identify these causes through discussion with those involved, preferably at meetings of the process circle. The performance indicators are important indices of a process's efficiency and effectiveness. They stimulate ideas, render the discussion more objective, and help to evaluate strengths and weaknesses.

Performance indicators are variables which measure the critical success factors. They provide process management with evidence of the effectiveness and efficiency of a process.

Performance indicator	Estimation method for UNTEL's sales process	Supporting application/ transaction
New customers	Number of newly acquired customers	SM/Determine the number of newly acquired customers in a period
Account management	Average number of sales representative visits per customer per year (excl. maintenance visits requested by the customer); account management only relates to the sub-process" account management"	(Manual evaluation)
Service speed	Maximum interval between customer order placement and delivery of an article (A-, B- or C-articles) to the customer	FA
Bad debts	Uncollectables as a % of turnover	FA
Processing costs per order	Average processing costs per order	(Manual evaluation)
Channel use: orders	Proportion of orders per UNTEL sales channel in the total number of orders. UNTEL's order channels: 1: Recording by sales support/order recording 2: Recording by sales representative 3: Online ordering 4: EDIFACT (via the catalogue) 5: EDIFACT (RICS)	SM/Determine the number, turnover and proportion of orders in the total number of orders per sales channel
Channel use: corrections	Proportion of corrections per UNTEL correction channel in the total number of corrections. UNTEL's correction channels: 1: Manual corrections 2: EDIFACT correction	SM/Determine the number and proportion of corrections in the total number of corrections per correction channel

Rate of order correction	Number of corrections in proportion to the total number of orders	SM/Determine the number of cancellation per sales representative in the period SM/Determine the number of cancellations per sales representative
Processing time: corrections	Average interval between receipt of the correction and dispatch of confirmation per correction channel	(Manual evaluation)

Fig. 2.7.2./3: Performance indicators for UNTEL's sales

(see List of Abbreviations for abbreviations used)

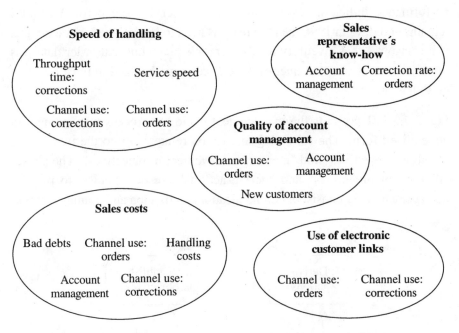

Fig. 2.7.2./4: Representing success factors by performance indicators

2.7.3.   Organization of Process Management

Once the process success factors are clear and the performance indicators have been derived the process organization needs to be built around them. This involves setting up a closed management cycle, and assigning authorization and responsibilities to positions and committees.

2.7.3.1.   Management Cycle for Process Management

In the course of its annual planning UNTEL establishes objectives for the sales process for the next three years on the basis of the performance indicators. For instance, it might decide that the service speed for A-articles should be 3 days in 1995, 1.5 days in 1996 and 1 day in 1997. The objectives enter into staff management and evaluation and from there into their pay.

The sales process adopts these objectives as given. From them it derives detailed process-internal performance indicators and sets its own process objectives. The sales management application delivers the actual values of the performance indicators every month. If the service speed for A-articles remains at 3 days in 1996 then the reasons need to be analyzed. For example, if it transpires that inventory levels were adequate, but that order data was often incomplete, so that queries were necessary, then action must be taken on this issue.

Fig. 2.7.3.1./1 presents the management cycle for process management in generalized form. The following discussion relates only to the two phases "establish objectives" and "measure achievement of objectives". The phases "implement objectives" and "derive actions" are not specific to process management; they consist of communication, motivation and training actions.

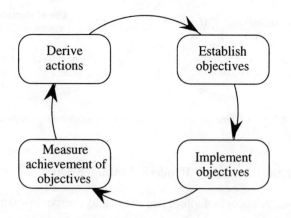

Fig. 2.7.3.1./1: Management cycle for process management

Establish Objectives

The term "objective" is often misunderstood. "Developing a Sales IS to increase speed" is not an objective from the business perspective; neither is a sales statistic. Objectives are neither process components nor actions, but timetables and assessable standards for process features.

One critical success factor for UNTEL's sales is processing speed. It is not sufficient to formulate the objective as "increase speed". What variable do you observe to evaluate the achievement of the objective? Take the example of service speed – is that measured by average order processing time or the number of orders which take more than three weeks to process? Let us assume we measure the first variable: Does it suffice to reduce the average processing time by one day? Or does the competitive situation require a reduction of at least a week? And on what timescale must this reduction be achieved?

An *objective* is operationalized if the agreed objective includes the following:
- Performance indicator (e.g. average order processing time),
- Target value (e.g. two weeks),
- Timetable for achieving the objective (e.g. end of the current year).

An operationalized objective can be assessed objectively.

Fig. 2.7.3.1./2 presents an extract from UNTEL's business objectives as an example of operationalized objectives.

Performance indicator	Units	Actual	Target		
		31.12.94	31.12.95	31.12.96	31.12.97
New customers		30	30	35	40
Account management		1.0	2.0	2.5	2.5
Service speed, A-articles	days	-	3	1.5	1
Service speed, B-articles	days	-	15	12	10
Service speed, C-articles	days	-	30	24	20
Bad debts	%	2	2	1.5	1
Processing costs per order	CHF	180	165	100	80
Channel use: orders	%				
Order channel 1:		40	30	20	20
Order channel 2:		60	40	35	20
Order channel 3:		-	10	15	20
Order channel 4:		-	10	10	13
Order channel 5:		-	10	20	27
Channel use: corrections	%				
Correction channel 1:		100	90	60	45
Correction channel 2:		-	10	40	55
Order correction rate	%	30	25	15	10
Processing time: corrections (both channels)	days	2.1	1.7	1.3	1.1

Fig. 2.7.3.1./2: Operationalized objectives for UNTEL's sales

Not every objective can be operationalized. "Improving UNTEL's brand image" is scarcely objectively assessable, but nevertheless worthwhile. We refer to such objectives as qualitative objectives. Operationalized objectives are always preferable to qualitative objectives.

Measuring Target Achievement

The values of the performance indicators can be measured either by computer or by hand, in their entirety or by sampling. For example, UNTEL measures service speed continuously, since the data required are available in the Sales IS. Processing time for corrections is not so easily measured, however, since not all the steps involved in a correction are associated with computer transactions. In this case UNTEL restricts itself to manual sampling.

If the performance indicators are clear and relevant over a longer period, the high level of computerization of operative flows renders it a simple matter to measure the actual values of the performance indicators. Often, existing computer applications already contain the raw data for many performance indicators: order data in the sales database, automatically recorded dialogue protocols (transaction use), journal files for data protection, etc. are sources of performance indicators that are scarcely used at present (see Section 2.13.).

Measuring performance indicators by machine has a stabilizing effect on process management, because it is cheap and independent of people. Manual measurement involves much effort, which in times of tight personnel capacity is often avoided because there is no operative pressure for it.

The measurement results are presented in a suitable form for management. Graphs are more informative than tables. The diagram showing the development of service speed for A-articles in Fig. 2.7.3.1./3 demonstrates a positive trend, for example. But it also indicates periodic exceptions which could be the sign of a weak spot.

In many cases it is possible to compare the objectives with corresponding values for other companies. Trade associations, management consultants or even cooperating partners can provide comparative values which can be used as benchmarks (guidelines from comparable situations).

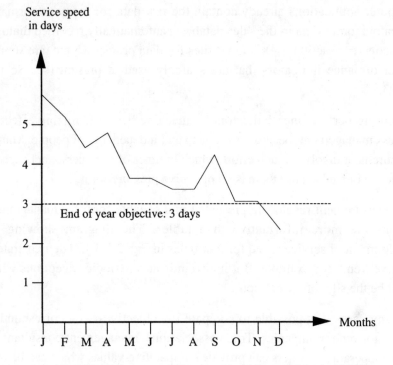

Fig. 2.7.3.1./3: Development of service speed for A-articles in UNTEL

Process Management of the Sub-Process

The management cycle formulates numerous tasks to be carried out repeatedly by various positions (controlling, process employees, process manager, line manager, etc.). Consequently we combine them into their own sub-process management.

Fig. 2.7.3.1./4 presents the activity chain for the sub-process "manage the sales process" in UNTEL. The process runs a few times a year - depending on the management rhythm - and in this sense is significantly different from a sub-process such as "order acquisition". It is standardized not because of the high cost component, but because of its great importance to the company. In many companies it is precisely management processes that are incomplete and consequently ineffective.

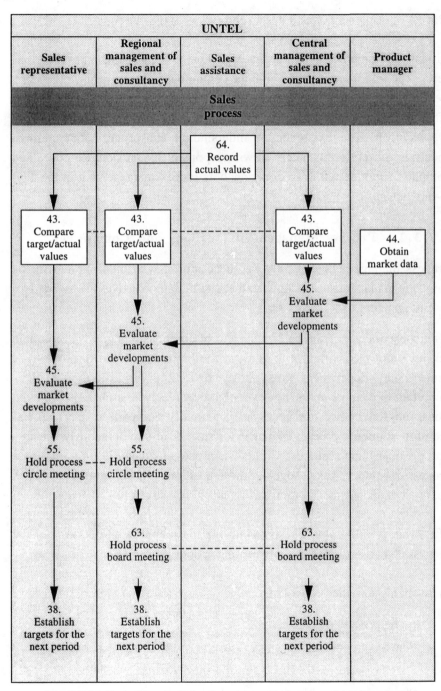

Fig. 2.7.3.1./4: Activity chain for the sub-process "manage the sales process"

Process management constitutes a sub-process in its own right.

Virtually all the process participants regard process management, as described here, as an important instrument in the continuous improvement of a process. Nevertheless, in the daily business the principles of process management are often lost, because the daily business itself generally has priority over its organization. The existence of independent sub-process management specifies the activities, their flows, responsibility and competence, and computer support, and in so doing anchors process management in the day-to-day business.

2.7.3.2.   Process Management Positions and Committees

Process management can only be successful if it is incorporated in the company management structure, so that conflicting objectives are avoided, or at least apparent.

As a consequence of the current system of commissioning, UNTEL's field service employees attempt to achieve the highest possible turnover. The central Sales department aims, above all, to stay within its budget. It is important to the customers, however, that they receive merchandise quickly. These objectives are not necessarily mutually compatible. UNTEL has therefore named a process manager for sales, and simultaneously set up a process board and a process circle. The process manager is supported by a process developer. Taken together these positions and committees establish the process management within the organizational structure.

The *process manager* is responsible for the planning and control of the process objectives, and for implementing actions.

In detail, his activities consist of:

- Planning process objectives
  - Plan the process critical success factors and check them periodically
  - Plan the performance indicators and check them periodically
  - Plan the process objectives
- Incorporate the process objectives in staff management

- Discuss the process objectives with those directly involved
- Motivation and training

• Monitor achievement of objectives
  - Develop and implement measurement instruments
  - Analyze and communicate measurement results

• Plan, implement and monitor actions for improvement
  - Collect ideas and develop improvement proposals
  - Provide personnel and resources for the implementation work
  - Plan, partially manage and implement project design projects

• Represent process interests
  - Inform the process board of process objectives and their achievement
  - Represent the process view in the management of the organizational units involved
  - Chair the process board meetings

• Organize process management
  - Set up and head the process circle
  - Create reporting mechanisms

The *process board* coordinates process management with the management of the functional areas.

It is composed of the process manager and line managers from the organizational units involved in the process. In UNTEL this involves the sales manager as process manager, the marketing manager and the logistics manager. The meetings serve to discuss and agree the planning of objectives and resources. The tasks of the process board are:

• To establish the critical success factors, performance indicators and objectives of the process

• To adopt and monitor resource and process cost plans

• To coordinate between the organizational units involved

• To decide on process design projects

If the responsibility for budgets and the authority to issue directives has been assigned to the process manager it is not essential to set up a process board. This presumes, however, that the functional company organization is replaced by a process organization, a serious step which is currently being discussed by many as visionary. It is not yet clear where it is appropriate to adopt a pure process organization that dispenses with the classical functional areas.

The *process circle* is composed of employees from the organizational units involved. Here the process participants have the opportunity to understand and evaluate their process in its entirety, to identify weak points and to initiate actions.

The process circle brings process development to the process participants. It is a motivational tool and combines the specialist knowledge of all the organizational units involved in the process. As a result it is in a position to assess the consequences of actions across organizational boundaries. The process circle is an important proponent of a process-wide, cross-boundary perspective. For example, if UNTEL's Marketing suggests the introduction of loyalty vouchers for customers, the process circle can easily identify the consequences for Sales, Sales Support and Logistics.

Process circles consist of five to ten employees, whose job responsibilities together represent the entire process, if possible. Process circles have no decision-making power; this remains with the line managers. If a company wants to ensure that the process is customer-oriented, the customer must also be represented on the process circle. However, there are not yet many examples of such thoroughgoing implementations.

The *process developer* supports process management in the process development.

The process developer is a specialist in either organization or information management (business engineer). He contributes the methodology, provides process development support, coordinates between processes and creates the links to the IT department. He can also carry out activities such as measuring the performance indicators, if this is not undertaken by Controlling.

In the UNTEL example, an external consultant acts as process developer. Given UNTEL's size, creating a staff position for this task is not justified.

2.7.4. Management Principles

There is scarcely a company that would be able to implement the process management proposals exactly as presented here. Consequently we have formulated a few principles of process management:

- *Customer orientation*
  The output to the process customer and the price it brings provide the scale of measurement for process structuring.

- *Cross-boundary approach*
  The process, and not the organizational unit, is the object of process management. This is in conflict with line management.

- *Teamwork*
  Process thinking means team thinking, since the basis of the process approach, integration across boundaries, can only be achieved through cooperation.

- *Continuous improvement*
  Processes are not static structures, but are constantly subject to new changes in environmental conditions and market requirements. Those involved in the process must adjust process objectives, flows and tools to these changes. The management mechanisms must contribute to this in the sense of Total Quality Management.

- *Clear competence and responsibility*
  In matrix organization terms the process view is orthogonal to the traditional, functionally-oriented organizational structure of the company. Given this, competence and responsibility need to be clearly defined.

- *Operationalized objectives*
  Operationalized objectives ensure more objective discussion. They render advances more visible and reduce resistance to change.

- *Management by objectives*
  Process and employee objectives should be tied together.

- *Incentive schemes*
  Performance-based pay or other incentives support the achievement of objectives.

- *Entrepreneurship*
  Processes are entities with independent responsibility for their results, in which employees can largely organize themselves within the framework of the objectives set.

2.7.5. Summary

Installation of process management requires:

- Critical success factors

- Performance indicators

- Process organization

Process management once running delivers:

- Process objectives

- Process status reports (tabular and graphic documentation of the measured results)

- Actions

2.8. Architecture Planning

Every company has numerous process flows. It must decide which are the most important, formulate them as independent processes and concentrate management attention on them. This is the task of architecture planning.

In UNTEL, for example, we find process flows for sales, logistics, software development, selecting suppliers, rebuilding a warehouse, or training sales representatives. In principle the process model could be applied to each of these process flows, but the costs involved could not be justified.

What are the process flows within UNTEL? Which are competitively decisive? And which flows can be combined into processes in the sense of the process method presented in Section 2.2?

Architecture planning is an organization design task at the business strategy level. It arises in connection with defining strategic business segments, analysis of competitors, the structural organization of the company or the assessment of potential alliances with other companies, etc.

For example, UNTEL is considering relocating logistics, together with other companies, in a subsidiary. The decision depends in large part on whether the logistic activities can be clearly separated from the sales activities and organized as an independent process. In the absence of the planned alliance in the logistics area, architecture planning would probably have considered other processes.

Architecture planning is a component of strategic development. It takes as its starting point business segments, product ranges, etc., derives the processes from them, and influences in its turn the business segments, product ranges, etc.

2.8.1.   Derivation of Process Candidates

Flow planning in Section 2.5. uses process outputs, customer processes, business objects, process types and segmenting as criteria for deriving activities and sub-processes. In deriving process candidates we concentrate on the customer needs (process outputs and customer processes), process types and segments.

Derivation from customer needs

Customer needs constitute the starting point for defining the process. The questions are:

- What outputs do our customers expect?
- In what flows does the customer need our outputs?

The customer needs are set against the market outputs, as UNTEL has defined them in its strategy:

- Consumer electronics and computer products
- Services (from customer service to merchandise management system)

The retailers consistently have two processes that communicate with UNTEL, procurement (trading in products) and service (repairs, etc.) (see Fig. 2.8.1./1). They see UNTEL from the perspective of these two flows and expect the best possible support, even if UNTEL sub-divides its outputs differently from the perspective of their production.

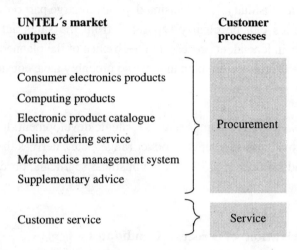

Fig. 2.8.1./1: Market outputs and customer processes

Although UNTEL's strategy sub-divides its market outputs into products and services (also reflected in the first version of the process architecture), the analysis of the customer processes indicates that this can scarcely meet customer needs. We therefore remove the provisional process architecture from the business strategy and sub-divide the market outputs in line with the customer processes.

If a customer process corresponds to the supplier process this facilitates the cooperation between the processes. The supplier is in a better position to deal with the customer in accordance with his needs.

In the past banks and insurance companies have organized their processes in line with their internal organization (divisions, sectors) and not with customer processes. One result is that an investment customer, for instance, receives separate statements for each product, which he then needs to consolidate himself for purposes of liquidity planning, taxation, assessing development, etc. His benefits would be higher if the bank processes mirrored his own processes.

Derivation from process types

What activities must UNTEL undertake to fulfil customer needs? It must procure products, develop its product range, present its product range to the customer, approach potential customers, advise on procurement, acquire and handle orders, etc. These are classical operational functions that can constitute sub-processes within other processes or processes in their own right. The sub-processes for creating and marketing a company's products and services are referred to as *value creation processes*. They are those sub-processes that must be executed between recognition of a customer need and fulfilment of that need.

UNTEL also has to employ and train staff, operate a warehouse, obtain or develop computer applications, etc. Processes that create and maintain the resources needed for output creation are referred to as *support processes*.

Finally it must monitor its finances, manage its personnel, develop its strategy and monitor its implementation. Such activities are combined under the term *management processes*.

Fig. 2.8.1./2 presents a process typology as a starting point for deriving process candidates (see also the discussion of core processes in [Krüger 1993]). This reflects the classical operational functions, which continue to be necessary even in a process-oriented company, but, in contrast to the classical organization, no longer create organizational boundaries but instead enter into processes.

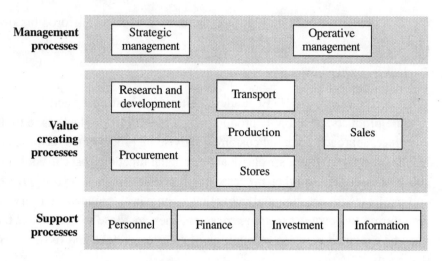

Fig. 2.8.1./2: Process typology

If UNTEL links up customer needs with process types it can derive the following process candidates:

- *Maintain product range process (for products)*
  Within UNTEL this process represents the "research and development" for the consumer electronics and computer products.

- *Sales process (of products)*
  UNTEL variants for the sales process type.

- *Logistics process (for products and customer service)*
  Combines the procurement, transport, production and storage process types.

- *Personnel development process*
  Personnel process type.

- *Organization and systems development process*
  Information process type.

- *Management process*
  "Strategic management" and "operational management" process types

- *Customer service process*
  The UNTEL customer service process combines all the value creation processes in customer service.

UNTEL dispenses from the start with independent processes for the finance and investment resources, since they are regarded as non-critical. Maintaining the product range, sales and logistics relate only to the customer's procurement process (see Fig. 2.8.1./1).

The *process types* are classes of operational sub-processes (activities, functions), that are needed to create the market outputs independent of the industry.

Sector-specific reference architectures are becoming increasingly common. Sometimes they are published [see Scheer 1994 or Mertens/Griese 1993 for the industrial firm]; sometimes they are available as products of software and consultancy firms [see SAP 1994].

Breakdown by segment

Internationally active companies usually organize their sales by country, so that they can adjust more easily to specific aspects of each country. Banks typically break down their products by product groups (or divisions). More recently there has been an increasing tendency to breakdown by customer segment such as business and private customers. As a matter of principle, it is necessary to check whether the processes identified thus far should be specialized by segment (see Fig. 2.8.1./3).

Further segmentation criteria might be sales channels, and technology used. Fig. 2.8.1./3 indicates how each possible combination causes the number of resulting processes, and hence the operational complexity, to grow exponentially.

The *breakdown* by customer and product segments, sales channels and regions generates simple, processes that can easily be optimized, since the specialization reduces the multiplicity of potential flows. In contrast, the *combining* of processes generates synergies in management, training and computerization, since these support functions must only support one instead of many processes.

Segmentation of processes generates simpler processes when viewed in isolation, but increases coordination costs and results in duplication within support functions.

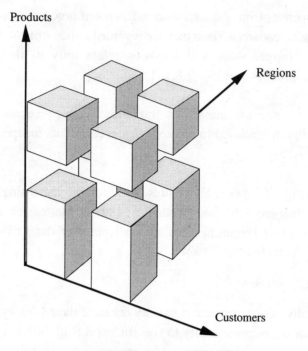

Fig. 2.8.1./3: Process segmentation

For example, it could be beneficial to UNTEL to sub-divide the sales process between small customers with little expertise in consumer electronics, and large customers with other advice requirements. From the perspective of the technology used, segmentation of the consumer electronics and computing business segments would be possible.

UNTEL decides not to break down processes by segments, since the additional costs are estimated as greater than the anticipated benefits.

Process candidates are derived from the customer needs, the sub-processes required to fulfil those needs, and potential segmentation.

2.8.2. Detailing and Checking the Process Candidates

Next we detail the process candidates and document their most important activities, outputs, and the customer's corresponding processes and activities (see Fig. 2.8.2./1).

Process candidates and their activities	Process outputs	Process customers and their activities

Maintain product range
    Market analysis
    Article selection
    Supplier selection
    Product range advice
	Supplier information
	Product information
	Product range data
	Product catalogue
		Procurement (customer)
		    Merchandise managemt.
		Sales (UNTEL)
		    Sales strategy advice
		    Article information

Sales
    Customer acquisition
    Customer care
	Sales strategy
	Framework contract
	Article information
	Order confirmation
	Procurement proposal
		Procurement (customer)
		    Strategic planning
		    Supplier selection
		    Merchandise managemt.

Logistics
    Procurement
    Delivery
    Invoicing
	Merchandise
	Dispatch confirmation
	Delivery note
	Invoice
	Transport order
		Procurement (customer)
		    Receipt of merchandise
		    Merchandise managemt.
		    Accounts payable

...	...	...

Fig. 2.8.2./1: Description of process candidates

It should be noted that the first column refers to process candidates and not processes; the third column refers to process customers. In accordance with the definition in the process model (Section 2.2.2.) these are themselves processes. So UNTEL's sales process is a customer of the potential process: "maintain product range", obtaining the outputs listed in the second column.

The description of process candidates is the basis for questions such as:

- Does there exist for every customer process a corresponding process that carries the responsibility for customer satisfaction?

- Can a process be simplified by breaking it down in accordance with the process customer's processes (e.g. by procurement and service)?

- Are costly and troublesome interfaces between processes generated?

- Do decisions with respect to segmenting the process still appear valid against a more detailed background?

- Is there duplication between processes?

UNTEL establishes that maintaining the product range and sales serve UNTEL customers' procurement process. In addition, maintaining the product range and sales need to communicate intensively. UNTEL therefore dispenses with the process "maintain product range" and integrates its activities into sales. In other companies, especially industry, however, maintaining the product range in the sense of research and development is an important, independent process.

The process candidates are detailed and checked.

2.8.3.   Selecting the Processes

Against this background we evaluate the process candidates using the following criteria:

- *Strategic significance*
  Does the process have a great impact on the company's critical success factors?

- *Core competence*
  Does the process represent a core competence that either exists or can be developed within the company? Core competence is that ability at the heart of the output-creating process for which the greatest know-how is available.

- *Potential*
  Is the process of great significance in cost terms (cost of execution, frequency of execution)? Does it offer the chance of significant increase in turnover? Thus, the potential may lie both in cost reduction and in improving turnover.

- *Standardizability*
  Can the process activities and flows be specified in generally valid terms?

- *Customer needs*
  Does each process fulfil some customer need, and does it carry sole responsibility for that fulfilment?

- *Comprehensive performance indicators*
  Are there performance indicators that are suitable for the entire process?

- *Process manager*

  Is there a management personality for the process that all those involved would accept, or could there be such a person?

- *Controllability*

  Can the process manager oversee the process in routine operation and coordinate all the interests involved?

Characteristics Process candidates	Strategic significance	Core competence	Potential	Standard- izability	Customer needs	Uniform performance indicators	Process manager	Controllabil- ity
Sales	●	◉	●	●	✓	✓	✓	✓
Logistics	●	◉	●	●	✓	✓	✓	✓
Personnel development	●	○	○	○	✓		✓	✓
Organization and systems development	●	○	●	●	✓		✓	✓
Management	◉	●	●	◉	✓	✓	✓	✓
Customer service	◉	●	●	◉	✓	✓	✓	✓

✓	fulfilled
○ ◉ ●	minor/moderate/absolute significance

Fig. 2.8.3./1: Evaluating the process candidates

Fig. 2.8.3./1 presents the evaluation of UNTEL's process candidates. UNTEL decides to define and structure the sales, logistics, management and customer service processes as independent processes in the sense of the process model in Section 2.2.

The process architecture in Fig. 2.8.3./2 documents the processes and their exchange of outputs.

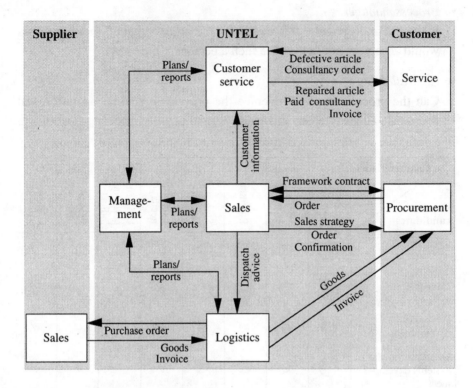

Fig. 2.8.3./2: UNTEL's process architecture

From the process candidates we select the strategic processes (core processes) and document them in the process architecture.

The *process architecture* gives an overview of the processes within the company, the most important processes of business partners, and the exchange of outputs between the processes. The nodes represent processes, the edges the flow of outputs, and the striped boxes cooperating companies.

2.8.4.   Summary

Architecture planning consists of the following steps:

- *Derivation of process candidates*
  The first step derives process candidates from customer needs, general process types and the segmentation of customers.

- *Detailing and checking*
  The second step details the process candidates, describes their most important activities and outputs, as well as the corresponding customer processes and activities, in order to check the process candidates.

- *Selecting the process*
  The third and final step evaluates the remaining process candidates using eight criteria, selects the competitively decisive processes and documents them as well as their interactions in the process architecture.

2.9.   IT Assessment

Information technology is the enabling technology for Business Engineering. In 1992 the IT industry had a turnover of more than 700 billion US$. Telecommunication (80% telephone) amounted to an additional turnover of 500 billion US$ [see CW 1993a].

The market volume combined with relative immaturity - compared with the chemical industry for instance - invests information technology with extraordinary dynamism in comparison with other technologies. Alongside continuous incremental improvements it has also generated fundamental innovations on a five-yearly basis. Since the 1970s these have been:

- the transition from batch to online processing,
- the replacement of isolated files with database management systems,
- the introduction of personal computers,
- the replacement of character terminals with graphic interfaces,
- the transition from in-house developments to package software
- internal and inter-organizational networking.

Not all these developments are complete, but each has generated a multiplicity of new business solutions. In the next five to ten years several significant developments are immanent, in consumer electronics for example.

2.9.1.   IT Map

The IT map summarizes the most important information technology developments from a process's perspective.

Package Software

Software packages that can be implemented in several enterprises, are referred to as package software (word processing, operating systems, accounting systems etc.). If the term is restricted to operational applications (accounting, sales, etc., see Section 2.2.2.5.) we usually speak of standard applications software.

Package software has already largely replaced the in-house development of applications, and will ultimately dominate in all areas. Individual software will be restricted to exceptional specialities, such as the direct private sale of entertainment media via VideoText. It is usually only a precursor to a standardized solution derived from it.

Architectural Change

The central mainframe computer with hundreds and thousands of terminals is still typical in practice. New applications, however, are being designed almost exclusively for distributed architectures with the following characteristics:

- Powerful workstations as clients at every workplace

- Mobile workstations (personal digital assistants, etc.) with data, speech and graphics communication

- Database, application, printer and communication servers as common resources on a network

- Networks within and beyond the organization in the megabit region (between one and several hundred million bits per second)

- Graphic user interfaces for new and many of the old applications

The economy will invest enormous sums in this architectural change over the next five years.

Multimedia

Document image processing is the first step towards new media in the presentation of information. A customer IS shows the user not only the traditional customer data but also a photograph of the customer, an electronic product catalogue presents not only technical data but also a photograph of a television or a video explaining the product. Electronic operating instructions instruct the purchaser of a television on its operation. The traditional telephone is extended to include moving pictures and conference capabilities. An architect can experience a house he has designed as virtual reality; he can place furniture inside it, install lights, and move through the rooms.

Communication

ISDN (Integrated Services Digital Network) for speech and data communication, GPS (Global Positioning System) for establishing locations, GSM (Global System for Mobile Communication) for mobile telephones and networks for data transmission are examples of the infrastructure that is being constructed for the information society. Powerful networks such as FDDI with videophone capabilities are already available within organizations.

Consumer Electronics

Electronic games, digital photograph albums, alarm units and digital televisions are examples of consumer electronics. At present innovation is arising primarily from the digital technology and associated possibilities. This is already well advanced and will open up huge new markets and transform business processing.

In the next five to ten years the economy is facing an even bigger advance in information technology innovations than in the last twenty years in total.

Organization design is concerned with the long-term reorientation of the organization. It must assess technological developments and their effect on the organization over the next three to ten years. The IT map [see Steinbock 1994] is a tool for compiling the information technologies that are relevant to a process, examining their interactions, positioning the technologies in time according to their state of development and recognizing or creating points of emphasis.

Fig. 2.9.1./1 presents an IT map for UNTEL's sales process.

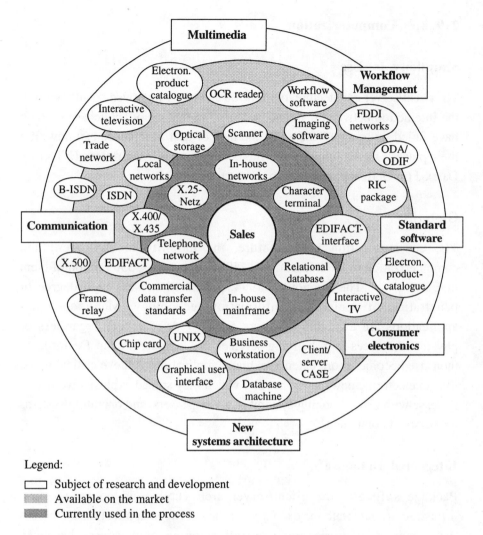

Legend:

☐ Subject of research and development
▨ Available on the market
�▦ Currently used in the process

Fig. 2.9.1./1: IT map for the sales process

It is not difficult to detect from Fig. 2.9.1./1 that there are numerous information technologies already on the market which the sales process does not yet make use of, so that a large unexploited potential may exist. Fig. 2.9.1./1 shows only those information technologies that are relevant to UNTEL's sales, it does not consider parallel computers or expert systems, for example. A comprehensive assessment of information technology developments can be found in [Steinbock 1994].

2.9.2.   Computerization Trends

Simplicity in Use

The client/server architecture, multimedia and many improved details simplify the interaction between man and machine, so that many applications which have failed up to now because of the lack of user acceptance can now find their place. One example is the replacement of Bildschirmtext (BTX) by Datex-J (in Germany) and later by interactive television.

Globality

The communication infrastructure, the mobility of equipment and computerization of the household (1 billion televisions, 350 million of them in Europe [see The Economist 1994, p.4]) will cause a high degree of penetration of society by information technology. Many computer applications are available 24 hours a day, 7 days a week regardless of physical distances (e.g. banking services or Computer Aided Design). As their use becomes more extensive, many applications achieve critical mass, like an electronic newspaper, beyond which they spread explosively, as was the case with travel booking systems, cash dispensers, and operating systems for personal computers.

Integrated Database

Package software, the client/server architecture and communication infrastructure facilitate the exchange of data between applications. Whereas the dream of enterprise-wide overall planning of databases has been abandoned for feasibility reasons, the capacity for cooperation between applications by means of data exchange has grown (see Section 3.9.). One example is the exchange of data between materials management (article master data), CAD (technical product description) and an electronic product catalogue (product description by sales).

Standardization

The basis for a large proportion of the developments has been generated by the standardization resulting from committees or market power. This ranges from technical standards relating to cabling, to application-specific standards, such as the content and format of a payment order. It has even generated organizational standards, for handling security trading for instance.

New and Improved Applications

The new potential of information technology will open up broad new application areas, above all in the private household. But the fact that existing applications will provide the basis for operational processes for many years yet should not be overlooked.

A rapidly growing number of IT applications will link individuals, teams, organizations and economic sectors via a global communication infrastructure.

Process vision cannot be allowed to stand still at the current state of IT use, but must retain a realistic view of IT developments.

2.9.3. Application Types

An additional tool in the search for innovation potential is an application typology. This classifies the IT applications currently available in the economy. It overlaps substantially with the IT map; however, it is based not on technology, but on applications.

Administration

Administration systems (transaction systems) are the classic IT applications. They support strongly structured operative administration tasks such as wage and salary accounting, production planning and control, payments and dispatch. In the past, administrative systems constituted well over half of all IT investments, and will in future continue to make up a major proportion. The following developments are to be expected:

- *Technical infrastructure*
  Central mainframe computers with comprehensive central databases and "dumb" terminals without their own processing intelligence and with little user comfort were the norm in the 70s and 80s. At the start of the 90s a

radical change began: The processing capacity and sometimes the data were distributed to many computers (servers) with specific functionality; the workplace computer (client) allows new forms of man-machine communication, which integrate not only text and data (e.g. the technical data for a product) but also graphics (e.g. a design drawing), audio and video (e.g. operating instructions) (multimedia). The comprehensive networking of economy and society means that this functionality will in future be available at any desired location (in the office, at home, while travelling), which is why the term virtual office has been coined.

In the UNTEL example replacement of the existing IT infrastructure is overdue, as the IT map shows.

- *Package software*
Nowadays well-developed package software is available on the market for large areas of administration. With package software a company buys well-tested expertise, but it also obtains a business toolbox which permits a variety of solutions, generally far more extensive than an in-house development could have offered.

In the course of the 90s package software became available for all sizes of operation, for nearly every sector, and for all operative functions. Package software has the best growth prospects of the entire IT market [see Frey 1990; Grobe 1992]. The emphasis is on sector-specific solutions, new technical concepts (client/server, multimedia etc.) and new functionality such as standard interfaces for inter-organizational integration (e.g. EDIFACT modules) or electronic product catalogues.

UNTEL decides on package software for electronic product catalogues, for merchandise management, and for data exchange between the retailers and UNTEL.

- *Integration*
Software solutions that handle all the operational requirements as an integrated whole, that is on the basis of an integrated database enterprise-wide data model), have proved to be the illusion of the 1980s. Companies have neither the time nor the resources for the modelling and implementation of such systems. They must be content to introduce and integrate the ready-made solutions of package software that rapidly appear

on the market. The greatest potential is still to be found in linking areas of activity that have thus far been separated, such as design with production or order processing with an electronic product catalogue; but the approach to mastering this challenge has changed. Cooperation between bought-in IT applications has replaced total integration on the basis of a single data model.

The electronic product catalogue is only possible for UNTEL if it can offer a simple interface to the existing product database provided by the parent company, include product descriptions from external suppliers, and create the links with the UNTEL-specific sales IS. However, if these conditions are fulfilled it could permit valuable business innovations, such as providing up-to-date article information for retailers or dramatically reducing the cost of including products from external suppliers in the UNTEL product range.

- *Operations control / Workflow Management*
  Up to now the management of workflows has been a human responsibility; the computer simply supported individual activities (e.g. recording of a credit application), but did not control the sequence of activities. Drawing the analogy with industrial manufacturing, this means that process workers have highly developed machines (applications) for executing their activities, but are organized like a handwork operation. Workflow Management Systems apply principles of controlling industrial production to administration (see Sections 2.6. and 4.11.), thereby developing huge potential.

Associated with the management of job processing is the aim of providing the individual responsible for performing a transaction with all the information needed for every task from a single source. The processor then no longer needs to understand a multiplicity of applications, but only his own workflow. He should obtain all the written information he needs to undertake an activity from the computer either as structured (coded) data, such as a customer's credit limit, or as unstructured (non-coded) data such as a customer's hand-written letter. Non-coded data are the subject of Document Image Processing (DIP), which is often closely related to Workflow Management.

A typical application area for UNTEL is sales. In a Workflow Management System with DIP the sales representative could manage all the customer information (customer data, correspondence, market research reports, etc.) and would obtain information about account management, such as the date of the next visit, reminders to check the framework contract or to respond to a customer query.

- *Inter-organizational Information Systems*
  Given the European and worldwide communications infrastructure we can expect a huge increase in inter-organizational applications. These range from the electronic exchange of documents such as delivery notes and payments (EDIFACT), through the exchange of offer data such as product information, to collaboration in design or the performance of obligations between customer and supplier. Communication and mobile computers allow new services to the customer. This applies particularly to the computerization of the private household and its link-up with broadband networks.

UNTEL can assume that within three years all retailers will be connected to the ISDN network and possess the necessary communication infrastructure. Via the computerization of the household, however, the option of direct sales to the end-consumer also arises.

- *Artificial Intelligence*
  In the late 1980s the expectations for artificial intelligence were grossly exaggerated. Now it is clear that expert systems, neural networks and fuzzy logic, as three specific instances of artificial intelligence, can lead to significantly better solutions when a number of easily measurable factors need to be combined in reaching a decision.

UNTEL is planning a configuration aid for household electronics, which would assist the end-consumer and the retailer in composing complete household systems. The configurer uses a set of rules in the form of an expert system.

Office

Office systems provide general operational support functions such as appointments management, spreadsheet systems, document processing and management, the analysis and presentation of information and interpersonal communications. They are predominantly document-oriented (non-coded information), not based on formatted databases (coded information) like transaction systems. They represent electronic tools without special reference to the specific application area.

- *Ad hoc organized teamwork*
  Initially, office systems supported isolated workplaces. Today they make new forms of cooperation possible: video-conferencing via the computer network and the business workstation (powerful personal computers), collectively used document databases, electronic mail, or tools for coordinating teamwork (meeting preparation, etc.).

  Within UNTEL an electronic conferencing system (e.g. on the basis of Lotus Notes) could support communication between Marketing, central Sales staff and sales representatives with respect to market processing. Problems, product information, etc., could be exchanged quickly and easily.

- *Weakly structured flows*
  Computerization using transaction systems has concentrated on the routine flows that can easily be standardized, such as order processing. But 80% of operative information processing is taken up with weakly structured processes. Examples might be selecting a supplier, assessing credit collateral, or an IT project. Groupware and workflow software support weakly structured flows, especially teamwork. Knowledge processes, such as the development of a new bank product, have up to now been the subject of little analysis in comparison with routine administrative flows.

  In UNTEL, typical examples of these kinds of tasks are the creation of market studies as a basis for customer-specific sales forecasts, the half-yearly reworking of the product range or a marketing campaign.

- *Multimedia*
  Office systems increasingly integrate the processing of transactions, text and graphics as well as audio and video sequences.

- *Mobile Computing*
  Miniaturization and networking have contributed to the ability of an employee to undertake a large part of his office work remote from his

workplace - while travelling for instance. For UNTEL this means that the sales representative can access all article data including current inventory levels, or an application for modifying customer or order data, while on a customer visit, for example.

Management

Management systems support the management process at all management levels and over all organizational boundaries. They provide information and tools for planning, decision-making, implementation and control. In data terms they are closely linked with the administration and office systems. The following trends can be observed:

- *Database for management systems*
  Management systems have thus far been based primarily on financial accounting. But nowadays the administration system databases contain a far more extensive and detailed representation of the entire operational activities, providing insight into the cost and output aspects. Workflow Management Systems can document the actual flows within the operation (see Section 2.13., "Organizational Monitoring"). The database permits process management (see Section 2.7.) on the basis of financial and direct performance indicators.

  Around 9,000 databases on offer worldwide [see Gale 1994] such as the Dow/Jones News/Retrieval Service throw light on markets and the company environment.

- *Analysis tools*
  Intelligent filters select internal company data and databases or external electronic news services on the basis of specific information requirements.

- *Comfortable user interface*
  Management systems are applications for occasional use, which demand an especially intuitive user interface.

For UNTEL this means that the performance indicators needed for process management can be extracted from the administrative and office systems without much effort.

Design and Knowledge

Computer Aided Design (CAD) is computerized design for mechanical engineering, architecture, etc. According to VDI Guideline 2222 design is "primarily an intellectually creative process, based on knowledge and experience, which aims to identify optimal solutions in the conception of technical products, their functional and structural form, and to produce the documentation needed for their manufacture." [see VDI 1977].

CAD supports the designer in drawing, technical specification, calculating, visualizing and simulating products, and generates the programs to control the manufacturing equipment. But, CAD also helps the designer to archive and reuse the finished designs, and thus is also a database of design know-how. Huge CAD potential is expected from the following developments:

- *Visualization through to virtual reality*
  Powerful workstations, especially parallel computers, open up new dimensions in visualization. CAD systems will make it possible to generate realistic pictures of products from the design, to link them up with video (multimedia), to represent movement (animation) and ultimately to use the product in virtual reality. For example, kitchen manufacturers could present a kitchen designed by a kitchen planner to the customer so that he can open cupboards, set up kitchen equipment, or test the lighting.

- *Integration*
  Design, Quality Assurance, Sales (e.g. electronic product catalogue), Cost Estimation and Service obtain their product data increasingly from a common engineering database. The appropriate standards (e.g. STEP, Standard for the Exchange of Product Model Data) are being created.

- *Cooperative design*
  In concurrent engineering several designers work on a product simultaneously - sometimes spread across different countries or continents - firstly in order to exploit specialist expertise from different locations and secondly to shorten development time. In simultaneous engineering, design tasks that were originally performed sequentially are undertaken by a team in parallel. Here too it is a case of increasing the speed of development, but also of mutual influence on design decisions.

- *Know-How Base*

  The product database, as referred to above, combines a company's knowledge of its products - from design data through to implementation experience gained from marketing - and supplements it with data from external databases. The product database becomes an operational expertise database and hence a critical resource. An independent discipline is arising to deal with the creation, maintenance, extension and collective use of team know-how.

- *Transference to design activities beyond technology*

  In the meantime we find CAD-equivalent applications in software development, organization design, publishing (of articles in daily papers to video films), in molecular design in chemistry, and in medicine in the design of implants. Even banks and insurance companies are beginning to assess and develop their products like engineers.

  Findings from technology can largely be transferred to this application area. It is a question of designing, visualizing, testing and managing objects such as software, organizations, business methods, etc.

What is the significance of the application type "design and knowledge" for UNTEL? In the consumer electronics area UNTEL can build up a knowledge base of equipment available on the market, of technical standards, of causes of breakdown on the basis of service experience, of market potential or consumer habits. It could develop or buy a configurer for planning household electronics on the basis of an expert system.

Process Control

Process control systems control and monitor technical processes such as a production line, chemical process, car motor, clock, traffic control system, cash dispenser, heating and air conditioning system. In contrast, Workflow Management Systems control administrative processes.

- *Integrated production control systems*

  The control centre exercises administrative and technical control over a group of machines. At present the networking of the control centre, the administrative system, other control centres and machine controls is in operation. This constitutes the backbone of Computer Aided Manufacturing (CAM).

- *Microsystems*

  At present microprocessors control refrigerators, car engines, lifts, etc. A new dimension is being opened up by so-called microsystems, which include miniaturized components alongside electronics. Using sensors, microsystems record data from the environment, process it using their microelectronic components, communicate with other microsystems if necessary and use actors to initiate actions. In medical technology, for instance, research is being carried out on microsystems that can be worn or implanted in the body to support body functions. One example would be an insulin microsystem that uses a chemical sensor to continuously measure and evaluate the blood sugar level, and to deliver small quantities of insulin as needed via a miniaturized pump (on the same chip). Potential uses of microsystems range from the private household through to industrial production.

In UNTEL's administrative processes there is little scope for implementing process controls. However, they do have enormous importance for the functionality of consumer electronics products.

The Private Household

Developments in consumer electronics, in equipment controls and in telecommunication are causing an information revolution of the private household. Consumer electronics acts as a path finder. It ensures acceptance and dispersion of the new technology. Household applications consist of consumer electronics (games, photography, audio and video), communications (speech, graphics and data), household equipment (security, heating, kitchen, etc.) training and administrative tasks (purchasing goods, using services, etc.). The information revolution in the household will in many sectors cause radical changes in customer relations, in sales channels, for instance.

UNTEL is profoundly affected by this aspect of the information revolution. It has described the implications for its products in its business strategy. Furthermore, the information revolution in the household could enable direct sales to the consumer (teleshopping), interactive advisory services (hotline etc.) and similar new services.

The *IT assessment* evaluates the potential opened up for the process by each application type.

This method of structuring information technologies and their applications does not generate an unambiguous, clearly defined and comprehensive structure. It is simply a means of making the multiplicity of information technology developments transparent to the user, in order to support the creative search for process innovations.

2.9.4. Procedure in IT Assessment

IT assessment consists essentially of four tasks:

* *Knowledge transfer*
  In order to recognize the application potential of information technology in IT assessment, the business and IT knowledge must be combined in the same minds. It is true that business and technical specialists work together in mixed teams, but they must still understand enough of each other's areas of activity to be able to communicate at all.

  In most companies this means first generating awareness of the need for collective IT assessment, then training the business representatives in information technology and the IT representatives in business issues.

* *The search for information technology of relevance to the process*
  Software catalogues, IT trade fairs, specialist journals for the business sector and for information technology, business associations and specialist consultants are the most important sources in the search for new solutions.

* *Process-specific IT map*
  Information technology has such a fundamental influence on new business solutions that each process vision should be based on the process-specific IT map.

* *Directory of ideas for each application types*
  Employees are frequently specialists in one or two types of application, and as a result do not see the potential of other types. Proceeding on the

basis of application types forces consideration of less familiar areas. The result of the analysis of application types is a directory of ideas (see Section 2.3.).

Process innovations on an IT basis usually generate temporary competitive advantage, while continuous process development can defend this advantage. There are, however, numerous examples of cases where IT-based innovations have raised lasting barriers to entry from competitors. Examples might be Reuters financial and information services, airline reservations systems or package software (e.g. SAP R/3).

2.10. Customer Relationship Analysis

The information revolution and the associated reorganization initially transformed individual operational activities (e.g. order recording) or areas (e.g. warehousing). Process-oriented reorganization now aims at flows that go beyond organizational boundaries, and are not restricted by company limits. Because inter-organizational processes have received little attention in the past it is precisely here that substantial potential lies.

In preceding sections the UNTEL example has uncovered many possibilities for innovations in customer relations. Order recording by the customer, the electronic product catalogue, the merchandise management system for retailers and direct deliveries to customers are some of the ideas that have been addressed (see Fig. 2.3.2./2).

The process vision, architecture planning and flow planning techniques regard the relationship of the supplier to the customer as one aspect among many (customer needs), whereas customer relationship analysis concentrates on this alone. Its aim is:

- to reveal customer needs from their own perspective,

- to increase the value of the supplier's market output,

- to check the distribution of activities between the supplier and the customer, and

- to strengthen customer ties or create barriers to entry for potential competitors.

Customer relationship analysis examines the relationship between two companies, not between two processes. In doing so it includes activities on both sides in the examination which up to now have not been the subject of the same process, but which perhaps should be.

2.10.1. Customer Activities

What customer activities can UNTEL support? The activity chain diagram for the sales process (see Fig. 2.2.1.1./1) indicates the following activities on the customer side: "develop sales strategy", "agree framework contract", "manage inventory", "determine requirements", "select suppliers", "select articles using the product catalogue", "place order " and "adjust order".

Customer Resource Life Cycle

With these activities the activity chain diagram in Fig. 2.2.1.1./1 takes into account the Customer Resource Life Cycle, as presented in Fig. 2.10.1./1 in general form and using the UNTEL example [following Ives/Learmonth 1984 and Schmid 1993].

The *Customer Resource Life Cycle* is the sequence of activities for which the customer requires our products and services.

A customer's needs arise out of his activities. From the supplier's perspective, those activities to which he could contribute something are of relevance. The Customer Resource Life Cycle is a tool for systematically recording these activities.

Process Typology

A second framework for identifying customer activities is the process typology in Fig. 2.8.1./2.

Using the Customer Resource Life Cycle and the process typology we obtain an activity catalogue for the customer (see the indented list in Fig. 2.10.2./1). The activity catalogue is not concerned with a specific process, department or area. Rather it identifies those activities that the supplier could support with goods and services. For reasons of clarity the catalogue is usually restricted to between 50 and 100 activities.

Activities in the Customer Resource Life Cycle	Examples of activities of UNTEL customer (retailers)
Identify requirements and possibilities for fulfilling them	Create product range (on the basis of consumer demand) Develop sales strategy
Obtain market information	Select suppliers Evaluate products on offer Evaluate services on offer
Select suppliers	Select suppliers
Specify quantity and characteristics of the demand	Inventory control Obtain market research reports Determine requirements
Ordering of a specific quantity from a specific supplier	Order placement
Payment or taking up of credit	Pay accounts payable
Receipt of products or services	Receive merchandise
Testing and acceptance	Technical merchandise control Check conformity with order
Use of products and services	Place merchandise in stores Present merchandise in saleroom
Monitor accessions and consumption	Stocktaking
Customer care	Advise consumers
Adjustment to new requirements	-
Maintenance and repairs	Customer service
Deal with remaindered stock	Warehouse clearance Disposal of old equipment
Accounting for consumption	Sales accounting

Fig. 2.10.1./1: Customer Resource Life Cycle

2.10.2. The Supplier's Activities

Corresponding to the customer activities are the activities of suppliers, who can offer outputs to meet the customer's needs. The right-hand side of Fig. 2.10.2./1 shows the supplier's activities using the UNTEL example. These activities arise primarily within the sales process, but can also be located in other processes in so far as they might be relevant to the customer.

Fig. 2.10.2./1: Customer relationship diagram (extract with examples of relationships)

2.10.3. Relationships

The customer relationship diagram (see Fig. 2.10.2./1) thus contains activities of mutual interest. In addition it shows existing relationships (solid lines) and potential relationships (broken lines). Here too, it is necessary to restrict attention to the most important relationships through which the supplier can influence the competitive situation in his own favour.

The aim of the customer relationship analysis is not the inclusion of as many relationships as possible in the diagram, but the derivation of process outputs with business potential. The most important result is a directory of ideas, as in the process vision (see Fig. 2.3.2./2).

2.10.4. IT Potential

Many innovations in customer relationships are based on information technology possibilities. If UNTEL wishes to provide the retailer with a self-service terminal in the salesroom, which the customer can use to sift through the range of video recorders using his personal catalogue of criteria, for instance, it is primarily the available information technology that determines the feasibility and economic efficiency of this idea. It is necessary to establish whether the package software for electronic product catalogues is suitable for such use, whether online access to the supplier's databases is available at reasonable cost, etc.

The IT map (see Section 2.9.) can provide suggestions for the customer relationship analysis but needs to be supplemented with detailed market research.

2.10.5. Analysis of the Customer Relationships

The evaluation of existing customer relationships and the search for new solutions are not so much an independent step within the customer relationship analysis, but rather a component of the derivation of activities and relationships. The checklist in Fig. 2.10.5./1 provides a few suggestions.

Ideal conception
• An ideal image of the cooperation between the customer and UNTEL (e.g. retailers as UNTEL subsidiaries)
• Removing restrictions on customer relationships through information technology (e.g. price changes only quarterly with paper price lists)

Outputs
• Additional outputs or output components (e.g. procurement proposal)
• Elimination of outputs (e.g. order confirmation in the case of online order recording)

Integration
• Synergies from the combination of activities - even with other companies (e.g. consumer credit together with a bank)
• Synergies from common processing of activities (e.g. "customer care" and "consumer questionnaires")
• Use of customer data (e.g. retailers' sales data)
• Customer use of our data (e.g. inventory levels from "inventory control")

In- and outsourcing
• Taking over customer activities (e.g. merchandise management for the retailer)
• Passing on activities to the customer (e.g. order recording)

Availability
• Temporal availability (e.g. 7 x 24 hour)
• Spatial availability (e.g. mobile to any location in Switzerland)
• Speed (e.g. of response to queries about article delivery)

Simplicity
• A single intermediary (e.g. a sales representative who deals with the customer from order acceptance, through processing to invoicing)
• A single contact ("one stop", e.g. order confirmation immediately on order acceptance)

Competition
• Achievement of the critical mass for competitive costs per transaction (e.g. for customer cards)
• Barriers to entry for competitors (e.g. worldwide product database from UNTEL International)

Customer
• Technical and human resource prerequisites for the customer (e.g. trading business network)
• Customer ties (e.g. providing software for merchandise management)

Fig. 2.10.5./1: Checklist for analyzing customer relationships

2.10.6. Summary

Customer relationship analysis investigates the inter-organizational, bilateral cooperation between the customer and the supplier with the aim of increasing the value of outputs, taking over new activities and binding the customer more tightly to the company. It proposes the following steps:

- Recording the customer's activities in relation to the supplier's market outputs

- Recording the supplier's activities in relation to the needs of the customer

- Establishing the existing and potential relationships between the activities of the customer and the supplier

- Investigating information technology possibilities

The obvious formal result of the customer relationship analysis is the customer relationship diagram; the most important result in content terms, though, is the directory of ideas as a contribution to the vision, architecture planning and flow planning.

The procedural method in customer relationship analysis can be applied to the supplier relationship analysis. In certain markets (e.g. automobile manufacture and its suppliers) this also plays an important role.

2.11. Activity-Specific Analyses

Process management derives performance indicators from a process's critical success factors and observes them. For cost reasons the emphasis is on the process as a whole, and scarcely the individual activities (see Fig. 2.7.2./3). In contrast, activity-specific analysis aims to undertake one-off recordings and evaluations, where the higher costs can be justified.

The success of process development rests partly on precisely this detailed analysis of a process's activities and their effects on the critical success factors. Reducing processing times, eliminating down time, reducing the frequency with which an activity is carried out, and lowering error rates are typical starting points for process-oriented organization design.

The improvement to UNTEL's sales process provides some examples:

- Order recording by the customer should replace costly order acceptance via the sales representative.

- The rate of corrections should be lowered.

- The customer should be able to select the speed with which he receives information about delivery dates and order confirmation in accordance with his own needs.

In order to locate starting points for improvements, organization design needs to investigate the individual process features down to the activity level. Just as in process management, the critical success factors generate the process features with the greatest potential.

Typical questions in the activity-specific analysis are:

- Where does the greatest potential lie?

- What does the administrative processing of an order cost?

- What is the effect of introducing a new product variant on costs?

- How long must the customer wait for a specific output?

Some quite elaborate tools have been developed to answer such questions. Of particular importance are process cost accounting (Activity Based Costing) [see Horváth/Mayer 1989] and simulation of activities [see Grund/Jähnig 1994]. Here we restrict the discussion to simple examples of activity-specific detailed analyses that are adequate for the design of many processes.

2.11.1. Processing Time Analysis

Processing time analysis investigates the time between requesting and receiving an output. Fig. 2.11.1./1 presents a simple investigation of the outputs sales advice, order confirmation and correction confirmation in tabular form for the existing sales process (average time in hours).

Output Activity	Down time	Trans- port time	Processing time	Total
Sales advice				
Advise customer on procurement	168	2	1	171
Order confirmation				
Receive order via sales representative			.5	.5
Record order	6	48	.25	54.25
Confirm order and send confirmation	6		.15	6.15
Note order (customer)		36		36
Total	*12*	*84*	*.9*	*96.9*
Correction confirmation				
Check order correction	6	36	.25	42.25
Check order correction	6		.25	6.25
Adjust order	2		.35	2.35
Confirm order correction and send confirmation	6		.15	6.15
Adjust order (customer)		36		36
Total	*14 - 20[1]*	*72*	*.75 - 1[1]*	*86.75 - 93[1]*

[1]   Depending on activities undertaken.

Fig. 2.11.1./1: Example of processing time analysis

It generates insights such as:

- If a customer requires advice on purchase (a sales representative visit) he obtains an appointment in a week on average. The journey time (transport time) and consultancy time do not enter into the customer's view.

- When a customer places an order with a sales representative in the existing situation he must wait 96.9 hours, i.e. 4.5 days, from calling the representative (or the representative's visit) for the order confirmation. UNTEL's processing time (0.9 hours) is insignificant compared with the lying and transport times (96 hours in total). The customer's activity "note order" is included in order to represent the preceding transport time.

- The situation is approximately the same for a correction confirmation. Processing time totals between 86.75 and 93 hours while the processing time is between 0.75 and 1 hour, depending on whether planning needs to check the order correction.

The totals present orders of magnitude, since various routes through the process are possible. It is a simple matter to derive graphical representations from the table showing at a glance the relationship between down time, transport time and processing time, or to incorporate ratios showing the proportion of processing time to other times (value creation proportion).

2.11.2. Cost Analysis

Cost analysis examines the costs of a process output and the share of the individual activities. Fig. 2.11.2./1 shows the breakdown of costs by activity for the same examples as used in the processing time analysis. The initiator of an activity we refer to as the cost source; its quantity is proportional to the costs incurred. The costs per operation include only those costs that are incurred for each instance of the cost driver. In the example they include processing time multiplied by the hourly rate of pay of the employee, the sales representative's travel costs, and the quantity-dependent IT costs (in the example 1,- CHF per transaction for average numbers of transactions performing the activity). The table gives the following information for process design:

- A customer visit costs 300.-- CHF, order confirmation (acceptance of an order) 74.-- CHF and a correction confirmation between 54.-- CHF and 84.-- CHF.

- Given the amounts involved the largest cost components are found in the activities "advise customer on procurements" and "receive order via sales representative". If it is possible to induce the customer to record his orders online himself, this would generate a considerable cost reduction, or alternatively would allow 1,500 additional visits by sales representatives for the same total cost.

As with processing times, graphics can also be used to show the cost relationships.

Output Activity	Cost source	Number	Costs / operation	Annual costs
Purchasing advice				
Advise customer on procurement	Sales rep. visit	3,000	300	900,000
Order confirmation				
Receive order via sales representative	Sales rep. orders	9,000	50	450,000
Record order	Sales rep. orders	15,000	15	225,000
Confirm order and send confirmation	Orders	15,000	9	135,000
Totals			74	810,000
Correction confirmation				
Check order correction (order recording)	Order corrections	4,500	25	112,500
Check order correction (Planning)	Substantial order corrections	1,000	30	30,000
Adjust order	Order corrections	3,000	20	60,000
Confirm order correction and send confirmation	Order corrections	3,000	9	27,000
Totals			54 - 84[1]	229,500[1]

[1]   Depending on the activities undertaken.

Fig. 2.11.2./1: Example of cost analysis

Processing time and cost analyses are two typical examples of activity-specific detailed analysis. Further analyses could be undertaken regarding the frequency of errors, for instance.

2.11.3. Summary

Activity-specific analysis investigates individual process features (usually performance indicators) down to the level of the activities involved. Simple, rough recordings and representations usually suffice to answer the central questions.

2.12. Benchmarking

Benchmarking aims to produce a measure for comparing the process and its parts.

How often should an UNTEL sales representative visit a customer in a year? What should it cost to process an order? Which market data should UNTEL make available to the retailers? What support can UNTEL offer its customers in restocking?

The benchmarking yardstick should provide two targets:

- *Realistic process goals*
  Process management should set process goals that are aimed at the achievable. These goals should not overburden the employee, yet they must allow the process to develop quickly enough.

- *Competitively adequate process goals*
  Quality is always relative. Even if UNTEL reworks its sales process repeatedly and is convinced by the achievements, the quality is still inadequate if its competitors are better. If UNTEL increases the number of visits a year to 6 (instead of 1 up to now), it is then much better than all its competitors. But if the customer does not pay extra or corresponding increases in turnover are not generated, then this "excessive" quality generates only costs.

The benchmarking results are incorporated primarily into the process vision, performance analysis and process management.

2.12.1. Subject Matter

Benchmarking develops targets for the features and parts of a process.

Features of a Process

Process management identifies a process's critical success factors. Performance indicators are features derived from these factors, and are used to develop benchmarking targets (see e.g. Fig. 2.12.1./1).

The performance indicators for the process are a benchmarking target. However, benchmarking may itself discover new performance indicators that have proved useful in other companies, and hence it can contribute not only target values, but also performance indicators.

Process feature:	Number of sales representative visits per year
Range:	Wholesalers of consumer electronics
Information source:	Electronic trade associations
Unit of comparison	Instances
NEUTREL AG	2.3
UNIO AG	2.7
MITECH AG	3.1
UNTEL AG	1.0

Process feature:	Processing costs per order
Range:	Wholesalers of consumer electronics
Information sources:	Staffing levels in sales companies Sales figures from market research institutes
Unit of comparison	Instances
NEUTREL AG	109
UNIO AG	181
MITECH AG	210
UNTEL AG	180

Fig. 2.12.1./1: Benchmarking of process features

Parts of a Process

Benchmarking attempts to identify standards not only for the process features, but also for the business solutions, that is the parts of the process [see Horváth/Herter 1992].

For the process output sales strategy UNTEL has decided that the customer should periodically receive a market analysis (see Fig. 2.4.3./1). But what should this look like? What is the experience with different approaches? Fig. 2.12.1./2 provides an impression of how benchmarking can contribute to the search for a solution.

Benchmarking can contribute solutions to all parts of a process, from the process outputs to the computer applications used (see Section 2.2.2., Process Model). The aim of benchmarking is to find the best solutions (World Class Benchmarking).

The search for the best solutions is of course a component of other organization design techniques. Benchmarking is distinguished by the fact that it aims to identify and document solutions to the most important parts of a process.

Process part:	Market analyses for customers
Range:	All sectors
Information sources:	Specialist sales journals
	Advertising material for market research institutes
Unit of comparison	**Value of the benchmarking variable**
Car manufacturers	In quarterly circulars the manufacturer gives the authorized dealers an overview of the development in registrations, market shares and other economic data relevant to car purchase (income distribution etc.). This information is assembled and prepared by a market research institute commissioned by the manufacturer.
Stationary wholesalers	As part of the half-yearly consultative discussions, the wholesaler provides the retailer with regional data on market developments. He prepares this information with the help of an online link to a market research database.

Fig. 2.12.1./2: Benchmarking a process part

2.12.2. Range

Benchmarking aims to break through company blindness by making the range of comparison explicit. It distinguishes between:

- *Company-internal benchmarking*
  UNTEL could determine, for example, the number of customer visits of the most successful sales representative. Internal benchmarking entails identification of the best values and solutions between comparable organizational units within the company (Best of Company).

- *Industry-internal benchmarking*
  In order to identify competitively adequate process goals, it is necessary to know the best within the industry (Best of Industry). A comparison of the "processing costs per order" (see Fig. 2.12.1./1) of the most important supplier is an important guideline for the sales process.

- *Inter-industry benchmarking*
  In assessing its order acquisition procedures UNTEL should not restrict

itself to solutions within the consumer electronics industry, but can perhaps adopt interesting solutions and target values from the furniture or car traders. Inter-industry benchmarking first identifies characteristics of its own industry and then seeks solutions from other industries with similar features (Best of World).

2.12.3. Information Sources

Some of the information sources for company-external benchmarking are [see Sabisch 1994]: data exchange between companies (reciprocal), visits to comparable companies (in other industries), joint customers, publications in specialist journals, company publications (annual report, prospectus, etc.), visits to trade fairs, business databases, benchmarks from consultancy companies, industrial organizations, trade associations and questionnaires.

2.12.4. Problems

The most important benchmarking problems are:

- Despite the multiplicity of information sources mentioned, precise details about a competitor's important variables are often difficult to obtain.

- Target values and solutions are only comparable to a limited extent. Processing costs per order, for instance, are only comparable if the sales processes are organized along similar lines. In Fig. 2.12.1./1 NEUTREL appears to be the next best competitor as a result of significantly lower costs. But if this is because it handles its sales using an external network of representatives the comparison can be misleading. NEUTREL possibly recognizes that it would achieve significantly higher sales using its own sales representatives.

- Benchmarking values are often susceptible to political misuse within a company, if, for example, only those variables are selected which present the company's performance in a positive manner, or if the background to comparative variables is inadequately explained.

A typical example is that of the computing costs as a proportion of total administrative costs. The more computer applications that are used to support administrative tasks and the more effectively they have lowered administrative costs, the worse the company will appear in terms of its computing costs. In addition, it is usually unclear which costs should be assigned to computing: only those of the computer department, or also those of the user departments; only task-related costs, or all business costs etc. Despite its obvious problems this ratio is used widely in many companies.

2.12.5. Summary

Benchmarking determines where a firm stands among its competitors and reveals the best performance of a process. It is the continuous comparison of a process with model standards. The results of benchmarking are:

• Comparative values (target values) for performance indicators, and

• Alternative solutions for the process parts.

2.13. Organizational Monitoring

Organizational monitoring is an instrument for understanding the organization as it actually exists. It uses data recorded by a company's applications to answer the following questions :

• How many orders are recorded by EDIFACT?

• How many orders require subsequent modification?

• Which data from the sales database are used by the regional managers?

• Does the "order acquisition" sub-process actually run as planned?

• Are the same activities undertaken repeatedly (corrections)?

What support has the organization specialist had up to now in answering such questions? Manual recording using checklists, control cards, etc. are time-consuming and depend on employees' subjective assessments. They are suitable for gaining a general overview of the existing state of a process, but are inappropriate for continuous process management .

Since a growing number of applications support operational flows and record data, an increasingly dense network of measurements is generated within the organization, which organizational monitoring can make use of for process development.

Organizational monitoring is a support technique. It provides performance indicators for process management, and an analytic foundation for process design and especially improvement.

2.13.1. Sources

Organizational monitoring uses the following data sources:

Systems Software Records

The operating system, the database management system, the online transaction processor, the network, the mail system and other components of systems software have monitoring functions, which collect a multitude of data about the operation.

The database management system, for example, keeps a protocol of all changes to the database (backup), in order to be able to reconstruct the database (recover) in the case of system breakdown. In addition, it provides information about the number of entities that have been newly incorporated in the customer entity set, how often existing orders have been modified and how many order positions are available.

There are also special monitors which record and evaluate additional operating data. One example is a transaction monitor for overseeing online operations (e.g. "The Monitor for CICS" [see Landmark 1988]). Fig. 2.13.1./1 presents an example of a protocol from such a transaction monitor.

Date	Start time	End time	Transaction	Terminal	Order number
26.7.	10.30	10.42	Display order	V0137	7062
26.7.	10.45	11.01	Modify order	V0137	7062
26.7.	18.00	18.07	Print order modification	BATCH	7012
					7027
					7062
27.7.	8.15	8.37	Display order	V0138	5172
27.7	9.05	9.10	Modify order	V0138	5172
27.7.	9.11	9.20	Display order	V0138	5172
27.7.	13.30	13.38	Modify order	V0138	5172
...	...	...	...	...	...
27.7.	18.00	18.12	Print order modification	BATCH	9006
					6731
					2175
					5172
...	...	...	...	...	...

Fig. 2.13.1./1: Protocol from a transaction monitor

A *monitor* keeps a protocol of certain activities on the computer and provides instruments for evaluating the records. It is either a component of systems software and applications (e.g. mail system) or an additional application on the computer.

Databases

Existing application databases deliver extensive information for process development. They reveal how long a customer has been listed in the sales IS, how many positions a specific customer's order has on average, how many customers are handled by a given sales representative, etc.

The applications can also display additional data for process management purposes. Examples are the name of an employee who modified an order, the date and time of order recording, and the data and time of order delivery.

Workflow Management Systems (WFMS)

The organizational monitoring sources mentioned thus far have been created for other purposes than organizational analysis and consequently can only be used to a limited extent. Sometimes they are so extensive (e.g. database backups) that they must be deleted daily or every few days; extracts have to be made for organizational monitoring - at a cost. Sometimes important links between the data are missing. Consequently it is impossible or extremely difficult to follow a complete procedure (e.g. a specific customer order) from creation to conclusion.

In contrast, a WFMS can display a flow starting from a specific event (see Section 4.11.1, "Functionality of WFMS"). Thus a WFMS for the workflow "accept EDIFACT order" (see Sections 2.2.1.2. and 2.6.) can reconstruct in detail what happened to the order from customer Meier AG of 30.8.1995, who undertook which activities, the sequence of activities, the transactions used, and the result. WFMS thus offer possibilities for organizational analysis that have thus far been unavailable.

The sources for organizational monitoring are records from all the software used in the company (operating system, mail system, WFMS, applications, etc.). In some circumstances applications must store additional missing data in the database.

2.13.2. Analysis

The performance indicators used in process management, and the problems that are central to process development, determine the kind of analyses to be undertaken in organizational monitoring. The following proposals are fundamental analyses that are relevant to most processes.

Transaction Analysis

Nowadays, practically every process can access a number of transactions from different applications. With the help of a transaction monitor it is possible to establish which transactions the process actually uses.

From the transaction analysis for the sales process (see Fig. 2.13.2./1) UNTEL can discover, for instance, that the "customer acquisition" sub-process is not running as planned, because the transaction "record potential customers" was only executed three times in the period under investigation.

In contrast, the number of cancelled orders is pleasingly low, as compared with the expected frequency (90 per year).

Transaction	Frequency
Start customer management transaction	400
Search/display customer address	250
Display potential customers	10
Record potential customers	3
...	
Cancel order	10

Fig. 2.13.2./1: Transaction frequency in the second quarter

Database Analysis

The database management system can deliver evaluations like those in Fig. 2.13.2./2. These are less informative regarding the activities undertaken, but reveal more about the results of the process, and how they affect the database.

The low number of alterations to the potential customer entities indicates to UNTEL that there are problems with the acquisition of new customers.

Entity type	Number of entities	Number of alterations
Potential customer	30	5
Customer	800	160
Order	45'000	7'000
Order position	150'000	13'000
...		

Fig. 2.13.2./2: Data volumes at 30.6 and alterations in the second quarter

Structural Analysis

Structural analysis checks the assignment of activities to positions (see Fig. 2.13.2./3) using an actual function diagram. The rows contain activities, the columns positions grouped by organizational units.

Organizational unit / Transaction	VU			Sales representative		
Terminal	V0137	V0138	...	SR011	SR012	...
Display orders of customer	32	25	...	15	12	...
Display order	51	46	...	20	21	...
...		...	... ...	...	...	...
Record order centrally online	155	210	...	5		
Record order online by customers						
Record representative order online		27		51	280	...
...		...	... ...	...	...	...
Cancel order	2	...	...	...	...	...
...		...	... ...	...	...	...
Determine customer turnover in the period				5		...
...		...	... ...	...	...	...

Fig. 2.13.2./3: Actual function diagram for the second quarter

The transactions must be used as proxies for the activities because a transaction can be used by several activities and the system`s software records do not indicate the activity. The organizational units are also not listed in the monitoring data; they must be substituted by network or terminal addresses.

There are two basic questions:

- Is a specific transaction used by the right position?

- Does a position use the right transactions?

Even this small extract from an actual function diagram permits typical insights:

- The sales representative with the network address SR011 records very few orders in comparison with his colleague with the address SR012.

- The sales representative with the network address SR012 does not use the transaction "determine customer turnover for the period". Either he does not know about it, or he finds it unhelpful and does not use it.

- At the network address SR011 the transaction "central online order recording" was undertaken five times (the authorization is restricted to Sales Support). Either a Sales Support employee has been working at the sales representative's workplace (very unlikely), or a sales representative has obtained a Sales Support employee's password in order to enter an order using the "central online order recording" transaction. In either case, this deviation from the target organization must be investigated further.

- The transaction "online order recording by sales representative" was used by sales representatives, as intended, but also by a sales support employee, again in conflict with the target organization.

Flow Analysis

Flow analysis checks the actual flow in the processing of tasks (see Fig. 2.13.2./4). The rows contain transactions (proxies for activities), and the columns the time of events. Flow analysis provides information about down time, processing times, repeated executions of the same activity, the frequency of routings through an activity chain, etc.

Fig. 2.13.2./4 shows the processing of two order corrections (see Section 4.4.2, "Entity Life History" on the representation). The correction of order 7062 begins on 26.7 at 10.42 with the transaction "display order". This gives rise to the transactions "order modification" at 11.01 and "print modification confirmation" at 18.07. If processing begins before the first transaction ("display order"), it escapes this analysis, since the information system has no measurement of it.

According to Fig. 2.13.2./4 the processing time for this task is 7hrs. 25mins. The long delay for both orders is a result of printing order confirmations only once daily at 18.00.

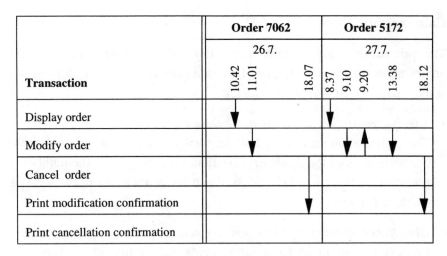

Fig. 2.13.2./4: Flows for two order corrections

The flow analysis also reveals that the "order modification" transaction was executed twice for the second order correction. The cause is not clear from the monitoring, and if necessary must be discussed with the employees.

Many kinds of flow representations are possible. Ideally the flows for each task could be condensed into an average flow and represented as an activity chain indicating the frequency of routings and times.

Analysing flows derived from systems software monitoring data poses the following problem: There are often no clear indicators (e.g. task number), which allow links to be created between the recorded events. Such links are needed to reconstruct the processing of an order from order recording through to delivery, for example.

A WFMS is based on a particular task and the activities associated with it. This data allows the reconstruction of actual flows.

The data from most information systems permit statements about the use of transactions, data volumes, alteration frequencies, the assignment of transactions to positions, and - though currently still within limits - about actual flows.

Comparisons

The preceding analyses have implicitly linked actual values for the organization with planned targets. There are various possibilities for arriving at these targets (see also Section 2.12.):

- *Target organization according to the design*
  The organization design can both implicitly and explicitly formulate the characteristics of the target organization. One example is the number of potential customers to be processed and hence included in the UNTEL database per year.

- *Objectives according to process management*
  Process management formulates target values for the performance indicators, such as the planned distribution of order recording between the various channels or processing times for order corrections (see Fig. 2.7.3.1./2).

- *Behaviour over time*
  Process management examines the development of specific performance indicators over time (e.g. the development of service speed for A-articles in Fig. 2.7.3.1./3).

- *Comparisons between organizational units*
  If a company has several organizational units that handle the same tasks, a comparison of their efficiency and the factors influencing it is of interest. The actual function diagram in Fig. 2.13.2./3 presents a direct comparison of the number of orders recorded by different sales support employees. If the function diagram was extended to include customers (grouped according to sales representative) a comparison of channel use in order recording by sales representative could be made.

- *Comparisons between companies*
  Comparative values for several performance indicators can be obtained outside the company. Since the number of new consumer electronic retailers each year can be recorded quite easily, the number of potential customers processed by UNTEL (see Figs. 2.13.2./1 and 2) could be compared with the actual potential.

Organizational monitoring must proceed on the basis of explicit or implicit targets concerning the organizational characteristics.

Monitoring Problems

Organizational monitoring is a powerful diagnostic tool, but its limitations must be recognized:

- High volumes in the processes to be investigated are a prerequisite for justifying the cost of monitoring.

- The limits to computerization in the company are the limits to monitoring: activities not supported by computer cannot be recorded.

- Monitoring can only give indications of possible weak points, it cannot explain their causes.

- Monitoring permits profound insight into an employee's work and allows detailed efficiency comparisons, which thus far have only been common in industrial manufacturing. It is the responsibility of the process circle and the process board to determine the instruments of process management and development.

2.13.3. Summary

The widespread penetration of the computer into operational flows creates a fine network of measurements. Organizational monitoring uses these broad databases, designed for other purposes, to derive statements about the actual organization. It offers a new set of tools for organizational structuring.

The formal results of organizational monitoring are the following evaluations:

- Transaction use

- Data and alteration volumes

- Actual function diagram

- Actual flow diagram

The insight provided by these analyses are incorporated in process management and process development.

2.14. Further Reading

Literaturstelle / Punkt	2.1. Ziele des Organisationsentwurfs	2.2. Prozeßmodell	2.3. Prozeßvision	2.4. Leistungsanalyse	2.5. Ablaufplanung	2.6. Workflowplanung	2.7. Prozeßführung	2.8. Architekturplanung	2.9. IT-Assessment	2.10. Kundenbeziehungsanalyse	2.11. Aufgabenbezogene Analysen	2.12. Benchmarking	2.13. Organisatorisches Monitoring
[BIFOA 1993]						X							
[Bleicher 1992]			X										
[Bossert 1991]				X									
[Brenner/Kolbe 1994]									X				
[Cooper 1990]							X						
[Corsten 1989]			X										
[CW 1993b]									X				
[Davenport 1993]	X	X					X						
[Eiff 1991]			X		X								
[Eversheim et al. 1992]					X								
[Ferstl/Sinz 1994]		X											
[Gaitanides 1983]		X											
[Garvin 1993]			X										
[Gerybadze 1988]			X										
[Gerybadze 1995]									X				
[Gomez/Probst 1987]			X										
[Haist/Fromm 1991]							X						
[Hansen 1992]									X				
[Harrington 1991]							X					X	
[Heilmann 1994]						X							
[Heinrich 1992]							X					X	
[Hinterhuber 1992]			X										
[Horváth et al. 1993]											X		
[Horváth/Herter 1992]												X	
[IIS 1993]									X				
[Ives/Learmonth 1984]										X			

Literaturstelle	2.1. Ziele des Organisationsentwurfs	2.2. Prozeßmodell	2.3. Prozeßvision	2.4. Leistungsanalyse	2.5. Ablaufplanung	2.6. Workflowplanung	2.7. Prozeßführung	2.8. Architekturplanung	2.9. IT-Assessment	2.10. Kundenbeziehungsanalyse	2.11. Aufgabenbezogene Analysen	2.12. Benchmarking	2.13. Organisatorisches Monitoring
[Kaplan/Murdock 1991]								X					
[Kargl 1990]				X									
[Krüger 1993]		X						X					
[Liebelt/Sulzberger 1992]				X									
[Malik 1991]			X										
[Malone et al. 1993]		X		X									
[Medina-Mora et al. 1992]		X								X			
[Mende 1994]						X					X		
[Mertens/Griese 1993]						X							
[Mertens/Plattfaut 1986]			X							X			
[Österle 1991]										X			
[Österle et al. 1994]													X
[Österle/Steinbock 1994a]									X				
[Österle/Steinbock 1994b]									X				
[Picot 1993]			X								X		
[Pieske 1992]				X								X	
[Porter 1988]			X										
[Porter/Millar 1985]			X										
[Prahalad/Hamel 1990]							X						
[Reiner 1993]				X									
[Rockart 1979]							X						
[Saxer 1993]							X						X
[Scheer 1994]		X						X					
[Scherr 1993]		X								X			
[Schildknecht 1992]							X						
[Schmid 1993]									X	X			
[Schmidt 1991]					X								
[Schumann 1992]			X										
[Seghezzi 1994]							X						
[Short/Venkatraman 1992]			X										

Literaturstelle	2.1. Ziele des Organisationsentwurfs	2.2. Prozeßmodell	2.3. Prozeßvision	2.4. Leistungsanalyse	2.5. Ablaufplanung	2.6. Workflowplanung	2.7. Prozeßführung	2.8. Architekturplanung	2.9. IT-Assessment	2.10. Kundenbeziehungsanalyse	2.11. Aufgabenbezogene Analysen	2.12. Benchmarking	2.13. Organisatorisches Monitoring
[Sommerlatte/Wedekind 1989]								X					
[Stalk/Haut 1990]											X		
[Steinbock 1994]									X				
[Steppan/Mertens 1990]										X			
[Striening 1992]							X						
[Vogler 1993]						X							
[Ward et al. 1990]		X											
[White/Fischer 1994]						X							
[Wiseman 1988]		X											
[Wunderer 1993]							X						
[Zeithamel et al. 1992]				X									

3. Data Design

Data design specifies which data are to be processed and stored by the system (see Fig. 3./1).

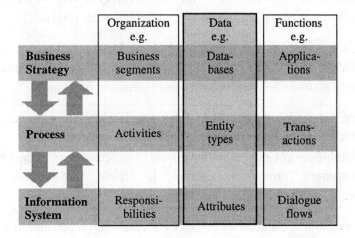

Fig. 3./1: Data design as part of Business Engineering

The strategic level of data design (data architecture) defines the process-independent databases a company wants to maintain, and specifies standards for the exchange of data between applications within and beyond the company.

The process and IS levels, to which the following discussion is restricted, use the data architecture as a framework. They specify in detail which data a specific process needs.

3.1. Data Design Objectives

Which machine-stored data does a company such as UNTEL need for the sub-process 'order acquisition'? What relationships must exist between the data? It is not difficult to list order data, such as customer number, name and address, credit limit, article number and description, order quantity and delivery date. But data design goes much deeper than this and has serious interdependences with the organization, as the following questions illustrate:

1. What customer and article data does UNTEL need? What does it cost to keep a sales projection per article group for each customer? How much time do the sales representatives need to estimate and update the sales projection? What are the savings in inventory storage costs generated by the improved planning accuracy based on sales forecasts?

2. Is it necessary to specify a period of validity for data such as delivery address or discount conditions, so that the old delivery address can apply up to 31.5.95 and the new one thereafter, for example?

3. Are the discount conditions for a specific customer, for a specific article, at a specific date, and for a specific order quantity unambiguous? Could it be that details of the conditions in the order, the customer's framework contract, the article, or other records are inconsistent?

4. Is a customer handled by one or by several sales representatives? Does a sales representative receive commission for each order obtained, a turnover commission, or a salary? Are delivery ratios calculated for customers and/or representatives?

5. Are customer data needed only in sales or also for accounts receivable (e.g. for invoicing)? What performance indicators does sales require from accounting? Does purchasing use the same article numbers and data as sales?

6. How does the structure of the sales product range appear? Do article descriptions conform to national standards in the electrical industry?

7. Should customers be able to enter their orders themselves at their business location and transmit them electronically to UNTEL? Do the existing formats of customer, article and order data conform to the EDIFACT standard, so that they can be incorporated in the new solution?

Data design is aimed at the following objectives:

- *Integration*

  The links between different areas such as Sales and Payrolling (question 4), Sales and Accounts Receivable (question 5) or Sales and Purchasing (question 5) create potential for operational processes. Integration is at present the most significant basis for restructuring business processes - both internally (questions 4 and 5) and externally (questions 6 and 7) - and consequently a central data design task.

  Integration does not mean that all applications access a common database in which all data is stored without any duplication. Integration implies that applications understand each other, so that the data to be exchanged between the applications are standardized. Thus smooth cooperation between Sales and Purchasing requires that both applications use the same article numbers (question 5) or are capable of reciprocal (automatic) assignment of article numbers.

- *Correctness*

  Data design must ensure that data are correct, so that the data correspond to reality and no inconsistencies arise between the data. For example, if the same data are recorded and stored at a single point, one source of inconsistency is excluded (e.g. questions 2, 3 and 4). Data design must formulate rules for correctness of data which are capable of monitoring the information system continuously. The more integrated and comprehensive an application is, the more reliant it is on correct data.

- *Generalization*

  The great challenge of data design is independence from any specific organizational form so as to be open to future reorganization. This means that the designer must be aware of organizational alternatives in advance. Data design can contribute to this by generalizing existing flows, forms, organizational rules, and specific business transactions. It should consolidate unnecessary organizational variants, differentiate special cases from standard cases, and structure the standard cases so that organizational variants are possible (e.g. in questions 4, 6 and 7).

- *Reconciliation with organizational design*

  Organization design provides the guidelines for data design. If UNTEL decides that a representative's commission is to be determined from order contribution margins (question 4) then contribution margins must be stored on an article-specific basis.

  Data design renders the organizational design concrete. If it is decided that sales targets are to be held for each customer, then each sales representative must enter a sales forecast for his customers, assuming they cannot be derived automatically (question 1).

  Data design can revise the organizational design. If data design gives concrete form to the method of determining sales representatives' commission (question 4), inconsistencies or new alternatives may become apparent.

- *Economic efficiency*

  The data design objectives listed have a common higher level objective: economic efficiency. Each data element (e.g. sales forecast per customer and article group) involves costs in both computing and application terms. For each data element, it is necessary to weigh up which costs (e.g. for monthly adjustment of sales forecast figures for each customer) are offset by which benefits (e.g. lowering storage costs by improving sales prognoses). In detailing the data (granularity) the data design has a decisive influence on costs (e.g. questions 1, 4 and 5).

Although data design is an information technology activity, it is primarliy a business activity. It demands a business expert with an entrepreneurial perspective, and a powerful set of tools for data modelling.

3.2. Data Model

The first step towards understanding a process's data structure is to develop a clear and easily communicable description of the data world. For this purpose we use a simplified form of the Entity Relationship Attribute (ERA) model [see Chen 1976].

3.2.1. Entity Type

Fig. 3.2.1./1 presents an extract from UNTEL's customer data as a table.

Customer

Cust. number	Name	Town	Street	Business type
...				
0815	Meier AG	Zürich	Bahnhofstr. 2	Specialist store
0830	F. Müller	Basel	Kornhausplatz 1	Dept. store
1213	Neukauf AG	Bern	Neuengasse 13	Specialist store
1720	Meier AG	Chur	Webergasse 20	Specialist store
8217	K. Kunz	Zürich	Dufourstr. 8	Mail order co.
...				

Fig. 3.2.1./1: UNTEL's customer data

The table describes five UNTEL customers. The description consists of the columns containing the customer number, name, town, street, and business type for each customer. Each row represents a customer. Each cell in the table contains an entry (for example, the entry, department store, in the business type column for row 0830).

If the customer data are maintained manually, the table corresponds to the card index, the rows to an individual card, and the columns to an item on the card. If the customer data are stored in the table of a spreadsheet program, then the data will be presented in a table such as Fig. 3.2.1./1.

Data design handles the customer data within a table, just like a spreadsheet, but has its own terminology. It refers to such a table as an entity set, and to the rows as entities. The entity set 'customer' contains the entities 0815, 0830, etc. The columns are referred to in data design as attributes; they describe customer characteristics. A given cell contains only a single attribute value (e.g. department store).

The following terms must be differentiated:

- *Entity*
  The customer 'F. Müller' is an entity. He has the customer number '0830', the name 'F. Müller', the town 'Basel', the street 'Kornhausplatz 1' and the business type 'department store'. Other entities in UNTEL's sales are the customer 'Neukauf AG' (real object), the order with the number 1300 (conceptual object) or the article 4711, i.e. the Accord CD player. The entity 'article 4711' does not represent a specific article (e.g. the Accord CD player with the serial number 00123005), but the set of all equipment referred to as the article 'CD player of the Accord type'.

An *entity* is an individual object in the real or conceptual world, which is unambiguously distinguishable from other objects.

- *Attribute*
  Customer number, name, town, street, and business type are the attributes (characteristics) of the entity type 'customer' (see below). The particular perspective determines which attributes are used to describe an entity type. A hospital, tax office, or financial institution, for example, would be interested in other attributes of the entity type 'customer' than those used by UNTEL.

An *attribute* describes a particular characteristic of an entity type. It has an unambiguous name.

- *Attribute value*
  Zürich, Basel, Bern and Chur are attribute values of the attribute 'town'. Zürich is the value of the attribute 'town' for the entity 0815 in the entity set 'customer'.

An *attribute value* is a concrete instance of an attribute (characteristic) of an entity.

- *Entity type*

  The entities 0815 and 1213 are of the same type; they are entities of the type 'customer'. The entity 3350 (sales representative Müller) is an entity of the type 'sales representative'; the entity 4711 (Accord CD player) is an entity of the type 'article'.

An *entity type* represents a class of entities with the same attributes, but different attributes values.

- *Entity set*

  Fig. 3.2.1./1 presents an extract from the entity set 'customer'. The entity set 'customer' contains all the entities in UNTEL's entity type 'customer'.

An *entity set* is the set of all entities of a specific entity type.

- *Identification key*

  If UNTEL credits the customer K. Meier from Zürich for a returned delivery, the application must be able to identify the customer unambiguously. If it credits the return to the customer with the name 'Meier AG', this would generate problems. There are several customers with the name 'Meier AG', so the attribute 'name' does not uniquely identify the customer.

  The application could use a combination of the attributes 'name' and 'town' to identify a customer. It is obvious that this also fails to guarantee unambiguity. To avoid this problem we have included the attribute 'customer number' in the table. The identification key 'customer number' is underlined in the table. The application ensures that each new customer receives a new number.

An *identification key* is an attribute or combination of attributes. It uniquely identifies each entity in an entity set, and does not change as long as the entity exists.

Fig. 3.2.1./2 summarizes the terminology.

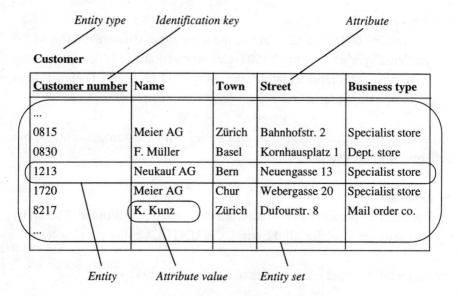

Fig. 3.2.1./2: Terminological summary

3.2.2.   Relationships Between Entity Types

An application must link entity types with other entity types. For instance, Sales must be able to establish which orders a particular customer has placed, and which customer belongs to a given order (see Fig. 3.2.2./1).

Which orders has Neukauf AG placed with UNTEL? In the entity set 'customer', Neukauf AG has the customer number 1213. The entity set 'order' also has the customer number as an attribute. The customer number 1213 appears once (in the excerpt shown), in the order with the order number 1301. Analogously, it can be established that the customer Meier AG from Zürich has placed the orders with the numbers 1300 and 1302.

Similarly, it is possible to answer the question of who the order 1301 belongs to, i.e. to pursue the relationship in the other direction.

The customer number attribute creates the relationship between the entity types 'customer' and 'order', and has therefore been included in the entity type 'order'. A relational attribute must be the identification key for one entity type ('customer'). The relational attribute, which is known as the *foreign key*, can be any attribute (key or non-key) contained in the other entity type ('order').

Customer

Cust. number	Name	Town	Street	Business type
...				
0815	Meier AG	Zürich	Bahnhofstr. 2	Specialist store
0830	F. Müller	Basel	Kornhausplatz 1	Dept. store
1213	Neukauf AG	Bern	Neuengasse 13	Specialist store
1720	Meier AG	Chur	Webergasse 20	Specialist store
8217	K. Kunz	Zürich	Dufourstr. 8	Mail order co.
...				

Order

Order number	Cust. number	Ordered by	Order date	Delivery date	Discount rate	Posn. no.[1]	Article no.[1]	Quan-tity
...								
1300	0815	Bohneis	13.03.95	30.04.95	3.50	1	4711	10
1301	1213	Mertin	14.03.95	15.04.95	2.00	1	3789	20
						2	4711	5
						3	4753	30
1302	0815	Grubli	15.03.95	30.05.95	3.00	1	2783	8
						2	2790	2
...								

[1] abbreviated here for presentational reasons

Fig. 3.2.2./1: Relationship between two entity types in tabular form

A *foreign key* in an entity type creates the relationship to another entity type. It is an attribute or a combination of attributes that serves as an identification key in another entity type.

The Entity Relationship Diagram (ER diagram) represents relationships between entity types in graphical form, as in Fig. 3.2.2./2.

For a given customer there may exist no, one or several orders. This is referred to as conditional-multiple *association*, which is represented in the ER diagram by the *cardinality* 'cn'. For a given order there is precisely one customer. The relationship is a single association; the cardinality is '1'.

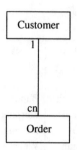

Fig. 3.2.2./2: Graphical representation of the relationship between the entity types 'customer' and 'order' in an ER diagram

The combination of these two associations forms a *relationship* between the entity types customer and order. Fig. 3.2.2./3 describes the possible kinds of cardinalities.

Cardinal-ity	Number of entities in the entity type E2 that are assigned to an entity in the entity type E1	Example (see Fig. 3.2.3./1)	E1 - E2
1 (simple)	precisely one	To each order (E1) there belongs precisely one customer (E2), i.e. for each entity in the order entity type there is precisely one related customer.	o—▶o o—▶o
c (condit-ional)	one or none	An order (E1) may be negotiated by a sales representative (E2) or not.	o—▶o o—▶
n (multiple)	at least one (n >= 1)	Each order (E1) must contain at least one article (E2).	o—▶o o⪤o o
cn (condit-ional-multiple)	one, none or several (cn >= 0)	An article (E1) may appear in one, none or several orders (E2).	o—▶o o—▶ o⪤o o

Fig. 3.2.2./3: Description of cardinalities

An *association* refers to a class of references from one entity type to another. It establishes how many entities of one entity type can be assigned to one entity of the other entity type. This is described in the ER diagram by the *cardinaltities* 1, c, n and cn.

Fig. 3.2.2./2 presents a 1:cn relationship (spoken as an 'one-to-c-n relationship').

A *relationship* between two entity types E1 and E2 consists of the association of E1 to E2 and the reciprocal association of E2 to E1.

3.2.3.   Notation

We describe an application's data with an ER-Diagram (see Fig. 3.2.3./1) and attribute lists (see Fig. 3.2.3./2).

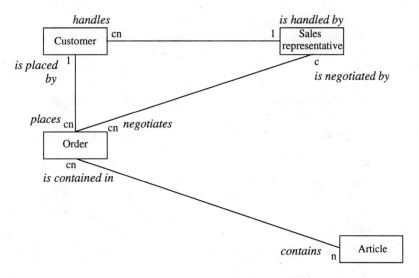

Fig. 3.2.3./1: Example of an ER diagram

Fig. 3.2.3./1 states:

• There are the entity types: 'customer', 'sales representative', 'order' and 'article'.

• A customer is handled by precisely one sales representative. A sales representative may handle none, one, or several customers.

• A customer places none, one, or several orders. An order is placed by precisely one customer.

- An order contains at least one article. An article may be contained in none, one, or several orders.

- A sales representative handles none, one, or several orders. An order may be handled by none or one sales representative.

Fig. 3.2.3./2 describes the attributes in the entity types in the form of attribute lists, separate from the ER diagram. The attributes that constitute the identification key are underlined. The foreign key is indicated by an arrow (->), followed by the name of the entity type to which the foreign key creates a relationship.

Sales representative
Representative number
Name
Town
Street
Rate of commission
Fixed allowance
Customer no. ->   Customer

Customer
Customer number
Name
Town
Street
Business type

Order
Order number
Customer no. ->   Customer
Ordered by
Order date
Delivery date
Discount rate
Position number
Article number ->   Article
Quantity

Article
Article number
Article description
Unit of measurement
Minimum stock level
Selling price

Fig. 3.2.3./2: Examples ofattribute lists

Fig. 3.2.3./3 shows an ER diagram in generalized form, while Fig. 3.2.3./4 presents an attribute list. In the ER diagram the meaning of a relationship between two entity types is usually self-explanatory. For this reason we often dispense with labelling the relationship with its name, but not with the cardinalities.

Fig. 3.2.3./3: General representation of an ER diagram

It should be noted that many different notations exist for data design [see Chen 1976; Vetter 1991; Zehnder 1989]. The notation presented here, however, has proved useful and is compatible with computerized tools available on the market for data design or systems design (CASE, Computer Aided Software Engineering).

Entity type
    <u>Key attribute 1</u>
    <u>Key attribute 2</u>
    <u>Key attribute ...</u>
    <u>Key attribute and foreign key attribute -></u>   Entity type 1
    <u>Foreign key attribute -></u>   Entity type 2
    <u>Foreign key attribute -></u>   Entity type ...
    Attribute 1
    Attribute 2
    Attribute ...

Fig. 3.2.3./4: General representation of an attribute list

The *data model* determines i) what entity types are needed by a computerized information system, ii) what relationships exist between the entity types, iii) what attributes an entity type possesses, and iv) which of them constitute identification keys and foreign keys. It is a special form of Chen's Entity Relationship (ERA) model [Chen 1976].

3.3.   Normalization

The ERA model provides a descriptive tool for data design. It allows the data environment of operational processes to be represented relatively effortlessly. The ERA model cannot judge the quality of data design, particularly with respect to the following properties:

- *Avoidance of redundancy*

  The entity type 'customer' contains the customer's address, while the entity type 'sales representative' contains the representative's address. If a representative is also a customer the address is held twice (redundantly). The problem this raises relates to data maintenance rather than wasted storage space. Any change of address requires alterations in two places. This is costly and error prone: it is all too easy to omit to change one of the addresses, resulting in inconsistent data records.

Redundancy means that the same information in the data is held in multiple locations. In other words: redundancy arises if parts of the data records (attributes, entity types) can be omitted without loss of information.

- *Simplicity*

  A sales manager has a spontaneous wish to follow the success of an advertizing campaign in the sales database. To do this he must be able to make queries by article group, by region, by order date, by delivery, etc. If the data have a simple structure he, or his assistant, will be able to do this with little effort.

  Simplicity means simple data processing (queries, storage, updating) and a natural design. The intelligibility of the data design is improved for everyone involved.

The normalization technique helps to avoid redundancy and to find simple structures. The following discussion formulates seven structural rules [see also Zehnder 1989, p. 49 ff.].

Data Design Rules

The *basic rule of normalization* states: The same information should only appear once in the data. Normalization serves to avoid redundant data records.

Contraventions of this rule arise, for example, when the same address is held once under customer and again under sales representative, or when the name of the customer appears not only in the entity type 'customer' but also in the entity type 'order'.

Rule 1: Foreign Key

Fig. 3.3./1 presents the ER diagram for the customer and the sales representative, and Fig. 3.3./2 presents the corresponding tables.

Fig. 3.3./1: ER diagram

Sales representative

Sales rep. no.	Name	Town	Street	Rate of commission	Fixed allowance	*Customer number*
...						
5050	E. Engel	Basel	Bahnhofstr. 19	2.70	2'000.00	*0830, 1213, ...*
8217	K. Kunz	Zürich	Dufourstr. 8	2.20	1'500.00	*0815, 8217, ...*
8218	A. Lang	Chur	Langstr. 10	2.10	2'000.00	*1720, ...*
...						

Customer

Cust. number	Name	Town	Street	Business type
...				
0815	Meier AG	Zürich	Bahnhofstr. 2	Specialist store
0830	F. Müller	Basel	Kornhausplatz 1	Dept. store
1213	Neukauf AG	Bern	Neuengasse 13	Specialist store
1720	Meier AG	Chur	Webergasse 20	Specialist store
8217	K. Kunz	Zürich	Dufourstr. 8	Mail order co.
...				

Fig. 3.3./2: Foreign key in the entity type 'sales representative' with cardinality 1

Since a sales representative handles more than one customer, the attribute 'customer number' (foreign key) has several values in the entity type 'sales representative'. Since each representative can have a different number of customers, each could have a different number of values for the attribute 'customer number' (in italics in Fig. 3.3./2). While this is technically feasible it gives rise to processing complexity.

Let us remove the attribute 'customer number' (which creates the relationship to the entity type 'customer') from the entity type 'sales representative', and introduce the attribute 'sales representative number' as a foreign key in the entity type 'customer'. Both entity types now have only one attribute value for each attribute, and the relationship between sales representative and customer is still retained (see Fig. 3.3./3).

Sales representative

Sales rep. no.	Name	Town	Street	Rate of commis- sion	Fixed allow- ance
...					
5050	E. Engel	Basel	Bahnhofstr. 19	2.70	2'000.00
8217	K. Kunz	Zürich	Dufourstr. 8	2.20	1'500.00
8218	A. Lang	Chur	Langstr. 10	2.10	2'000.00
...					

Customer

Cust. number	Name	Town	Street	Business type	Sales rep. no.
...					
0815	Meier AG	Zürich	Bahnhofstr. 2	Specialist store	8217
0830	F. Müller	Basel	Kornhausplatz 1	Dept. store	5050
1213	Neukauf AG	Bern	Neuengasse 13	Specialist store	5050
1720	Meier AG	Chur	Webergasse 20	Specialist store	8218
8217	K. Kunz	Zürich	Dufourstr. 8	Mail order co.	8217
...					

Fig. 3.3./3: Foreign key in the entity type 'customer' with cardinality cn

In order to simplify relationships from the start we formulate *Rule 1*:

The foreign key is always contained in the entity type with the cardinality c, cn or n.
(In a 1:1 relationship the foreign key is contained in either of the entity types.)

Rule 2: Unstructured Attributes

Rule 1 renders the solution in Fig. 3.3./2 inadmissible because the attribute 'customer number' contains several values per entity. The entity type 'order' in Fig. 3.3./4 involves a similar problem. An order can contain several positions (articles) which means that the attributes 'position number', 'article number' and 'quantity' appear repeatedly. Here the attributes are said to have an internal structure.

Order

Order number	Cust. number	Ordered by	Order date	Delivery date	Discount rate	Posn. no.	Article no.	Quan-tity
...								
1300	0815	Bohneis	13.03.95	30.04.95	3.50	1	4711	10
1301	1213	Mertin	14.03.95	15.04.95	2.00	1	3789	20
						2	4711	5
						3	4753	30
1302	0815	Grubli	15.03.95	30.05.95	3.00	1	2783	8
						2	2790	2
...								

Fig. 3.3./4 Order entity set containing attributes with internal structure

There are two basic possibilities for implementing this data structure:

- Each order constitutes an entity (see Fig. 3.3./4). This entity 'order' contains multiple position data, namely for each position. This avoids redundancy, but generates a complex structure for processing.

- Each order position constitutes an entity. In this solution each order position must include the complete order data (order number, customer number, ordered by, order date, delivery date, and discount rate). This means that the order data are recorded repeatedly (redundantly). Alterations - to the delivery date, for example - must be made in several entities, resulting in increased costs and the danger of errors.

If we separate the entity set in Fig. 3.3./4 into an entity set 'order header' (which contains only those data that arise once for each order) and an entity set 'order position' (which contains only data that arise once for each order position) then we obtain two entity types containing exclusively simple attributes (see Fig. 3.3./5). We have generated two entity types with only simple attributes (see Figs. 3.3./5 and 6) from a single entity type with structured attributes.

Order header

Order number	Cust. number	Ordered by	Order date	Delivery date	Discount rate
...					
1300	0815	Bohneis	13.03.95	30.04.95	3.50
1301	1213	Mertin	14.03.95	15.04.95	2.00
1302	0815	Grubli	15.03.95	30.05.95	3.00
...					

Order position

Order number	Posn. no.	Article no.	Quan- tity
...			
1300	1	4711	10
1301	1	3789	20
1301	2	4711	5
1301	3	4753	30
1302	1	2783	8
1302	2	2790	2
...			

Fig. 3.3./5: Order header and order position with simple attributes

We establish the basic principle: an entity's attributes are not allowed to have internal structure, i.e. an attribute may not be composed of several values or itself appear more than once. *Rule 2* states:

If an entity type contains an attribute with internal structure we must delete this attribute and extend another entity type, or introduce a new entity type, to accommodate it.

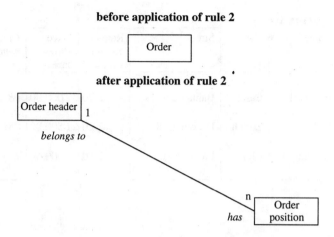

Fig. 3.3./6: ER diagram before and after application of Rule 2

Rule 3: Only Simple Relationships

In Fig. 3.3./1 we assumed that each UNTEL customer was handled by precisely one sales representative. In future, however, products from the entertainment and computing areas will be sold via different representatives. Since many customers order products from both the entertainment and the computing areas this will mean that they are handled by two different representatives. A cn:n relationship arises between the entity type 'customer' and the entity type 'sales representative' (see Fig. 3.3./7). The creation of this cn:n relationship gives rise to attributes (foreign keys) with internal structure in either the entity type 'customer' or the entity type 'sales representative' (see Fig. 3.3./8).

Fig. 3.3./7: ER diagram after the new Sales organization

Rule 2 demands unstructured attributes. Extending one or the other of the existing entity types without contravening Rule 2 is not possible. To represent the n:cn relationship, a new entity type 'customer management' needs to be introduced. The resulting ER diagram is presented in Fig. 3.3./9 (resolving multiple relationship).

Sales representative

Sales rep. no.	Name	Town	Street	Rate of commission	Fixed allowance	*Customer number*
...						
5050	E. Engel	Basel	Bahnhofstr. 19	2.70	2'000.00	*0830, 1213, ...*
8217	K. Kunz	Zürich	Dufourstr. 8	2.20	1'500.00	*0815, 8217, ...*
8218	A. Lang	Chur	Langstr. 10	2.10	2'000.00	*1720, ...*
...						

or

Customer

Customer no	Name	Town	Street	Business type	Sales rep. no.
...					
0815	Meier AG	Zürich	Bahnhofstr. 2	Specialist store	8217
0830	F. Müller	Basel	Kornhausplatz 1	Department store	5050, 8301
1213	Neukauf AG	Bern	Neuengasse 13	Specialist store	5050, 8301
1720	Meier AG	Chur	Webergasse 20	Specialist store	8218
8217	K. Kunz	Zürich	Dufourstr. 8	Mail order co.	8217
...					

Fig. 3.3./8: Possible entity sets after the new organization

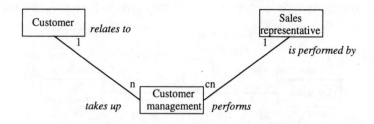

Fig. 3.3./9: ER diagram with the new customer management entity type

The entity type 'customer management' (see Fig. 3.3./10) resolves the n:cn relationship. It contains the customer number and sales representative number as foreign keys. Together these two foreign keys generate the identification key, since each entity can only be determined unambiguously when they are applied collectively.

In future UNTEL will determine each sales representative's rate of commission individually for each customer transaction. Consequently, the rate of commission attribute is eliminated from the entity type 'sales representative' and incorporated in the entity type 'customer management'.

Sales representative

Sales rep. no.	Name	Town	Street	Fixed allow-ance
...				
5050	E. Engel	Basel	Bahnhofstr. 19	2'000.00
8217	K. Kunz	Zürich	Dufourstr. 8	1'500.00
8218	A. Lang	Chur	Langstr. 10	2'000.00
...				

Customer management

Cust. number	Sales rep. no.	Rate of commis-sion
...		
0815	8217	2.20
0830	5050	2.70
0830	8301	2.50
1213	5050	2.20
1213	8301	2.40
1720	8218	3.00
8217	8217	1.00
...		

Customer

Cust. number	Name	Town	Street	Business type
...				
0815	Meier AG	Zürich	Bahnhofstr. 2	Specialist store
0830	F. Müller	Basel	Kornhausplatz 1	Dept. store
1213	Neukauf AG	Bern	Neuengasse 13	Specialist store
1720	Meier AG	Chur	Webergasse 20	Specialist store
8217	K. Kunz	Zürich	Dufourstr. 8	Mail order co.
...				

Fig. 3.3./10: The entity sets 'sales representative', 'customer management' and 'customer'
after resolution of the n:cn- relationship

Let us examine a further example: A sales representative not only handles customers, he also acquires orders. A representative can acquire none, one or several orders (entity type 'order header'). Conversely, an order is negotiated by either none or precisely one sales representative (see Fig. 3.3./11).

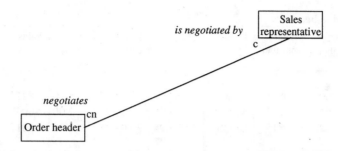

Fig. 3.3./11: ER diagram for order acquisition by sales representatives

If the relationship between the order header and sales representative is created by introducing the order number in the entity type 'sales representative' (see Fig. 3.3/12), this obviously contravenes Rule 2, since the attribute 'order number' appears more than once.

Sales representative

Sales rep. no.	Name	...	Order number
...			
5050	E. Engel	...	...
8217	K. Kunz	...	1300, 1302, ...
8218	A. Lang	...	...
...			

Fig. 3.3./12: Entity type 'sales representative' displaying inner structure in the attribute 'order number'

In contrast, if the identification key from the entity type 'sales representative' is included in the order header as a foreign key, the attribute 'sales representative number' is then stored at most once (see Fig. 3.3./13). The entities contain either the number of a sales representative or no value (null value) in the foreign key 'sales representative number'. 'Null value' is represented by the symbol 'null'.

Order header

Order number	Cust. number	Ordered by	Order date	Delivery date	Dis- count rate	Sales rep. no.
...						
1300	0815	Bohneis	13.03.95	30.04.95	3.50	8217
1301	1213	Mertin	14.03.95	15.04.95	2.00	null
1302	0815	Grubli	15.03.95	30.05.95	3.00	8217
...						

Fig. 3.3./13: Entity set 'order header' withnull values in the attribute 'sales representative number'

Working with null values increases the demands made by queries, and is undesirable in foreign keys (referential integrity, see Section 3.6.). Consequently, to represent the c:cn relationship, the entity type 'sales representative order' must be introduced (see Fig. 3.3./14). It creates the relationship between the entity types 'order header' and 'sales representative' and contains the identification key of both entity types as foreign keys (see Fig. 3.3./15).

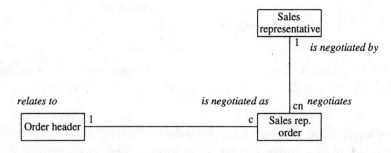

Fig. 3.3./14: Normalized ER diagram for order acquisition via sales representatives

It should be noted clearly: Only simple relationships, i.e. 1:1, 1:c, 1:n and 1:cn relationships, may exist between entity types. A new entity type always results from the resolution of non-simple relationships. *Rule 3* thus states:

Only simple relationships are permitted between entity types. Non-simple relationships need to be resolved by the introduction of a new entity type.

Sales representative

Sales rep. no.	Name	Town	Street	Fixed allow- ance
...				
5050	E. Engel	Basel	Bahnhofstr. 19	2'000.00
8217	K. Kunz	Zürich	Dufourstr. 8	1'500.00
8218	A. Lang	Chur	Langstr. 10	2'000.00
...				

Sales rep. order

Sales rep. no.	Order no.
...	
8217	1300
8217	1302
...	

Order header

Order number	Cust. number	Ordered by	Order date	Delivery date	Discount rate
...					
1300	0815	Bohneis	13.03.95	30.04.95	3.50
1301	1213	Mertin	14.03.95	15.04.95	2.00
1302	0815	Grubli	15.03.95	30.05.95	3.00
...					

Fig. 3.3./15: Entity sets for order acquisition by sales representatives

Rule 4: Resolution of Direct Recursions

UNTEL breaks down its product range into a hierarchy of article groups. Fig. 3.3./16 presents a data structure in tabular form which corresponds to the ER diagram in Fig. 3.3./17. To clarify this concept the article group structure is shown.

It is characteristic of the hierarchy that one article group can have several lower groups, but only one upper group.

The data structure in Figs. 3.3./16 and 17 creates this relationship merely by referring to the upper article group. The entity type 'article group' thus contains the article group number once as identification key and once, or not at all, as foreign key. This foreign key refers to its own entity type, the article group. This is known as direct recursion.

Article group number	Article group description	Article group number upper group
0001	Product range UNTEL AG (Switzerland)	zero
0020	├── Consumer electronics	0001
2030	│ ├── Audio	0020
2345	│ │ ├── Tuner	2030
2346	│ │ ├── Amplifier	2030
2347	│ │ ├── Cassette recorder	2030
2446	│ │ │ ├── UNTEL Highlife 3000	2347
2447	│ │ │ ├── NONAME Slimlife 30	2347
3550	│ │ │ └── ...	2347
3601	│ │ ├── CD player	2030
3602	│ │ ├── Speakers	2030
3603	│ │ └── ...	2030
3666	│ ├── Video	0020
3667	│ │ ├── Colour TV	3666
3668	│ │ ├── VHS camera	3666
3669	│ │ ├── Camcorder	3666
3670	│ │ ├── VHS recorder	3666
3671	│ │ └── ...	3666
3672	│ ├── Communication	0020
3673	│ └── Accessories	0020
0030	└── Computing	0001
3674	│ ├── Hardware	0030
3675	│ ├── Software	0030
3777	│ └── ...	0030

Fig. 3.3./16: Entity set 'article group' with built-in hierarchical representation

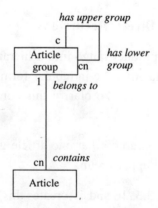

Fig. 3.3./17: ER diagram with built-in hierarchical representation

This solution appears simple and elegant at first sight, but on closer examination it brings with it the following problems:

- The integrity condition that an entity can only refer to already existing entities (referential integrity, see Section 3.6.) can not always be guaranteed for recursions. If we delete the article group 0020 (consumer electronics), then the article groups 2030 (audio), 3666 (video), 3672 (communication) and 3673 (accessories) will refer to an upper article group that no longer exists.

- The highest article group (0001) has a null value in the foreign key. This gives rise to the processing complications already mentioned under Rule 3.

An alternative solution might be to list the lower article groups (e.g. consumer electronics article group (0020) with the foreign keys 2030 (audio), 3666 (video), 3672 (communication) and 3673 (accessories)). Once again the foreign keys (the lower article groups) refer to their own entity type. This solution generates attributes (foreign keys) with structure, which is prohibited by Rule 2.

A third possibility might consist of a combination of both the above solutions, resulting in foreign keys with null values and attributes with structure simultaneously in the entity type 'article group'.

Consequently, we resolve the recursion by introducing a new entity type containing the hierarchical information (i.e. the upper and lower relationships between article groups)(see Fig. 3.3./18).

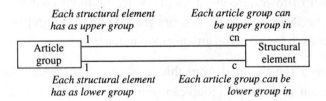

Fig. 3.3./18: Hierarchy representation without recursion in the ER diagram

Article group

Article group number	Article group description
...	
0001	Product range UNTEL AG (CH)
0020	Consumer electronics
2030	Audio
2345	Tuner
3666	Video
...	

Structural element

Article group number upper group	Article group number lower group
...	
0001	0020
0020	2030
2030	2345
0020	3666
...	

Fig. 3.3./19: Entity group 'article' with separate hierarchy representation

The entity type 'article group' no longer contains information about the relationship between its entities. Each hierarchy relationship between two article groups now corresponds to one entity of the structural element type (see Fig. 3.3./19).

UNTEL's management decides to introduce a multimedia article group. This will contain articles from both the entertainment and the computing areas. An article group must therefore be able to have a number of upper groups as well as a number of lower groups. This gives rise to minor changes in the data structure, because now there is more than one upper-group article group number for each lower-group article group number

- A network is generated from this hierarchy. The cardinality 'c' in the association 'each article group can be a lower group in' becomes 'cn' (see Fig. 3.3./20).

- The attribute 'lower group article group number' is no longer adequate as an identification key. It must be extended to include the upper-group article group number to ensure that it remains unambiguous.

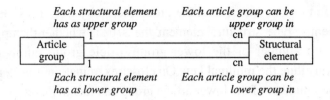

Fig. 3.3./20: ER diagram for the article group structure (network)

The separation of structure (hierarchy or network) and elements (article groups) increases an application's transparency and flexibility.

Rule 4 states:

Direct recursions are resolved by introducing a new entity type.

Rule 5: Minimal Identification Key

The identification key uniquely identifies each entity of an entity type. What happens in the entity type 'sales representative' (see Fig. 3.3./15) if the sales representative number, name, and town are used as the identification key, even though the sales representative number alone is sufficient for his unambiguous identification?

The entity type 'customer management' requires the identification key 'sales representative' as a foreign key to generate the relationship to the sales representative. If the identification key 'sales representative' includes the name and town as well as the representative number then the foreign key would also have to include these attributes. The result would be redundancy of these data with the problems mentioned in making alterations.

In addition, the sales representative's town could not be changed in the event of a change of business location, because an identification key may not be modified (see Section 3.5.). In the case of a change in location, the sales representative would have to be recorded anew. This is particularly problematic for entities with a relationship to this sales representative (e.g. the orders he has negotiated).

For these reasons identification keys should contain a minimal number of attributes. The minimal key may not always be as easily identified as in this example. Let us consider the article group hierarchy from Figs. 3.3./18 and 19. In the entity type 'structural element' the issue is whether the upper-group article group number or the lower-group article group number or both together constitute the minimal key. On closer examination it is clear that the article group number of the lower article group can identify every relationship between a lower and higher-level article group. The lower-group article group number thus constitutes the minimal key.

However, if the article groups form a network (see Fig. 3.3./20) both the upper and lower article group numbers are needed to uniquely identify every entity. Together they constitute the minimal key.

Rule 5 is formulated as follows:

An identification key must be a minimal identification key. This means that no attribute of the key can be omitted without destroying the unambiguous identification of the entities.

Rule 6: Dependency of the Identification Key

Before examining the entity type 'sales representative' once more, let us complete the address details by including the post code (see Fig. 3.3./21).

Sales representative
Sales rep. no.
Name
Post code
Town
Street
Fixed allowance

Fig. 3.3./21: Modified entity type 'sales representative'

In Rule 6 we pose the following question: Is each attribute exclusively dependent on the identification key? The name of the sales representative is obviously dependent on the representative's number. There is no other attribute in the entity type that would uniquely reveal the representative's identity.

But this is not the case for the town. The town can also be identified from the post code (simplified assumption). The attribute town can thus be determined from an attribute that is not in the identification key. Consequently, the statement that the town Chur has the post code 7000 appears more than once in the data record, creating redundancy. We therefore define a new entity type 'town' for each attribute in the entity type 'sales representative' that is not dependent on the identification key (see Fig. 3.3./22 and 23).

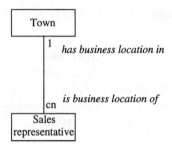

Fig. 3.3./22: ER diagram with the new entity type 'town'

Sales representative		**Town**
Sales rep. no.		Post code
Name		Town
Post code->	Town	
Street		
Fixed allowance		

Fig. 3.3./23: Attribute list with the new entity type 'town'

Another example: UNTEL is examining whether each order position in an order can have its own delivery date. This would mean that the attribute 'delivery date' must appear in the entity type 'order position' (see Fig. 3.3./24).

Order header		**Order position**	
Order number		Order number ->	Order header
Customer no. ->	Customer	Position number	
Ordered by		Article number ->	Article
Order date		Quantity	
Discount rate		Delivery date	

Fig. 3.3./24: Attribute 'delivery date' in the entity type 'order position'

However, to simplify the flows, it is determined that there can only be a single delivery date for all positions in a given order. Of course it would be possible to leave the delivery date in the entity type 'order position'. Then the same delivery date would apply to all positions belonging to a given order number. In this case only part of the identification key, the order number, is sufficient to establish the delivery date. The attribute 'delivery date' is thus not dependent on the entire identification key. It describes a characteristic of another entity type, namely the order header. It must therefore be deleted in the order position and included in the order header (see Fig. 3.3./25).

Order header
Order number
Customer no. ->   Customer
Ordered by
Order date
Delivery date
Discount rate

Order position
Order number ->   Order header
Position number
Article number ->   Article
Quantity

Fig. 3.3./25: Attribute 'delivery date' in the entity type 'order header'

Both the cases described are summarized in *Rule 6* :

All the attributes in an entity must be dependent on the identification key alone, and on the identification key in its entirety. Attributes to which this does not apply must be deleted and included in another, possibly new, entity type.

Rule 7: Generalization/Specialization

In UNTEL's Sales IS, independent entity types have been created for the business partners: customer and sales representative (see Fig. 3.3./26). The two entity types contain similar attributes (customer number, sales representative number), identical attributes (name, post code, street) and diverse attributes (business type, fixed allowance).

Customer		**Sales representative**	
Customer number		Sales representative number	
Name		Name	
Post code->	Town	Post code->	Town
Street		Street	
Business type		Fixed allowance	

Fig. 3.3./26: Entity types 'customer' and 'sales representative'

Within this framework, if an UNTEL sales representative orders articles for his own use he is both a sales representative and a customer. The attributes 'name', 'street', and 'post code' will be stored redundantly. Consequently, we combine the attributes common to the two entity types, 'customer' and 'sales representative' (name, post code, street) into a single generalized entity type: 'partner'. Since a sales representative is always an UNTEL partner, whereas a partner can (but need not be) a sales representative there is a 1:c relationship between sales representative and partner. The same applies to the relationship between partner and customer (see Fig. 3.3./27).

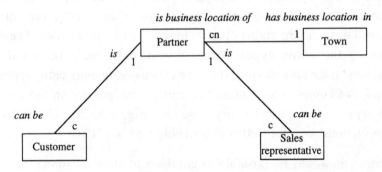

Fig. 3.3./27: Generalization of customer and sales representative in the ER diagram

The entity type 'partner' needs an identification key. So we extend it to include the attribute 'partner number'. The partner number enters into the entity types 'customer' and 'sales representative' as a foreign key. The foreign key is called either 'partner number-customer' or 'partner number-sales representative'. Since the partner number uniquely identifies each entity within customer and sales representative, the original identification keys, customer number and partner number, are removed (see Fig. 3.3./28).

Partner
    <u>Partner number</u>
    Name
    Post code->Town
    Street

Town
    <u>Post code</u>
    Town

Customer
    <u>Partner-no. customer</u> -> Partner
    Business type

Sales representative
    <u>Partner-no. sales rep.</u> -> Partner
    Fixed allowance

Fig. 3.3./28: Attributes of the entity types after generalization

The entity type 'partner' is a generalization of the entity types 'customer' and 'sales representative'; alternatively, customer and sales representative are specializations of partner.

Usually each entity can be assigned to precisely one entity type. This is the case in UNTEL for the entities in the entity types 'supplier' and 'sales representative'. The two entity types are *disjunct*, i.e. an entity can only be assigned to one of the two entity types. Because a sales representative can also be a customer, the two entity types 'customer' and 'sales representative' *overlap*, i.e. there are entities that belong to both entity types. The same applies to the entity types 'supplier' and 'customer'. To avoid data redundancy in the entities concerned, we create *overlapping* entity types that combine the common attributes. The entity type 'partner' in the example above represents a global entity type (see Fig. 3.3./29). The following discussion does not refer further to the entity type 'supplier'.

Of course, it would be possible to continue to store customer and sales representative data separately and to ensure that the other entity type is also amended in programs that record, update, or delete customer or representative data . In our simple example this would already involve six programs (record customer data, amend customer data, delete customer data, record sales representative data, amend sales representative data and delete sales representative data).

Disjunct entity types   **Overlapping entity types**

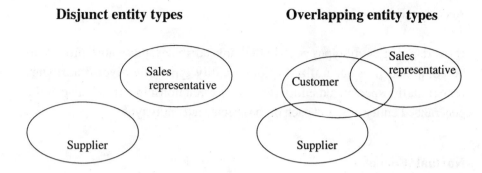

Global entity type

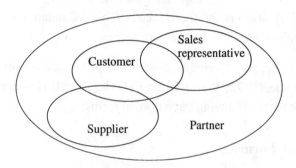

Fig. 3.3./29: Forming a global entity type

The necessary modifications would be correspondingly costly and error-prone if, for example, at some later date, customer and sales representative telephone and fax numbers were to be included in the data records. The solution suggested above means that only the entity type 'partner' would need to be extended to include the attributes 'telephone' and 'fax number'.

Generalization/specialization helps avoid redundancies in the data and in programs. Entity types are created with the greatest possible generality, in which the generally applicable attributes are combined. On this basis more specialized entity types are defined by the attributes that apply to them alone. This avoids data redundancy that can arise from several specializations (e.g. sales representative and customer). At the same time it prevents the same functionality (e.g. amending addresses) having to be provided redundantly in several programs. Generalization/specialization is an important component of object-oriented data modelling (see Section 3.4.).

Accordingly, *Rule 7* states:

If overlapping entity types contain the same attributes, those attributes are to be combined in a generalized (global) entity type. The diverse attributes remain in the specialized entity types. A 1:c relationship exists between the generalized entity type and each of the specialized entity types.

Normal Forms

The seven normalization rules formulated above provide practical instructions for designing low-redundancy, simple data structures. If all seven are followed we obtain an ERA model (see Fig. 3.3./30), in which the only redundant information is the foreign keys. This redundancy is necessary to create the relationships between the entity types.

This section is headed 'Normalization' but goes beyond normalization as a theory [see Meier 1992; Vetter 1991; Zehnder 1989]. However, the seven rules give rise to the following three normal forms:

First Normal Form

An entity type is in *first normal form*, if its attributes possess only simple attribute values.

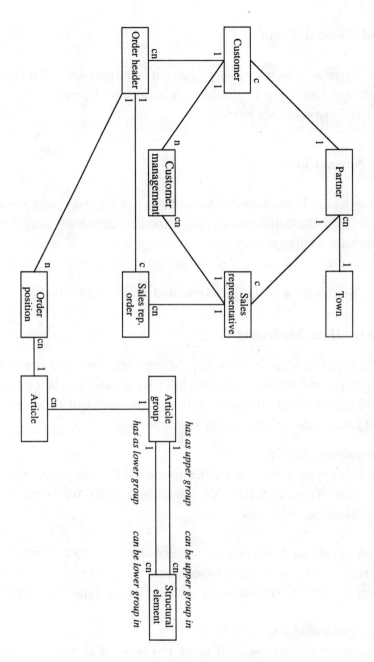

Fig. 3.3./30: Normalized ER diagram for UNTEL's Sales

Second Normal Form

An entity type is in *second normal form*, if it is in first normal form and each attribute not belonging to the identification key depends on the entire identification key, and not just part of it.

Third Normal Form

An entity type is in *third normal form*, if it is in second normal form and no attribute can be identified via a non-key attribute. Entity types in third normal form are referred to as *normalized*.

3.4.   'Semantic and Object-Oriented Data Modelling'

Semantic Data Modelling

The ERA notation in Section 3.2. differentiates between entity types, relationships, and attributes. Cardinalities are given for relationships, but only one type of relationship is recognized. If we analyze data design we can see that certain kinds of relationship arise repeatedly:

- *Categorizing abstraction*
  The entity type 'partner' is a generalization of the entity types 'customer' and 'sales representative'. 'Customer' and 'sales representative' are specializations of 'partner'.

Categorizing abstractions combine common features of entity types into new, global entity types. Common attributes appear in the more general entity types while special attributes remain in the specialized entity type.

- *Aggregative abstraction*
  If an order contains several order positions, it is an aggregation of components.

Aggregative abstractions assign several entities from one entity type to a higher-level entity type.

Semantic data modelling [see Hull/King 1987; Ortner/Söllner 1989; Scheer 1994] extends the ERA model to include categorizing and aggregative abstractions. As an example of other approaches we present a simplified form of the ASDM (A Semantic Data Model) notation [Lindtner 1991], since this is based on the ERA notation used in Section 3.2 (see Fig. 3.4./1).

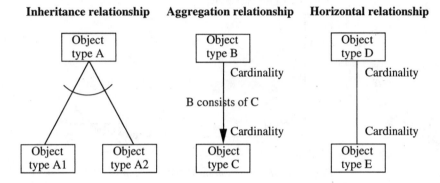

Fig. 3.4./1: ASDM notation

Lindtner refers to entity types as object types and differentiates three types of relationship:

- The categorizing abstraction is called the inheritance relationship. The inheritance relationship expresses the fact that the object types (entity types) A1 and A2 contain the same attribute A, in addition to their specific attributes.

- The aggregate relationship describes the aggregative abstraction. It expresses the idea that one object type is composed of several objects of another object type.

- Lindtner refers to all other kinds of relationship as horizontal. The cardinality is indicated only in aggregate and horizontal relationships .

Fig. 3.4./2 presents an excerpt from UNTEL's ER diagram in the ASDM-notation. It should be noted that the object type (entity type) 'order header' is replaced by 'order', since an order (and not an order header) is made up of order positions. The object type (entity type) 'order' contains the same attributes as were previously assigned to the 'order header'.

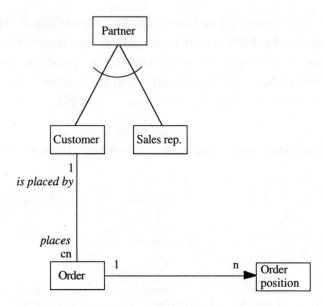

Fig. 3.4./2: ER diagram in ASDM notation

As the example shows, semantic data modelling increases the informational (semantic) power of the ER diagram. However, the notation is more complex and hence more difficult to explain in practice. Furthermore the most widely used database management systems (DBMS) do not support the relationship types in the semantic data model. For these reasons this book restricts itself to the minimal notation of the ERA model.

Object-Oriented Data Modelling

Object-oriented data modelling goes one step further: it stems from object-oriented programming and describes the data and the (program) functions (see Section 4.1.) that use the data. In the object-oriented approach, the entity type is called a class (object type), while the entity is an object (instance of a class). The functions for manipulating the data (read, amend) are called the methods of class. Objects communicate with each other via messages. If an order is to be amended, a message must be sent to the object 'order'. To amend an order position the object 'order' sends a message to the object 'order position'. The object 'order position' then calls up the method 'order position amendment'. The message corresponds roughly to calling up a function.

The object-oriented approach plays an important role, especially in programming; however, its significance for process and IS design is often overestimated. The most important extensions to the techniques discussed here are:

- Object-orientation differentiates between the relationships identified in semantic data modelling, i.e. inheritance, aggregation and horizontal relationships.

- Object-orientation combines objects and the methods that use them into classes. A class's methods can only access attributes from that class. The techniques used in this book design data and functions separately, and then use independent tools to describe how functions access objects (see Effect Model in Section 4.4.1.). Fig. 3.4./3 illustrates the difference, whereby the class data have been equated with entity types for simplicity's sake.

Object-oriented modelling consists of classes (entity types), attributes, relationships, methods (functions) and messages (function call-ups) [see Ferstl/Sinz 1990]. In the simplest case the methods are described by listing the attribute and method names.

Some of the methods presented in this book, such as effect modelling, the entity life history, or the design and breakdown of processes in the organization, use techniques from the object-oriented approach. These techniques, however, are most often used to identify the functions for a given object. More adventurous concepts in the object-oriented approach have not yet been sufficiently tested for use in the design of organizations and their information systems. For a more thorough treatment of the object-oriented approach see [Booch 1994], [Jacobson et al. 1993] and [Ferstl/Sinz 1990; Ferstl/Sinz 1991], for example.

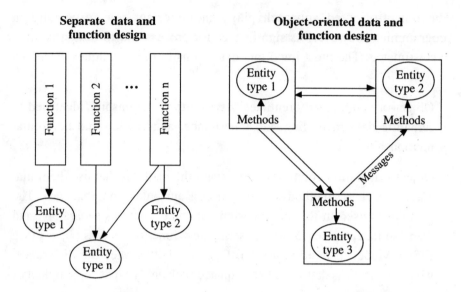

Fig. 3.4./3: Separate versus object-oriented data and function design

3.5. Keys

In data design, keys are assigned for various reasons. In addition to the identification key and foreign key from Sections 3.2.1. and. 3.2.2, there are also descriptive keys, primary and secondary keys, sort keys and match codes. A new function that accelerates data access is added to the logical functions of the keys that identify entities and create relationships.

Identification Keys

A customer sends an order by means of an EDIFACT message (see Section 2.6.2). He uses his customer number to identify himself. This is the identification key for the customer entity type. This ensures that the order is assigned to the correct customer (see Section 3.2.1.).

An *identification key* is an attribute or combination of attributes. It uniquely identifies each entity of an entity type and does not change during the life of that entity.

The identification key is a simple way of generating an unique reference to an entity in an entity set. In an EDIFACT message, for example, it avoids the otherwise laborious identification by name, address, etc. In accessing a database it creates an unambiguous relationship between the entities.

The identification key in the customer example (partner-number customer or partner number, see Fig. 3.3./28) is an *artificial key*. An artificial key contains no information about the characteristics of the customer or partner, it merely serves to provide a unique reference. Artificial keys use groups of numbers and/or letters. Identification keys must display three characteristics:

- *Uniqueness:*
  The identification key uniquely identifies each entity in an entity set.

- *Continuous allocation:*
  New entities (e.g. new customers) obtain their identification key immediately.

- *Brevity and simplicity:*
  An identification key should be brief and simple to write.

Descriptive Keys

In the past UNTEL AG has used descriptive article numbers (see Fig. 3.5./1).

A *descriptive key* consists of one or more statements about an entity's contents.

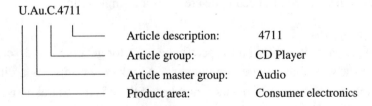

U.Au.C.4711

Article description:	4711
Article group:	CD Player
Article master group:	Audio
Product area:	Consumer electronics

Fig. 3.5./1: Example of a descriptive key

Using the customer's identification number, the sales representative could quickly identify the article type, the article's group and upper group, and the article's location within the product range. He could easily find his way around the product catalogue, which was organized in accordance with this key. Warehouse staff could easily find the correct storage bay, since the warehouse was organized in line with the product range. The article number provided information about what was inside a closed box, without it having to be opened. Even Sales Support staff who had to produce statistics about the sales success of particular parts of the product range could easily do so using the article number. The key thus contained information which allowed the product to be classified. In this case we speak of a *classification key*.

However, a descriptive key can generate problems:

- *Exhaustion of the key*
  In the upper article group for audio equipment, C denotes CD player. But since 'cassette recorder' also starts with 'C', the mnemonic aid provided by the key is disrupted. If the upper article group for audio equipment contains more than 26 article groups, the range of alphabetic values is exhausted. The key must be extended, which involves high costs, since order forms may need to be reprinted, for example.

- *Reorganization of the key*
  The structure of the product range must meet business needs (for example, it must allow regrouping if the market demands it). Relabelling articles, reorganizing the warehouse, reprinting the product catalogue in response to changes in the key involve substantial costs.

- *Network structures*
  If UNTEL AG wants to be able to combine articles into new article groups spontaneously this will not be possible with descriptive keys, since several article numbers would need to be created for a single article.

- *Uniqueness*
  In many cases it is difficult to specify the rules for generating a descriptive key in a way that ensures uniqueness. A typical example is a citizens identification number or passport number: if there is no central assignment of numbers it can easily happen that the same number is assigned several times, and consequently citizens are not uniquely identifiable.

Computerization renders descriptive keys unnecessary and avoids their problems. All the assistance provided by a descriptive key can be offered by the computer if the information in the key is included in the appropriate attributes. The database can then be used to print listings (indices, see below) by article group, article description, etc. for the product catalogue. In future the electronic product catalogue will be available, and hence much more conveniently accessible. Sales Support staff can easily formulate a query using SQL (see Section 3.10.2.) or a similar query language. The warehouse can be chaotically organized, i.e. merchandise is simply stored wherever the most suitable space is available. The computer tells the warehouse staff or the warehouse robot control where the goods are to be found. The label on the box contains not only the article number, but an article name and, if necessary, a more detailed description.

For these reasons descriptive keys are fundamentally to be avoided. There are exceptions to this rule, however. One example is the 13-digit European Article Number (EAN) (see Fig. 3.5./2). This is a descriptive identification key for retail articles within Europe.

Components ('attributes')	Country identifier	Company number	Company's article number	Check digit
European Article Number	76	12345	67890	0
Example	Switzerland	Neue Suppen AG	Special mushroom	

Fig. 3.5./2: European Article Numbers

The first two digits are the country identifier, five are used for the company number and five for the article number from that company. The final digit is a check digit. The five-digit article number can identify a maximum of 99, 999 articles per company. The product range in large companies can in some cases exceed 99,999 articles, since different colours and package sizes can multiply the volume. This would mean that the descriptive key is exhausted. The problem has been solved by giving companies with more than 99,999 articles several company numbers. This also gives rise to problems, because all the applications that have assumed a unique company number for each company must now be revised.

Nevertheless descriptive keys are necessary in certain situations. Continuous numbering of all European retail articles would require each company to request a new article number from a central office for every new article. Even on the basis of a European communication network, which does not yet exist in this form, such a procedure would be cumbersome and costly.

Primary and Secondary Keys

The sales applications access customers most frequently using the customer number, since all relationships with the customer are created via the customer number. To ensure speedy program execution, it is necessary that the customer number can be found quickly. Consequently the customer number is defined as the primary key.

The *primary key* consists of an attribute (attribute combination), in accordance with which the database management system (DBMS) organizes and optimizes data storage. Normally the identification key is the primary key.

UNTEL's Sales must also be able to identify the customer quickly by name. Therefore the attribute name is defined as the secondary key. The DBMS creates an index to handle this. An index is an auxiliary file containing the logical address (in the above case the attribute name) and the physical address of the corresponding entity. If a specific name is being sought, it is no longer necessary to search the entire database, but only the index. If an index is created for a primary key it is called the primary index, and for a secondary key it is a secondary index.

The *secondary key* is an attribute for which an index is created, in addition to the primary key.

Primary and secondary keys have functions within a database similar to the table of contents and index in books. The table of contents is the primary introduction to a book and defines the structure of the book. It usually identifies chapters uniquely. In addition, books have indices for key words, figures, authors, etc. The indices allow information to be found quickly when factors other than the structure are uppermost. If a book has no author index and an author wants to discover whether he has been correctly cited he must read the book sequentially from beginning to end. The same applies to accessing entities in a database if the access is to be made via an attribute that is neither a primary nor secondary key.

The more indices there are, the more speedy access possibilities are available. It must be recognized, though, that each secondary index increases the computer work-load whenever an entity is added, amended or deleted.

Sort Keys

The sales department requires a list showing customers sorted by annual turnover (see Fig. 3.5./3).

Customer

Partner-no. customer	Name	Town	Street	Annual turnover
...				
0815	Meier AG	Zürich	Bahnhofstr. 2	2'000'500.00
0830	F. Müller	Basel	Kornhausplatz 1	1'803'000.00
1213	Neukauf AG	Bern	Neuengasse 13	1'800'050.00
1720	Meier AG	Chur	Webergasse 20	1'345'450.00
8217	K. Kunz	Zürich	Dufourstr. 8	1'200'200.00
...				

Fig. 3.5./3: Customer list and size of turnover

The *sort key* is an attribute (attribute combination) that determines the sequence of entities in a list or table.

Search Key

If a customer places an order with UNTEL by telephone, he usually gives his name. The employee types in this name and obtains a list of customers with that name. By asking additional questions (about town, street ...) he reduces the list until the customer is uniquely identified. He typically uses the secondary key for this. If he has to access an attribute that is not defined as a primary or secondary key, the computer must search the entire database entry by entry, which in practice gives rise to waiting times of several minutes and a heavy computer work-load. It is recommended, therefore, that indices be created for search keys.

The attribute (attribute combination) used to search for an entity is called the *search key*.

Match Code

Customer search is a very frequent procedure in order recording. Usually the details needed to identify the customer are incomplete. For example, a customer called Maier or Mayer from Zürich is being sought. In a search using the search key, the order recording staff must display all customers called either Maier or Mayer and then select those from Zürich. Many software packages offer a special form of search key for this task, known as match codes. These simplify the search for the user and accelerate it for the computer.

A match code consists of several abbreviated attributes, in Fig. 3.5./4 the code includes name, town and street. The employee only needs to enter parts of the given attributes. The more accurate the search data (e.g. 'Zü' in Fig. 3.5./4 instead of 'Z', or details of the street name), the quicker the selection is.

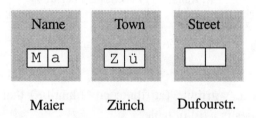

Fig. 3.5./4: Example of a match code entry

A *match code* consists of several search values, ordered in a particular sequence.

3.6.   Integrity Conditions

A database is correct when all the values in the database correspond to reality and do not contain inconsistencies. This means, for example, that a returned delivery is credited to the correct customer, or that it is possible to establish at any time what articles still have to be delivered to a customer. The DBMS can ensure the accuracy of the database if we prescribe rules for that correctness.

Integrity conditions are rules about the permissibility of attribute values. They help ensure the absence of inconsistencies in the database.

A returned delivery must be credited to the particular customer who paid for the delivery. If the staff responsible for accounts receivable can refer to the customer number, and the customer number is unambiguous, we can assume that the correct credit will be made (see identification key in Section 3.2.1.).

The *first integrity condition* states:

Unambiguity condition: Each entity type must have an identification key that uniquely identifies each entity.

On the basis of the unambiguity condition, the DBMS ensures that when a new entity is included it is given a value for the identification key and that this value only appears once in the entity set.

For UNTEL to be able to ensure that incoming orders are delivered to the right customers it must be able to identify unambiguously who placed the order. Each order must be assigned to precisely one customer. The order and customer data are in different entity types ('customer' and 'order header'), between which a relationship exists via the attribute 'partner number-customer'. The 'partner number-customer' is the identification key in the entity type 'customer' and the foreign key in the entity type 'order header'. The foreign key 'partner number-customer' provides the reference to the entity type 'customer'.

If the foreign key contains an attribute value that has no counterpart in the customer identification key the order cannot be assigned to a customer. An attribute value in the foreign key (partner number-customer in the order header) is only useful if the corresponding entity in the referenced (customer) entity type exists.

From this we can derive the *second integrity condition* :

Referential integrity: Every attribute in a foreign key must exist as an attribute value in the identification key of the referenced entity type.

The DBMS monitors the correspondence between identification and foreign keys on addition and deletion of entities. For example, it only allows an order header to be recorded if a value is given in the foreign key which appears as the identification key in the customer entity set (e.g. the value 0815 for Meier AG in Fig. 3.2.1./1).

If we consider the two entity types - 'customer' and 'order header' - in isolation, an order header can be deleted without problem, since the entity type 'customer' contains no attributes from the order header as foreign keys. In contrast, problems do arise if the customer 'Meier AG' is deleted: the entity type 'order header' contains the 'partner number-customer' as foreign key. Orders 1300 and 1302 would then contain the 'partner number-customer' of a no longer existing customer and could not be assigned. There are two possible solutions to this. Process requirements determine which of the two should be chosen:

- *Restrictive deletion:* A customer can only be deleted from the records if he has no outstanding orders. This means that the deletion operation will not be carried out as long as the entity to be deleted (customer 'Meier AG') is referenced by another entity (orders 1300 and 1302).

- *Continued deletion:* In this case the entity 'Meier AG' and all the orders from Meier AG - that is orders 1300 and 1302 - are deleted. Continued deletion means that when an entity is deleted all entities of another entity type which reference that entity are also deleted. Similarly, all order positions would be removed if the order header were deleted.

A sales quantity of -5 or 3.4 televisions makes no sense. The attribute sales quantity may only contain positive whole numbers. The set of values that an attribute can assume is called the domain. The *third integrity condition* states:

Domain condition: Each attribute is assigned a domain. The attribute may only assume values that appear in this domain.

We normally employ the data types from the DBMS in use to define the domain. Integrity condition 14 in Fig. 3.6./2 uses the data type 'NUMBER (5.2)' to specify that the order discount rate is a number with three digits before the decimal point and two after. Integrity condition 15 uses the data type 'INTEGER (9)' to permit sales quantities of only whole numbers.

Thus, the integrity conditions give concrete form to, and supplement, the results from Sections 3.2. through to 3.5. They are needed to transfer the data design to a DBMS, and are incorporated in the documentation of entity types. To illustrate we formulate the integrity conditions in Fig. 3.6./2 for the ER diagram in Fig. 3.6./1. In the case of referential integrity the column 're. entity type/attribute' indicates in which entity type the foreign key is the identification key, and what the identification key is called there.

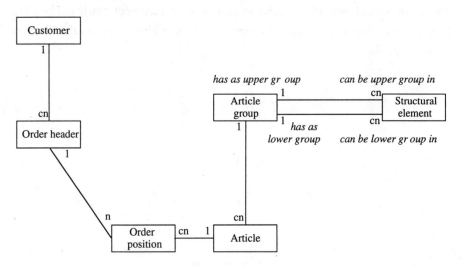

Fig. 3.6./1: Excerpt from the ER diagram for the Sales IS

These integrity conditions are based on the relational data model, which in third normal form contains the integrity conditions 'unambiguous identification key' and 'referential integrity'. Integrity conditions 1 to 6 in Fig. 3.6./2 specify the underlining of the identification key in the indented lists and tables. The referential integrity conditions (numbers 7 - 12) give substance to references of the form 'attribute name -> name of the referenced entity type' in the attribute lists (see Section 3.2.3.). Integrity conditions 13 to 15 contain additional statements that have not yet been available. They determine the attribute domains.

Although the integrity conditions discussed render the notation presented in Section 3.2.3. more precise, they scarcely add any further information. For some years academics have been trying to formulate more meaningful statements about the data in integrity conditions. One example might be: 'the total value of a customer's outstanding orders may not exceed the credit limit.' However, the proposed solutions have not been accepted. The reasons are associated with the computer work-load involved in checking such complex conditions, and the complexity of finding an exact formulation.

An advance in this direction is currently expected from object-oriented databases. Here the system designer writes a method (program function), for including orders, and one for changing the credit limit. These methods then check the stated integrity condition and prevent incorrect entries. They are linked to the database so that all programs are only able to access the data via these methods.

Integ. condition no.	Entity type	Attribute	Integ. condn.	rel. entity type/ attribute
1	Customer	Partner-no. customer	identified	
2	Order header	Order number	identified	
3	Order position	Order number Position number	identified	
4	Article	Article number	identified	
5	Article group	Article group no.	identified	
6	Structural element	Lower-group article group number Upper-group article group number	identified	
7	Order header	Partner-no. customer	referenced	Customer/partner-no. customer
8	Order position	Order number	referenced	Order header/order number
9	Order position	Article number	referenced	Article/article number
10	Article	Article group no.	referenced	Article group/ article group number
11	Structural element	Upper-group article group number	referenced	Article group/ article group number
12	Structural element	Lower-group article group number	referenced	Article group/ article group number
13	Order header	Order date	Date of order recording <= Delivery date	
14	Order header	Order discount rate	NUMBER (5.2), 0 <= Order discount rate <= 100	
15	Order position	Sales quantity	INTEGER (9), Sales quantity > 0	

Fig. 3.6./2: Integrity conditions

3.7.   Code Tables

UNTEL sub-divides its customers into segments (see Fig. 3.7./1),

- in order to address each segment individually in advertising,

- in order that sales analysis can compare UNTEL's sales figures with industry sales figures from market research institutes

- in order that pricing policy can differentiate between the segments.

Customer segment
Specialist store
Discount store
Department store
Mail order company
Employee

Fig. 3.7./1: UNTEL's customer segments

The entity type 'business type' in the entity type 'customer' must fulfil these requirements. It is often the case that different departments find different customer classifications of relevance (e.g. by payment behaviour, industry, customer segment or sales quantity). The customer classification (coding) must be mutually agreed upon by the departments. If this cannot be achieved, separate attributes must be provided.

UNTEL was able to achieve internal agreement on the business types listed above. They became an internal UNTEL standard. Now it is necessary to ensure that every sales representative and Sales Support employee who records potential customers uses the values listed in Fig. 3.7./1 for the business type. To achieve this the permitted customer segments are defined in the form of codes in a code table (entity table) (see Fig. 3.7./2) and the data model is extended to include the entity type 'business type', so that each customer is assigned exactly one value (code) from the business type (see Fig. 3.7./3). The entity type 'customer' thus no longer contains the name of the business type, but only its number (attribute code) as a foreign key.

Business type

Code	Code description
1	Specialist store
2	Discount store
3	Department store
4	Mail order co.
5	Employee

Fig. 3.7./2: Business type code table

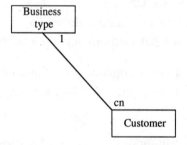

Fig. 3.7./3: ER diagram for business type and customer

A *code table* (central table, static table, domain table) defines all the possible entities of an entity type in a complete listing.

Of course, it would be possible for the programs (transactions; see Chapter 4.) to record and modify customer data to ensure that only the permitted business types are used, instead of setting up a code table. But then these programs would need to include the information in the code table. Alterations to the business types would then require alterations to several programs. But even if the alteration was restricted to a single program, it would still be simpler to alter a code in a code table than a program. We therefore formulate the following rule for data design:

If an attribute's domain consists of a specification of values with prescribed semantics, a code table should be established.

Alterations to these kinds of codes belong to the most time-consuming information system maintenance. They can affect reporting (e.g. sales planning and control), procedures (e.g. commissioning), activity distribution, programs etc., which make reference to the codes. Companies pay correspondingly great attention to the design and maintenance of their code tables. Consequently, many companies have their own application for code table management.

3.8.   Providing Data History

On 1 July 1995 the customer 'Meier AG' moves his place of business from Zürich to Basel. He informs UNTEL of his change of address in advance, at the end of April. In the data model developed so far UNTEL can only store one address and as a result has the following options:

- It records the new address immediately. This means that all deliveries made between the end of April and 1 July are sent to the new (but not yet valid) address.

- It files the letter informing of the change of address for resubmission on 30 June and only then changes the address. This involves additional administrative expenses and brings with it the danger that the alteration will be forgotten.

UNTEL must therefore be able to store more than one address for the same customer, of which only one applies at a particular date. The data model must be extended to include time-specific attributes (here address dates). In such a case we speak of providing data history.

Providing *data history* means that a data model allows for time-specific attributes.

Providing Data History via an Additional Entity Type

UNTEL extends the data model with an entity type for 'customer data not in effect'. 'Customer data not in effect' contains all customer data that do not apply at present, i.e. all data that are either no longer valid, or not yet valid. If customer data are recorded that only apply in future they are stored in 'customer data not in effect'. A batch transaction (see Section 4.6.) checks periodically (e.g. every evening or once a week), whether data stored in 'customer data not in effect' have become applicable, and if so transfers them to the entity types 'customer', 'partner' and 'town'. In contrast, the old data are removed from 'customer', 'partner', and 'town' to 'customer data not in effect'.

There is a 1:cn relationship between 'customer' and 'customer data not in effect' (see Fig. 3.8./1). Since the entity set 'customer data not in effect' can contain several entities from the same customer, the 'partner-number customer' no longer suffices as identification key. We therefore extend the identification key with the attribute 'valid from' (see Fig. 3.8./2).

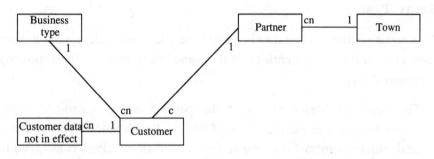

Fig. 3.8./1: Providing data history via an additional entity type

Business type	**Partner**	**Town**
Code	Partner number	Post code
Code description	Name	Town
	Post code-> Town	
	Street	

'customer data not in effect'	**Customer**	
Partner-no customer ->Customer	Partner-number customer ->	Partner
Valid from	Valid from	
Business type	Business type code->	Business type
Name		
Post code		
...		

Fig. 3.8./2: Attribute list of entity types for providing customer data history

In the entity type 'customer' there is only one entity per customer, which means that the identification key can be retained. Nevertheless, we extend the attribute list to include the attribute 'valid from' so that data can be stored with the correct 'valid from' date when they are transferred from customer data to 'customer data not in effect'.

The proposed solution gives rise to redundancies: the customer 'Meier AG' in the above example has changed his address but not his company name. Nevertheless, the company name is stored redundantly in both entity types 'partner' and 'customer data not in effect'. Since all the entities in 'customer data not in effect' are correct and will not be altered for this change of address, this redundancy can be tolerated.

Providing Data History via Additional Entities in the Same Entity Type

An alternative to providing data history via an additional entity type is to keep past, current and future entities in the same entity type, as the following examples show:

- The customer 'Meier AG' (with the 'partner-number customer' 0815) moves his place of business from Zürich to Basel. Sales representatives deal with customers from their region. The town of Zürich is assigned to the central Swiss region, whereas Basel is assigned to the south/west Switzerland region. As a result a different sales representative, namely Mr. E. Engel with the 'partner-number sales representative' 5050, is responsible for Meier AG from 1 July. Customer management must be altered from 1 July.

- A further example of the need for data history in the case of account management arises if a sales representative's rate of commission is specified for each customer relationship and is altered from time to time.

In both cases we store the altered relationship between customer and sales representative as an additional entity in the entity type 'customer management' (see Fig. 3.8./3). Since entities are neither deleted nor overwritten, past, current and future account management are held in the same entity type 'customer management'. Of course, the entity type 'customer management' needs to be extended to include the attribute 'valid from'.

This means that for a specific customer/sales representative combination several entities can exist in the entity set 'customer management'. The identification key consisting of the partner numbers of the customer and the sales representative is no longer unambiguous and must therefore be extended to include the attribute 'valid from' (see Fig. 3.8./3).

Customer management

Partner-no. customer	Partner-no. sales rep.	Valid from	Rate of commis- sion
0815	8217	1.1.95	2.20
0815	5050	1.7.95	2.30
0815	5050	1.9.95	2.40

Fig. 3.8./3: Additional entities in the entity type 'customer management' generated by providing historical data

As we can see, this now raises the issue of which sales representative deals with a given customer at a given time. Referring to the example in Fig. 3.8./3 we first identify all the entities with the 'partner-number customer' 0815, and then check the attribute 'valid from' for all four entities to establish those entities valid at a particular date (see Section 3.10.2.1 on read-only access to data).

If we use a common entity type for past, current and future entities, substantial costs are involved in identifying the entity that is currently valid. Since the account management data are relatively seldom used (e.g. for calculating sales representatives' commission) and do not change frequently this solution is justifiable.

But this is not the case for historical customer data. The currently valid customer address, for example, is needed to record and amend orders, to print order confirmations, delivery notes, invoices and reminders, and to dispatch merchandise. If in each of these cases we had to go through the operational procedure described above, the computer work-load, and user waiting time would rise dramatically. In this case, therefore, we store the 'customer data not in effect' in an independent entity type and check periodically using a batch transaction which data are currently valid, instead of checking the validity of each entity 'customer' every time customer data is accessed.

A normalized data model can be extended in two ways to provide data history:

1. All attributes requiring a history can be duplicated and summarized in an independent entity type. In this new entity type the identification key must be extended to include the attribute 'valid from'.

2. Current and historical data are stored in the same entity set. The identification key must be extended to include the attribute 'valid from'.

3.9. Data Integration

The data design techniques discussed thus far have been applied exclusively to a limited application area, such as UNTEL's Sales IS. As a result they have implicitly excluded an important problem, namely the integration of separately-developed or separately-operated applications with respect to their data. In practice, every company lives in a heterogeneous application world in which new developments must work alongside existing in-house applications and purchased package software. Furthermore, cooperation with suppliers' and customers' applications is becoming increasingly prevalent.

Let us consider two examples from UNTEL:

• Before accepting an order, UNTEL checks whether the customer is within his credit limit, i.e. whether the sum of all outstanding invoices together with the value of the order reaches or exceeds his credit limit. The Sales IS administers a customer's credit limit and order data, while invoices and payments are booked by the accounts receivable application in the financial IS. Before accepting an order, the Sales IS thus requires information about outstanding debts from the accounts receivable application.

• Many UNTEL customers use a software package for retailers. This prints their orders to suppliers, including UNTEL. The customers send the orders by Fax to UNTEL, where Sales staff enter the order into the Sales IS. The same occurs in reverse with the delivery note and invoice. The Sales IS and the customer exchange data on paper. In future UNTEL plans to handle this exchange electronically as far as possible.

Data integration links applications via the exchange of data.

Data integration is an important source of process restructuring (see Section 1.1.). From the organizational design perspective the following questions relating to data integration must be answered:

- What type of data integration is suitable for the process?

- Should data exchange occur synchronously or asynchronously?

- What data does an application need from another application?

- Which transactions are needed for the data exchange?

3.9.1. Types of Data Integration

Manual exchange of data between applications - between UNTEL and the retailers, for example - means repeated (redundant) recording of data, and the associated danger of recording errors, loss of time and increased costs. It is only economically feasible where the demands on data integration are small (e.g. few data to be exchanged). We do not regard this as data integration, but distinguish the following types:

Integration of the Data

It is not difficult to extend the data model for the Sales IS in the first example to include information about the customers' outstanding debts (see Fig. 3.9.1./1).

The outstanding debts are the sum of customers' open invoice positions, that is, those invoice amounts that have not yet been offset by payments. The highly simplified data model takes into account the fact that order address, invoice address and payment address may differ (especially in the case of branch organizations), and that part payments or collective transfers are possible. If the Sales IS data model is extended in this way, and if the Finance IS uses the same database, then the Sales IS can read current outstanding debts from the database at any time. Conversely, the Finance IS has access to the sales data, for invoicing, for example.

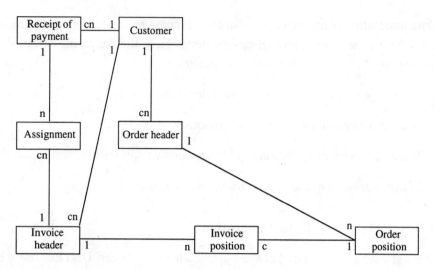

Fig. 3.9.1./1: Introducing the entity types 'invoice header', 'invoice positions', 'receipt of payment' and 'assignment'

Similarly, in the second example it is possible to link the customer directly to the Sales IS: the retailers record their orders themselves from their place of business to the Sales IS. Since this involves checking the availability of the articles wanted and conformity with the credit limit, the orders received no longer need to be confirmed by UNTEL. With this type of data integration customers must be provided with transactions that can directly access UNTEL's data from their workplace. Of course, customers must not be allowed to see their competitors' order data, which requires a system of authorization (see Section 4.10.) to limit their access to the data in the Sales IS. The solution described allows UNTEL to offer its customers access to up-to-date and complete data, i.e. improved process outputs. At the same time the administration of the order acquisition process is simplified (neither data recording by Sales staff nor sending of order confirmations is required).

In both the integration of the Sales IS with the Finance IS and the accessing of Sales IS data by transactions from the customers' workplace, several applications use the same data. This form of data integration is referred to as *integration of the data* .

In *integration of the data* various applications use the same data (and hence the same data model).

'Integration of the data' has the following advantages and disadvantages [see Hackstein/Köhl 1991, p. 31; Thoma 1993, p. 223 f.]:

⊕ Integration of the data opens up great potential for processes, by ensuring that the data required are immediately available (see the example of Getzner Textile AG in Section 1.1.).

⊕ The data are free of redundancy and hence consistent.

⊖ The design of the data model must fulfil the requirements of all the applications involved. The number of applications and the speed with which they change make this an illusion in most companies.

⊖ Alterations to one application which affect the data model can have implications for the other applications involved.

⊖ Applications running on different computers must have direct access to the common data via a network, which in many cases leads to unjustifiable network costs and access times.

⊖ The technical infrastructure (network, database server, etc.) must be compatible.

⊖ Package software or other already existing applications have their own data model which will not typically be consistent with the new application's data model.

Many companies have in the past attempted to create an enterprise-wide, integrated data model. For the reasons listed above they have had to satisfy themselves with integrated databases for manageable sub-areas, and as a consequence use the following form of data exchange for integrating applications.

Integration via the Data

In UNTEL's case the integrated database between the Finance IS and Sales IS in the first example is ruled out because the Finance IS already exists, runs on its own ageing computer and is to be replaced next year by package software.

As a result customers' outstanding debts are stored in both the Sales IS and the Finance IS, i.e. redundantly. The invoices and payments received are recorded only in the Finance IS. In the Sales IS we do not store all the invoice and payment data, but only the outstanding debts. Thus we extend the entity type 'customer' with the attribute 'outstanding invoice positions' (see Fig. 3.9.1./2).

Customer
    <u>Partner-no. customer</u> ->   Partner
    Valid from
    Business type code ->   Business type
    Credit limit
    Outstanding invoice positions

Fig. 3.9.1./2: Extending the entity type 'customer' to include the attribute 'outstanding invoice positions'

A transaction computes the outstanding debts daily and makes them available to the Sales IS, which then enters the data into its database. There is partial inconsistency between booking the invoices or receipt of payments and incorporating the data in the Sales IS database, since not all alterations are taken into account. As a result an order might be turned down because the credit limit has been exceeded, even though payment has been received in the meantime. Since this very seldom arises, UNTEL decides in favour of the solution described.

In the example of order recording by the customer, data integration without direct access to the Sales IS data is again possible: A customer records the order data in the merchandise management system database. The order data are then transmitted via the network to the UNTEL's Sales IS. For each order, a transaction checks whether the customer is within his credit limit and whether all the order positions are available by the delivery date. If both are fulfilled, the order data are entered into the UNTEL database and the customer is sent an electronic order confirmation (see also Section 3.9.4.). Otherwise the customer is sent a refusal - again electronically. Hence the customer cannot tell, at the time of order recording, whether UNTEL will accept the order. He (or the customer's information system) only discovers this on receipt of the order confirmation or refusal. The time interval between order recording and receipt of the confirmation/refusal thus depends on the data transfer time, the point at which the data is transferred (e.g. immediately after order recording) and the point at which the Sales IS checks the incoming order.

In both of the cases described above the applications hold their own data. In order to ensure the consistency of data held redundantly in more than one information system, the data concerned must be exchanged. We refer to this as integration *via the data*.

In *integration via the data* applications hold their own data records. Redundant data are kept consistent by means of data exchange (controlled redundancy). Between alteration of the redundant data in one of the applications involved and the next data exchange, the database of the other application is inconsistent with respect to these data.

Data can be exchanged via magnetic tape, diskettes, networks, etc. Here, however, we are less interested in the technical aspects of the solution than in the organizational consequences of 'integration via the data':

⊕ Integration via the data is relatively simple and can be achieved at little cost.

⊕ The databases can be modelled and implemented independent of each other. Only the data to be exchanged between the databases needs to be standardized.

⊕ In comparison with data exchange by Fax or manual data recording, time-consuming activities can be avoided.

⊖ Integration via the data demands precautions - especially organizational ones - for handling inconsistency (e.g. in the outstanding invoice positions attribute), when detected.

⊖ These precautions which could prevent radical changes to flows, easily arise in the example of data exchange between UNTEL and its customers.

⊖ If the requirement for up-to-date data is high the costs of data exchange rise dramatically.

⊖ Extra costs are involved in the maintenance of redundant data.

3.9.2. Synchronous and Asynchronous Data Exchange Between Transactions

Data exchange demands additional functionality from the information system (see Section 4.3.). If the retailer records the order data using the 'customer online order recording' transaction in UNTEL's Sales IS, then only this transaction is involved. However, if the retailer places the same order using EDIFACT, then at least two transactions are involved: one transaction that sends the data and one transaction that receives, checks and stores the data in the Sales IS. In Fig. 3.9.2./1 an additional transaction is added to evaluate the answer.

From the organizational perspective this means that the processing of the retailer's transaction 'place EDIFACT purchase order' is complete without waiting for a response from UNTEL's receiving transaction, i.e. without knowing whether the order has indeed been accepted. In the Sales IS the transaction 'receive and check EDIFACT purchase order' checks the EDIFACT order received with no temporal dependence on the customer's transaction.

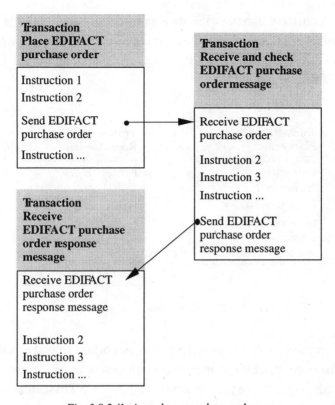

Fig. 3.9.2./1: Asynchronous data exchange

The sending and receiving transactions need not be simultaneously capable of communication, the data being transferred are put into intermediate memory. This type of data exchange is comparable to sending orders by mail. It is termed *asynchronous* .

In *asynchronous data exchange* each transaction completes its processing on dispatch of the message without waiting for an answer. The communicating transactions need not be simultaneously capable of communication.

However, if a consumer is standing in a retailer's shop and wants to know if a certain television can be delivered in two days, asynchronous data exchange is inadequate, as too much time elapses between sending the order and UNTEL's response.

For on-the-spot information the retailer needs synchronous data communication (see Fig. 3.9.2./2): this records the order in the retailer's system, which then transfers the data immediately to UNTEL's Sales IS where it initiates a transaction and awaits the response indicating whether the television is available. The Sales IS checks the availability of the television and sends a response.

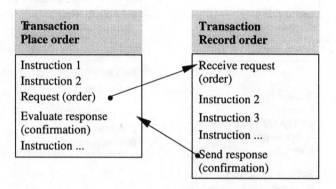

Fig. 3.9.2./2: Synchronous data exchange

From the organizational perspective it is important that the retailer can perform the order placement operation immediately and in its entirety. The retailer needs only a single transaction to do this. If UNTEL cannot accept the terms of the order, the retailer receives this information immediately.

In this case data exchange occurs *synchronously* (synonym: *request-response*). Synchronous data exchange is equivalent to order placement by telephone: the customer rings up and asks whether an article is available (request). While he waits the Sales staff check whether the desired article is available and that the credit limit is not exceeded. The Sales staff reply to the customer (response).

In *synchronous data exchange (request-response)* the sending transaction interrupts processing and only continues when the response has arrived from the receiving transaction. This requires that both types of transaction are simultaneously capable of communication.

From the organizational perspective synchronous data exchange is equivalent to accessing an integrated database.

3.9.3.   Data Exchange Requirements

Data design formulates the requirements on data exchange from the organizational, rather than the technical perspective. The designer needs only to be able to assess the possibilities for the process.

Data Model

The content of the data exchange needs to be determined independent of its form. What does this mean in the case of 'integration of the data' and 'integration via the data'?

Data exchange using 'integration of the data'

If the Sales and Finance IS use the same data model, the design of the data model must take into account the requirements of both information systems. How diverse these requirements can be has already been indicated in the simple example of the credit limit check: In the Finance IS the booking of invoices and payment receipts affects revenue accounts, accounts receivable, etc., whereas in the Sales IS only the sum of outstanding debts is relevant. In designing the data model it is necessary to decide how the data model handles the accounts from accounts receivable, and whether it contains an outstanding invoice position attribute for each customer (see Fig. 3.9.1./2) or whether the Sales IS calculates the outstanding debts from the data in accounts receivable each time it checks a credit limit.

Using 'integration of the data' the data model must take into account the requirements of all the applications involved.

Data exchange using 'integration via the data'

Using 'integration via the data' the applications involved have their own data models, which may be very different. We differentiate two possible ways of describing the data to be exchanged:

1. *Data exchange on the basis of one of the two data models*
   We formulate the requirements on the contents of the data exchange on the basis of one of the two applications, for example, UNTEL's Finance IS. If the Sales IS does not obtain the data from an integrated database ('integration of the data'), it will additionally need the

customer's identification key. But it only needs those customers' outstanding debts that have changed since the last data exchange. This requirement can be framed as an SQL statement (see Section 3.10.2.) on the basis of the Finance IS data model, as in Fig. 3.9.3./1.

> SELECT   debtor number, outstanding invoice positions
> FROM   debtor
> WHERE   alteration date >= date of last reconciliation

Fig. 3.9.3./1: 'Outstanding invoice positions' interface'

This SQL statement defines the data to be exchanged. The execution of the exchange itself is the task of transactions (see Chapter 4.). The interface description (Section 3.9.5.) is thus the starting point for deriving the transactions (see Section 4.3.) and determining their effects (see Sections 4.3. and 4.4.1.).

If applications do not communicate via an integrated database, the requirements can be formulated as an SQL statement on the basis of the data model of one of the two transactions. The relevant data types and code tables are those of the data model selected.

2. *Data exchange via a neutral data model*
    Thus far in Section 3.9.3. we have considered internal data exchange. In this case the designers of the applications involved can agree on one of the applications. In the case of 'integration via the data' between the customer's retail system and the Sales IS, the customer is particularly keen to avoid entering into bilateral interface agreements that would bind him to UNTEL. What he wants is a generally applicable data model for data exchange that is accepted as a market standard. EDIFACT is a very widespread standard (see Section 3.9.4.). A data exchange standard is also useful internally to reduce the multiplicity of data models for data exchange.

If two applications communicate via a neutral data model we formulate the requirements on the data needed using the commonly recognized data model. The data types and code tables of the data model selected are the relevant ones.

Since the EDIFACT standard is not documented as a relational data model, the data to be exchanged cannot be expressed without further ado in SQL.

Semantics and Syntax of the Data

One objective of the interface specification is to avoid having to know about the cooperating applications or their data models in detail, and to restrict attention to the data to be exchanged. In some circumstances this objective is difficult to attain. Do we know, for example, from the data model and SQL statement in Fig. 3.9.3./1 whether the Finance IS has an attribute for outstanding invoice positions, and, if so, whether customer credits are reflected there? We must have an understanding of the transactions that manipulate these data. This means that we must know the application well enough to be able to determine precisely the semantics and syntax of the data to be exchanged. A verbal description of the entity types and attributes can only give an intuitive understanding of the semantics.

Data semantics are determined by the transactions that manipulate the data.

Up to now we have assumed that the identification keys for debtor and customer are the same. If this is not the case, the debtor number from the Finance IS must be converted into the customer number from the Sales IS. This is merely an example of the manifold conversions that are needed because different applications model the same or similar data differently.

Data conversion transforms the data from one data model into the data of another data model.

Figures 3.9.3./2 and 3 present two variants of data conversion. In the first case the designers agree on one of the two data models for the applications involved. In the examples in Fig. 3.9.3./2 the sending application uses (broken lines) the finance data model to generate (directional lines) the message. The receiving transaction must convert the data from the finance data model into the data of its own data model (sales).

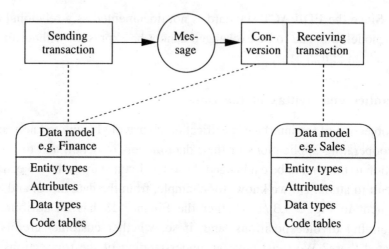

Fig. 3.9.3./2: Conversion in the receiving transaction

The exchange of EDIFACT orders between the retail system and UNTEL's Sales IS is more cumbersome. The retailers and their suppliers have agreed to exchange data using the EDIFACT standard. In other words, they will use the neutral data model of the EDIFACT standard. This additional data model requires a further conversion. First the retail system converts the order from his data model into the EDIFACT model, then UNTEL's Sales IS converts the EDIFACT model into its own data model (see Fig. 3.9.3./3). Furthermore, the message has the EDIFACT format.

Data exchange in the case of 'integration via the data' means that the value of an attribute from one application is transferred to an attribute in the other application. If the data types or code tables (domains) differ, the value must be converted.

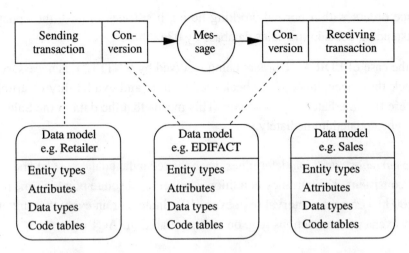

Fig. 3.9.3./3: Conversion in the sending and receiving transactions

If there is no clear correspondence between the domains of the two attributes, conversion by machine is not possible. For example, if UNTEL's article descriptions use a Japanese material classification which does not correspond to the European one, conversion requires the manual treatment of material codes that cannot be assigned by machine.

In addition, data models have diverse depths of structure. For instance, the retail system stores delivery dates for each order position, whereas UNTEL only recognizes a delivery date for a complete order (see Section 3.3., Rule 6). If a retailer sends an order with several different delivery dates, the Sales IS must sub-divide this order into several part orders each with the desired delivery date; as a result the sense of the order as a whole, as it was placed by the customer, is lost. If UNTEL wants to avoid the problems that this raises, it can involve costly adjustments to the applications.

Updating

UNTEL stores the data relating to outstanding debts redundantly, for the reasons we have discussed. From the perspective of the 'order acquisition' sub-process, it is necessary to decide how up-to-date these data need to be. Since payments received by the bank are delivered electronically overnight, UNTEL is able to book all payments received up to the end of the previous day within the financial accounting system by 07:00 hr. Since customers only place orders within normal working hours, it suffices to have the updated outstanding debts in the Sales database by 08:00 hr.

In the case of EDIFACT orders being received by UNTEL, it is necessary to check their acceptance (i.e. check credit limits and availability of articles ordered) immediately upon receipt. This means that the data in the Sales IS must be updated immediately.

The *currency condition* determines when the redundant data must be updated, i.e. consistent. The currency condition is either an absolute point in time (e.g. 08:00 hr.) or a time interval (e.g. every 10 minutes) or an event that initiates data exchange transactions (e.g. on receipt of an EDIFACT order).

3.9.4.   Data Standards

In the 1980s public institutions and many industries defined numerous standards for inter-organizational data exchange (for a few important examples see Fig. 3.9.4./1).

These standards typically regulate,

- which documents are to be exchanged (e.g. order, order confirmation, and invoice),

- what attributes these documents must and may contain (e.g. customer name and address) and

- how these data are structured within the document (e.g. sequence of sender, addressee, order number, etc.).

'Working Party 4 on Facilitation of International Trade Procedures' of the United Nations Economic Commission for Europe (UN/ECE WP.4) defined the UN/EDIFACT standard, which now provides the basis for all standardization work.

The example of a (simplified) order confirmation, which is called a 'purchase order response message' in EDIFACT, can illustrate the EDIFACT standard. Fig. 3.9.4./2 shows the original text, Fig. 3.9.4./3 illustrates the EDIFACT coding and Fig. 3.9.4./4 depicts the structure of an EDIFACT file.

Standard	Industry/ Institution	Explanation
UN/EDIFACT United Nations / Electronic Data Interchange for Administration, Commerce and Transport	United Nations	see below
SWIFT Society for Worldwide Interbank Financial Telecommunication	Banking	System for transmitting messages about international banking transactions
SEDAS Standardregelungen für einheit-liche Datenaustauschsysteme	Trade	Standard for data exchange in German retailing
ODETTE Organisation for Data Exchange through Teletransmission in Europe	Automobile industry	Message standards and file transfer protocols for the automobile industry
ANSI ASC X12 ANSI Accredited Standards Committee X12	American National Standard Institute	US-American norm for electronic data exchange
TRADACOMS Trading Data Communications Standards	Article Numbering Association	Telecommunication standards for retailing in England

Fig. 3.9.4./1: Some standards for inter-organizational data exchange

Documents are sent as EDIFACT transfer files to business partners. A transfer file consists of message sets (several messages of the same type) or messages of different types. An EDIFACT message contains all the information needed to represent a business document. It is composed of a series of segments. A segment is a data record consisting of data elements (attributes) or groups of data elements. At the start of the transfer file, message set, message and segment there always appears an identifier, also called a header, and at the end a separator. If several identical segments appear the repeat factor is given. This indicates how often the segment in question occurs (see Fig. 3.9.4./4).

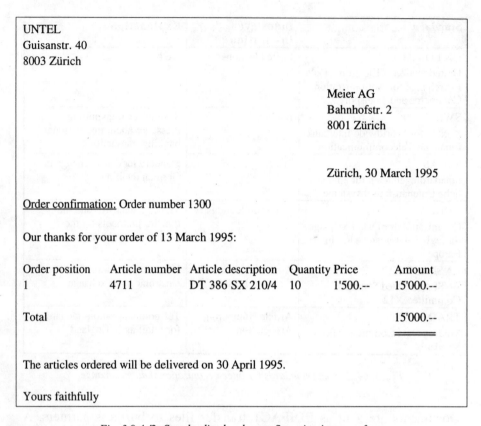

UNTEL
Guisanstr. 40
8003 Zürich

                                            Meier AG
                                            Bahnhofstr. 2
                                            8001 Zürich

                                            Zürich, 30 March 1995

Order confirmation: Order number 1300

Our thanks for your order of 13 March 1995:

Order position	Article number	Article description	Quantity	Price	Amount
1	4711	DT 386 SX 210/4	10	1'500.--	15'000.--
Total					15'000.--

The articles ordered will be delivered on 30 April 1995.

Yours faithfully

Fig. 3.9.4./2: Standardized order confirmation in paper form

The EDIFACT standard contains a data model for the inter-organizational exchange of business data, which can be presented in the same notation as used in the previous sections of the chapter on Data Design. However, in addition to the data model, EDIFACT also comprises a syntax for data streams for describing the data to be transferred in a specific EDIFACT message. This usually contains only some of the entity types (messages and segments) and attributes (data elements) from the complete data model of the EDIFACT standard.

The communication between enterprises via EDIFACT messages is not yet very widespread in Europe. On the one hand, individual EDIFACT message types are too complex for some sectors; on the other the possibilities offered by EDIFACT must often be adapted to industry-specific business practices. Several sectors have therefore decided to develop their own subsets of

EDIFACT, such as ODETTE (see Fig. 3.9.4./1). However, subsets compromise the standardization character of the EDIFACT norm, and make it more difficult to use standardized conversion software.

Example	Explanation
`UNA:+.?'`	Segment for defining separators, need not necessarily be sent
`UNB+UNOA:2+UNTEL+MEIER AG+950313:1600+1168'`	Header segment of the transfer file; where UNOA = standard and version + sender + recipient + date and time (13.03.95 at 16:00 hr) + identification
`UNH+1+ORDRSP:1:911:UN'`	Start segment of an individual message
`BGM+231+235791113'`	Basic invoice data, here the system assigns the purchase order response number
`DTM+137+19950313:102'`	Date of purchase order response
`RFF+VN:1300'`	Reference details, in this case the order number
`DTM+8:19950313:102'`	Date of customer order
`NAD+BY+++UNTEL+ GUISANSTRASSE 40+ ZUERICH+8003'`	Name and address of sender
`NAD+ST+++MAIER AG+ BAHNHOFSTRASSE 2+ ZUERICH+8001'`	Name and address of recipient
`UNS+D`	Listing of the individual positions
`LIN+1+6+4711:SA'`	Position 1 with article number
`IMD+++ZZ:::DT 386SX 210/4'`	Article description
`QTY+113+10+PCE'`	Order quantity 10 (PCE = unit, does not appear in document)
`DTM+191+19950430:102`	Delivery date
`PRI+CAL:1500:::1:PCE'`	Price per unit (PCE)
`UNS+S`	End of the listing
`MOA+9:15000'`	Total
`UNT`	Termination segment of message
`UNZ`	Termination segment of the transfer file

Fig. 3.9.4./3: Standardized order confirmation (purchase order response message) in
EDIFACT format

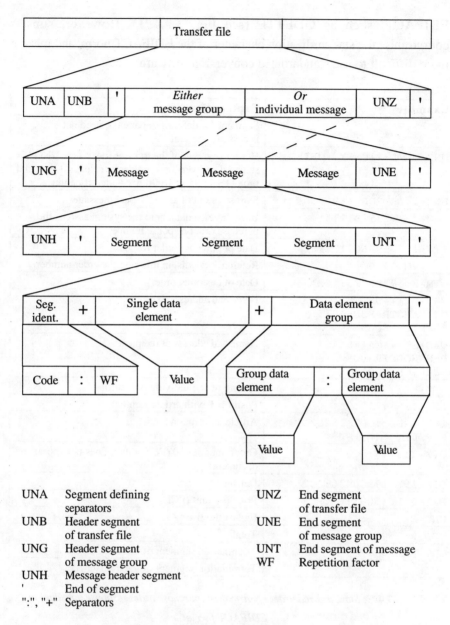

UNA	Segment defining separators	UNZ	End segment of transfer file
UNB	Header segment of transfer file	UNE	End segment of message group
UNG	Header segment of message group	UNT	End segment of message
UNH	Message header segment	WF	Repetition factor
'	End of segment		
":", "+"	Separators		

Fig. 3.9.4./4: Structure of an EDIFACT transfer file

The EDIFACT standard consists of the following norms and directories:

• UN/EDIFACT Message Directory: At present slightly more than 30 message types (documents such as payment order, invoice, transport/shipping order and customs declaration) are available for banking, trade and industry, transport and customs. It is estimated that about 120 message types will be needed to undertake all the planned EDI operations.

- UN/EDIFACT Segment Directory: Listing of possible segments (e.g. name and address segment).

- UN Handbook of Trade Data Elements (ISO 7372): Data elements (attributes) for defining EDI messages.

- UN/EDIFACT Code Lists: Internationally agreed code tables, for example for countries, currencies, and payment conditions.

- UN/EDIFACT Syntax Rules (ISO 9735): Rules for structuring both data elements in segments, and segments in messages.

3.9.5. Description of Interfaces

The result of the data exchange specification is both an interface description (see Fig. 3.9.5./1) [see Böhm et al. 1993, p. 221], and a description of the transactions for data exchange (see Chapter 4).

3.9.6. Summary

Integration represents one of the greatest areas of potential in restructuring flows. It is made possible by the global availability of information via electronic data exchange, within and between organizations. The complexity of operational information processing makes enterprise-wide 'integration of the data' an illusion. Instead the (controlled) redundancy of data between applications is tolerated, and procedures for exchanging data are established ('integration via the data').

The process determines the requirements on data exchange. It establishes

- which data are to be exchanged
- whether transmission occurs synchronously or asynchronously
- with what temporal delays will the exchange take place

To specify the data to be exchanged, reference is made to a data model. In the case of inter-organizational data exchange an industry-specific or general data exchange standard is often used as a data model.

Interface with the Finance IS	
Description:	
Daily entry of customers' outstanding invoice positions (outstanding debts) from the Finance IS.	
Generating application: Accounts receivable application	*Consuming application:* Customer management
Transaction: 'Report outstanding invoice positions'	*Transaction:* 'Enter outstanding invoice positions'
Excerpt from the data model: Finance database SELECT debtor number, outstanding invoice positions FROM debtor WHERE alteration date >= date of last reconciliation	
Redundant attributes in the data model: Partner database	Customer outstanding invoice positions
Type of data exchange:	Synchronous data exchange
Transfer file:	Outstanding invoice position messages
Data medium:	Network
Frequency:	Each working day
Quantity (number):	300 data records per day
Currency condition / *trigger (event):*	<= 8.00 am. on the day of booking receipt of payment / completion of the transaction 'book payments received' in the Finance IS

Fig. 3.9.5./1: Interface with the Finance IS

3.10. Implementing the Data Model

This chapter on data design has thus far been concerned exclusively with the conceptual or logical data model; the data design has not taken the IT solution into account. In an IS development project the data design is followed by the design of the database within a specific database system. The data model serves as a plan for the database.

A *database system* consists of data records (database) and software components for data management, known as a database management system.

In practice the terms database, database system and database management system (DBMS) are often used synonymously.

DBMSs are currently founded on three basic models of physical data storage - the hierarchical model, the network model and the relational model (see [Date 1986] or [Schlageter/Stucky 1989], for example). We restrict ourselves here to the relational model and present a few new approaches from the object-oriented model.

The *relational model* uses only entity sets (relations, tables), entities (objects, lines) and attributes (columns) [see Codd 1970]. Relationships are generated by the use of foreign keys.

Since we have presented the techniques of data design on the basis of the relational model, implementing the result of the data design in a relational DBMS presents few difficulties. The explanation of the implementation of UNTEL's Sales IS refers to the relational DBMS ORACLE 7.0.

The following brief treatment of data model implementation and database use is intended merely to give the reader some insight into the consequences of data design decisions. For a more detailed treatment see [Schlageter/Stucky 1989] and [Zehnder 1989], or the courses and training material from suppliers of DBMSs.

3.10.1. Data Definition Language

To transfer the conceptual data model into a concrete DBMS we use a Data Definition Language (DDL).

The *Data Definition Language* specifies the entity types, their attributes, integrity conditions and further guidelines for database management.

The DDL commands depend on the DBMS being used. Fig. 3.10.1./1 presents an example of creating the article entity type using the DBMS ORACLE 7.0.

CREATE TABLE Article (Article number CHAR (16) NOT NULL
                        PRIMARY KEY,
                        Article description CHAR (32),
                        Selling price NUMBER (9.2))

Fig. 3.10.1./1: DDL commands to create the ARTICLE entity type

This command creates the entity type with the name 'article' and the attributes 'article number', 'article description' and 'selling price'. The data type of the attribute is always given after the attribute name. The attribute 'article number' is the primary key and may not be 'null', i.e. it must have a value.

3.10.2. Structured Query Language

A database accession generally relates to only a certain subset of the entire data, i.e. specific attribute values of specific entities from a specific entity set. The following examples illustrate this:

- To record an order we write the attribute values of the new order header and the associated order positions in the corresponding entity sets.

- To modify the selling price of the CD player CDW 23, we alter the value of the attribute 'selling price' in the entity with the article number 2783.

- To create a complete list of articles, we need the values of the attributes 'article number' and 'article description' for all article entities.

Relational DBMSs use the Structured Query Language (SQL) for data manipulation (Data Manipulation Language, DML), i.e. to create, read, modify and delete entities within entity sets. SQL is specified in ISO Standard 9075:1992 and consists of both Data Manipulation Language and Data Definition Language. The following discussion relates to the Data Manipulation Language and differentiates between read (see Section 3.10.2.1.) and write access to data (see Section 3.10.2.2.).

The *Data Manipulation Language* is used to create, read, modify and delete entities.

Order header

Order number	Partner-no./ customer	Ordered by	Order date	Delivery date	Discount rate
...					
1300	0815	Bohneis	13.03.95	30.04.95	3.50
1301	1213	Mertin	14.03.95	15.04.95	2.00
1302	0815	Grubli	15.03.95	30.05.95	3.00
...					

Order position

Order number	Posn. no.	Article number	Quan- tity
...			
1300	1	4711	10
1301	1	3789	20
1301	2	4711	5
1301	3	4753	30
1302	1	2783	8
1302	2	2790	2
...			

Article

Article number	Article description	Selling price
...		
2783	CD player CDW 23	300.00
2790	CD player CDP 10	200.00
3789	Television FSp 34	600.00
4711	DT 386 SX 210/4	1'500.00
4753	LT 386 SX 60/2	1'450.00
...		

Fig. 3.10.2.1./1: Entity sets for generating evaluations

3.10.2.1. Read Only Access

To define subsets of a database in SQL, the relational database model uses the three set operators, projection, selection and join.

Projection

Let us start with the entity sets shown in Fig. 3.10.2.1./1. Foreign keys appear against a grey background. Projection is the selection of specific attributes. UNTEL's sales manager requires a list of all articles in the article entity set with their article numbers and descriptions. In SQL he formulates:

SELECT   article number, article description
FROM   article

This command generates the subset shown in Fig. 3.10.2.1./2. SELECT specifies the attributes of the subset. This specification of particular attributes is called *projection*. Using SELECT all attributes would be designated. FROM specifies the entity set from which the attributes and attribute values originate: in this example article is the subject of selection.

Article number	Article description
...	
2783	CD player CDW 23
2790	CD player CDP 10
3789	Television FSp 34
4711	DT 386 SX 210/4
4753	LT 386 SX 60/2
...	

Fig. 3.10.2.1./2: Result of the selection

Projection selects specific attributes from entity sets. SQL carries out projections using the command 'SELECT <attribute name(s)>'.

Selection

In a further evaluation the sales manager requires a list of all articles whose article number is below 3790. The list should contain both the attributes 'article description' and 'price', and be sorted by article description. In SQL we write:

SELECT	article description, price
FROM	article
WHERE	article number < 3790
ORDER BY	article description

With the help of WHERE individual entities can be selected from an entity set. Fig. 3.10.2.1./3 presents the results of the query. It is a *selection* of entities that fulfil the condition following WHERE (here: 'article number < 3790'). The command ORDER BY sorts the selected entities according to the attribute specified, in this example by article description.

Selection identifies those entities in entity sets that fulfil the given conditions. The corresponding SQL command is: 'WHERE <condition(s)>'.

Article description	Selling price
...	
CD player CDP 10	200.00
CD player CDW 23	300.00
...	
Television FSp 34	600.00
...	

Fig. 3.10.2.1./3: Result of the selection

Join

The third evaluation of the information in the database involves listing all articles appearing in orders sorted by order number. The list includes the attributes article number, article description and order number. The information required is contained in different entity sets. Since attributes with the same name can appear in different entity sets, we must specify the entity sets from which they should come when selecting the attributes. We do this by putting the name of the entity set before the attribute name, separated by a period. The SELECT and FROM commands then read:

SELECT	article.article number, article.article description,
	order position.order number
FROM	article, order position

Since the query relates to two entity sets (article and order position) these two entity sets need to be linked by the relationship between them via the foreign key and the corresponding identification key: The foreign key must have the same attribute value as the identification key. We speak of a *join operation*. In SQL the command reads:

WHERE   order position.article number = article.article number

If the entities are to be sorted by order number, the complete query reads:

SELECT   article.article number, article.article description,
              order position.order number
FROM   article, order position
WHERE   order position.article number = article.article number
ORDER BY   order position.order number

As a result we obtain the entity set in Fig. 3.10.2.1./4.

Article number	Article description	Order number
...		
4711	DT 386 SX 210/4	1300
3789	Television FSp 34	1301
4711	DT 386 SX 210/4	1301
4753	LT 386 SX 60/2	1301
2783	CD player CDW 23	1302
2790	CD player CDP 10	1302
...		

Fig. 3.10.2.1./4: Result of the join operation

The *join operation* links entities from different entity sets that belong together. Entities belong together when entity set 1 has the same value in its identification key as entity 2 has in its foreign key. The SQL command reads:

'WHERE <entity set 1.attribute entity set 1> =
<entity set 2.attribute entity set 2>'.

More Complex Example

We can summarize the procedure for defining subsets using SQL with the help of a more complex example: UNTEL's sales manager requires a list of all articles (article number and description) that have been ordered by Bohneis.

Manually, we would proceed as follows: In the first step we would search for the name Bohneis in the attribute 'ordered by' for the entity set 'order header'. In the extract presented it appears once, namely in the order with the number 1300. The order number is the foreign key in the entity set 'order position'. We discover that the article 4711 was ordered in the order number 1300. The article number is the foreign key in the entity set 'order position' and the identification key in the entity set 'article'. Now we search for the article description for article 4711 in the entity set 'article'. As a result we obtain the entity set in Fig. 3.10.2.1./5.

Article number	Article description
4711	DT 386 SX 210/4

Fig. 3.10.2.1./5: Result of the complex example

The SQL procedure can be viewed as analogous to the manual search: In the first step we specify the attributes to be presented in the evaluation. Since the query relates to more than one entity set we must specify the entity sets from which the attributes and attribute values are to be taken:

SELECT   article.article number, article.article description

Then we determine which entity sets will be needed for the query:

FROM   order header, order position, article

Only articles ordered by Bohneis are to be presented. We must therefore search for the value Bohneis in the attribute 'ordered by' in the entity set 'order header'. Since the name Bohneis is a chain of characters (and not a number) we must write it in SQL within two apostrophes:

WHERE   ordered by = 'Bohneis'

Now we need to identify the order positions contained in the Bohneis order header, and the articles ordered from these order positions. We use the foreign key to do this:

WHERE   order header.order number =
             order position.order number
WHERE   order position.article number = article.article number

Linking together all the parts of the command we obtain the following query. Since all three conditions must be fulfilled, the WHERE clauses must be linked by AND .

SELECT   article.article number, article.article description
FROM   order header, order position, article
WHERE   ordered by = 'Bohneis'   AND
             order header.order number =
             order position.order number   AND
             order position.article number = article.article number

The result is the entity set presented in Fig. 3.10.2.1./5.

Using the three SQL operations, projection, selection and join we can form any desired subset from the entity sets. It is of no fundamental significance whether we want to read only or amend the subsets (see Section 3.10.2.2.) A SQL command for reading data consists of the following components:

SELECT	*<attribute name(s)>*	select the attributes ...
FROM	*<entity set(s)>*	from the entity set(s) ...
WHERE	*<conditions(s)>*	under the condition(s) ...
ORDER BY	*<attribute name(s)>*	sorted by ...

3.10.2.2. Write Access

Section 3.10.1. showed the creation of an entity set using the article example. Section 3.10.2.1. described queries to a relational database. Section 3.10.2.2. now presents the SQL commands for write access, i.e. for creating, modifying and deleting entities.

Creating an Entity

A Sales employee wants to record the article 'CD player CDW 23' with the article number 2783 and selling price 250.00. To do this he must record an entity in the entity set 'aricle' with the value 2783 for the article number, 'CD player CDW 23' for the article description, and 250.00 for the selling price. In SQL this can be done using the command:

INSERT INTO article
                VALUES (2783, 'CD-Player CDW 23', 250.00)

The command INSERT INTO specifies the entity set in which the entity should be included; VALUES specifies the attribute values. The attribute values must be entered in the same sequence as the attributes were set up with the DDL. Otherwise the attributes concerned must be specified in brackets after the name of the entity set (e.g. INSERT INTO article (article number) VALUES ('3000')).

Modifying an Entity

The price of the CD player CDW 23 is altered from 250.00 to 300.00. We write:

UPDATE   article
SET   price = 300.00
WHERE   article number = 2783

The UPDATE command specifies the entity set for modifying the data. SET alters the attribute value of the given attribute (price) and WHERE specifies the entity to be altered.

Deleting an Entity

If the CD player CDW 23 is to be removed from UNTEL's range we write:

DELETE
FROM   article
WHERE   article number = 2783

DELETE FROM defines the entity set, and WHERE the entity that is to be deleted from the entity set.

User-friendly DBMSs spare the user the explicit formulation of SQL commands. They conceal the read only and write access behind computer-led dialogue. The logic of the underlying set operations must nevertheless be understood by the database user.

3.10.3. Denormalization

Despite all the advances in computing power (especially storage media, channels, databuses, and processors), the costs of computer resources and the speed of applications (response times) will continue to play a role for the foreseeable future. Normalization generates simple, low redundancy data models with significant advantages for systems development. But occasionally it gives rise to unacceptable computer costs or response times. As a result, the real world sometimes abandons pure, normalized data models in the interests of the operating efficiency of applications.

Combining Entity Types

In Section 3.3. the partner data were split between the entity types 'partner' and 'town' on the basis of normalization Rule 6 (Fig. 3.10.3./1). However, many applications require the attributes that have been distributed between the two entity types to be together (e.g. recording, displaying, or altering customer address data or invoicing). Each time an application needs to access a customer address, including the town, this split means high additional expense for the DBMS by using the join operation on the two entity sets.

```
Partner                          Town
   Partner number                   Post code
   Name                             Town
   Post code->     Town
   Street
```

Fig. 3.10.3./1: Normalized data model

If we reverse the normalization undertaken in Rule 6 and recombine the partner and town entity types (see Fig. 3.10.3./2), the DBMS now needs to access only one entity set.

Combining entity types improves run time efficiency, by avoiding join operations.

> **Partner**
> Partner number
> Name
> Post code
> Town
> Street

Fig. 3.10.3./2: Denormalized data model

If two entity sets A and B, as in Fig. 3.10.3./3, are in a 1:c, 1:cn or 1:n relationship they can be combined in two ways:

1. All or some of the entity types to which the :1 relationship exists, are incorporated in the entity type to which the :c, :cn or :n relationship exists. In the example in Fig. 3.10.3./2 all the attributes in the entity type 'town' are incorporated in the entity type 'partner'. This solution means that the data in the earlier entity type 'town' now appears several times in the entity type 'partner'.

2. The attributes of the entity type to which a :c, :cn or :n relationship exists are incorporated in the entity type to which a :1 relationship exists. In the example of the entity types 'partner' and 'town' this generates an unnatural solution, since now a variable number of partners exist for any town.

   This solution is conceivable though where attributes from the entity set 'order position' are included in the entity set 'order header'. This means that the entity type 'order header' must either reserve a fixed number of order positions or provide a variable number of attributes for storing the order positions.

The problems with this solution have already been treated in the discussion of normalization Rules 1 and 2 (Section 3.3.).

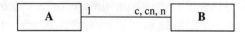

Fig. 3.10.3./3: Starting point for combination

Splitting an Entity Type

In future UNTEL wants to store a verbal description of the technical data and a picture of the article. This means that the entity type 'article' needs to be extended to include the attributes 'verbal description' and 'article picture'. The article pictures are stored as BLOBs (Binary Large Objects). However, these attributes require a great deal of storage space and are rarely used; for example, a customer or sales representative wants to obtain information about a new article's technical details. Typically, however - as in order recording - the attributes 'verbal description' and 'article picture' are not needed.

Storage of the verbal description and the picture in an independent entity type 'article description' (Fig. 3.10.3./4) permits access to the technical data when queried, but not on order recording. Access is more efficient because less unnecessary data are 'carted around'.

Fig. 3.10.3./4: Splitting the article entity type to avoid projection operations

If attributes take up a lot of space and are rarely needed, or their attribute values are typically needed together, they can be split off into an independent entity type and linked via a 1:c or 1:1 relationship with the original entity type.

Splitting the attributes from one entity type between two entity types improves run-time efficiency, by avoiding projection operations.

Splitting entity types can be based on the frequency with which individual entities in an entity set are used. At UNTEL, for example, spare parts are ordered relatively infrequently. If all spare parts are stored in an independent entity type 'spare parts' and all other articles in a entity type 'sales articles' (see Fig. 3.10.3./5), the access to sales articles will be quicker.

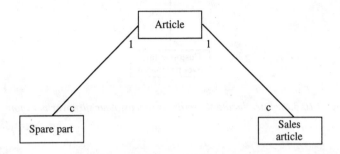

Fig. 3.10.3./5: Splitting the article entity type to avoid selection operations

The entity type 'article' now contains only the identification key 'article number'. The attributes 'article description', 'unit', 'minimum inventory levels' and 'sale price' are now stored in the appropriate entity type 'spare part' or 'sales article'. We do not abolish the entity type 'article', however, so that articles of both types can still be accessed, as is required for order position, for example.

Specialization of an entity type, which involves splitting it into two entity types, improves run-time efficiency by anticipating the selection operation.

Derived Attributes

UNTEL produces monthly turnover statistics for each customer. Turnover per customer is the sum of all orders delivered to the customer in one month. Calculating this sum requires many access operations to identify all the orders filled for a given customer in the month (entity types 'order header' and 'order position'). For each order position the order quantity has to be multiplied by the price, which requires additional access to the entity type 'article'.

It might be appropriate to store current customer turnover in an entity type 'customer turnover per month' (see Fig. 3.10.3./6). Customer turnover is derived from existing attributes. We therefore speak of derived attributes.

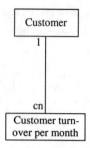

Fig. 3.10.3./6: Introducing the entity type 'customer turnover per month'

Introducing derived attributes improves run-time efficiency in that the results of calculations are stored and need not be recalculated for each new use.

There are arguments against introducing the entity type 'customer turnover per month':

- Recalculation of customer turnover requires many access operations, as described above, and hence puts a load on the computer system. However, if the turnover statistics are generated using a batch transaction (see Section 4.6.) during the night, the data access has no repercussions on response times during UNTEL's business hours.

- On introducing the entity type 'customer turnover per month' the turnover data must be continuously updated e.g. when orders are filled or merchandise is returned. This is costly in data maintenance terms. If data maintenance is forgotten, the data become inconsistent (the turnover that results from the calculation described above no longer agrees with that in the entity type 'customer turnover per month').

Holding derived attributes thus involves considerable maintenance costs and consistency problems. On the other hand, results that have been calculated are not thrown away, which renders the repeated execution of the same calculation unnecessary.

The objectives of normalization are simplicity and lack of redundancy, not operational efficiency. Denormalization aims at the operational efficiency of the data model from the perspective of a specific application. The price of this is redundancy, which has the following disadvantages:

- Denormalization optimizes the data model for a specific application as well as specific hardware and software components. It thus reduces flexibility in face of changing business requirements and technical possibilities.

- Denormalization often leads to more complex data structures.

For these reasons, we avoid denormalization as far as possible. Deviations from normal form should only be considered when an application's performance with the normalized data model is fundamentally inadequate, and the technical hardware and software possibilities have been exhausted. The need for denormalization of data models depends heavily on the DBMS used. The DBMS can in itself drastically reduce access costs by optimizing physical storage. In addition, it is to be expected that special database servers with parallel processors will push run time efficiency considerations further into the background in coming years.

Denormalization avoids cumbersome access operations by structuring the data in a suitable form for access, or by including derived data in the database. By combining entity types it avoids a join operation, by splitting entity types either a selection or a projection, and by using derived data the repeated execution of the same calculations.

3.10.4. Digression: 'Object-Oriented Model'

For some years, object-oriented DBMSs have been the subject of research, and an increasing number of products are available on the market. Object-oriented databases are currently used primarily in technical applications, such as Computer Aided Design (CAD). As the development of relational databases and other fundamental software concepts has shown, typically about 15 years are needed from the first idea to widespread practical implementation. Extensive use of object-oriented DBMSs in operational transaction systems can therefore be expected by the end of the 90s at the earliest.

In contrast to relational DBMSs, there does not yet exist a uniform database model for object-oriented DBMSs. The following statements outline a few characteristics and trends:

- Object-oriented DBMSs combine the program functions (methods) with the data. A class consists of attributes and methods. The attributes in a class can only be accessed by the methods in that class. To query an article description, for example, the article class would have to possess a method 'display article description'. Queries using SQL would not be possible.

- In relational DBMSs only entity sets are provided for data storage. Object-oriented DBMSs, however, should make it possible to define other data structures. This includes the definition of new data types (e.g. network) and the specification of new methods permitted for these types (e.g.'establish link').

- In the relational model complex entity types must be broken down into several entity types (see Normalization in Section 3.3.). Object-oriented DBMSs, however, allow composite objects, i.e. the attributes of one object can themselves be objects.

- Object-oriented DBMSs support the concept of generalization and specialization (see Section 3.4.), in that a class can inherit the attributes and methods of a wider class.

- In relational DBMSs all entities have an identification key. In object-oriented DBMSs, all objects are also assigned independent, immutable object identifiers by the DBMS, which are unrelated to their current identification key.

3.11. Further Reading

Literaturstelle	Punkt									
	3.1. Ziele des Datenentwurfs	3.2. Datenmodell	3.3. Normalisierung	3.4. Exkurs "Semantische und objektorientierte Datenmodellierung"	3.5. Schlüssel	3.6. Integritätsbedingungen	3.7. Codetabellen	3.8. Historisierung von Daten	3.9. Datenintegration	3.10. Implementierung des Datenmodells
[Böhm et al. 1993]		X	X					X	X	X
[Booch 1994]				X						
[Carmichael 1994]				X						
[Chen 1976]		X								
[Codd 1970]										X
[Date 1986]										X
[Ferstl/Sinz 1990]				X						
[Ferstl/Sinz 1991]				X						
[Ferstl/Sinz 1994]		X		X						
[Frank 1991]									X	
[Gabriel/Röhrs 1994]	X	X	X	X		X				X
[Grill 1987]		X	X		X					X
[Gutzwiller 1994]	X						X			
[Hackstein/Köhl 1991]									X	
[Hansen 1992]		X	X							X
[Heinrich/Burgholzer 1990]		X	X		X					
[Hübner 1993]									X	
[Hughes 1991]										X
[Hull/King 1987]				X						
[Jacobson et al. 1993]				X						
[Lindtner 1990]				X						
[Martin/McClure 1988]		X	X							X
[Meier 1992]		X	X			X				X
[Ortner/Söllner 1989]				X						

Literaturstelle / Punkt	3.1. Ziele des Datenentwurfs	3.2. Datenmodell	3.3. Normalisierung	3.4. Exkurs "Semantische und objektorientierte Datenmodellierung"	3.5. Schlüssel	3.6. Integritätsbedingungen	3.7. Codetabellen	3.8. Historisierung von Daten	3.9. Datenintegration	3.10. Implementierung des Datenmodells
[Pálffy 1989]										X
[Plattner et al. 1990]									X	
[Pomberger/Blaschek 1993]				X						
[Raasch 1991]		X	X	X		X				
[Scheer 1994]		X		X						X
[Schlageter/Stucky 1989]		X	X							X
[Schönthaler/Németh 1990]		X		X						
[Schwarze 1994]		X	X			X				X
[Thoma 1993]									X	
[Vetter 1991]	X	X	X			X		X		X
[Zehnder 1989]	X	X	X		X	X				X

4. Function Design

Function design specifies the computer functions (applications and transactions) that support the processes and their activities (see Fig. 4./1).

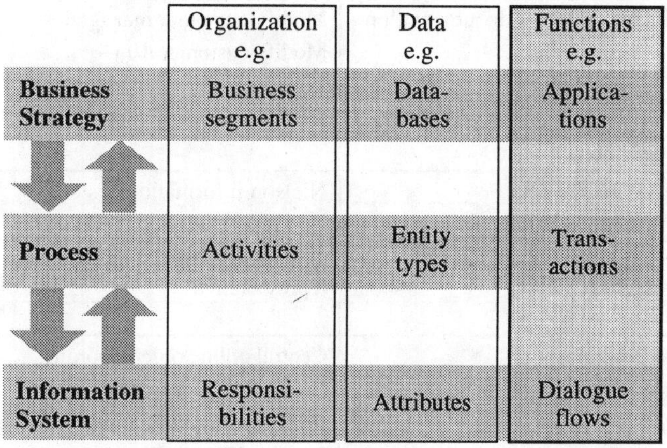

	Organization e.g.	Data e.g.	Functions e.g.
Business Strategy	Business segments	Data-bases	Applica-tions
Process	Activities	Entity types	Trans-actions
Information System	Responsi-bilities	Attributes	Dialogue flows

Fig. 4./1: Function design as part of Business Engineering

The strategy level function design (application architecture) defines the applications that a company wants to have, independent of specific processes. Here we concentrate on the function design for the process and IS levels. This specifies which transactions are available to support activities, and what effect they have on the data. At the IS level, the function design specifies details of the solution such as dialogue flow or screen masks.

4.1. Objectives of Function Design

Organization design (Chapter 2.) determines the activities in a process, and function design determines the computer support for these activities. Fig. 4.1./1 presents the breakdown of the sales process into its activities (left column) and the transactions that the function design envisages for them (right column).

Process
    Sub-process
        Activity
	Applications / Transactions

Sales	
Customer acquisition	
Prepare consultative discussion	Record potential customers
...	...
Account management	
Maintain customer documentation	Modify customer management Modify customer data ...
...	
Order acquisition	
Prepare market data	Nielson information system ...
Receive order via sales representative	Online order recording by sales representative ...
Order recording	Central online order recording ...
Order confirmation	Print order/modification confirmation Receive EDIFACT purchase order message ...
...	...
Order adjustment	
Order adjustment	Order modification Order cancellation ...
...	
Manage sales process	
...	...

Fig. 4.1./1: Activity-function breakdown of the sales process

The following list presents a sample of questions often asked in the course of function design:

1. What transactions are needed by the activity 'receive order via sales representative'?

2. How often is the activity 'customer acquisition' undertaken per day on average? Is it worthwhile developing and maintaining independent transactions for this activity?

3. Can an order be modified once the order confirmation has been printed?

4. Which transactions from existing applications can be used? Can the sales manager enter region-specific prices in the existing product-range management application, or does he need a new transaction in the order-management application to handle this?

5. Is a sales representative allowed to initiate the transaction 'calculate regional turnover for the period'? Or may only the sales management do this? How are access rights to transactions assigned?

6. What does the screen mask for order recording look like? What machine assistance does the sales representative need when entering an order?

7. What standards must be observed in the dialogue structure?

8. Can the article number for an article that the sales representative has sought and found be transferred automatically to the order position, or must he type it in again?

9. What rules (customer-specific prices, region-specific discounts, campaign prices, etc.) must be observed in establishing prices?

The objectives of function design are:

- *Integration*
  A user employs transactions from various applications at his workplace. It can be a significant obstacle to the work if different styles of applications are used (question 7).

  More important than the integration of user support is integration of the contents (question 8). If the applications are not reconciled with each other, the user often has to enter the same information (e.g. a customer's change of address) in several applications.

- *Unambiguous guidelines for software development and selection*
  Function design must formulate the requirements on software so clearly and unambiguously that the implementation can be checked against the design (questions 3, 5, 6, 7, 8, 9).

- *Generalization*
  As in data design, it is primarily the designer's responsibility to recognize organizational variants in advance and ensure flexibility. A high rate of transaction reuse lowers software costs (question 4). A good example of this is package software.

- *Efficiency*
  Each computer function involves development, maintenance, training, support and operating costs. These must be weighed against the expected benefits (question 2, 4).

- *Reconciliation with the organization design*
  Like data design, function design proceeds from the organization design (questions 1, 2, 5). To reap the organizational benefits, organization design must already have the possibilities for computer support in mind when deriving the activities.

Solutions to business management problems also have precedence over information technology issues in function design.

4.2.   Function Model

The transaction 'WITHDRAWAL WITHOUT RECEIPT' at a cash dispenser supports the bank customer in performing the activity 'withdraw cash'. *Transactions* are operations performed by computer; they form the basis for computerized information processing. Transactions are central to the function design process.

What happens when cash is withdrawn from a cash dispenser? First we insert a cash card in the machine, then we enter our personal identification number. Thereafter we can choose between various services (see Fig. 4.2./1).

If we press button 'A' we select the function 'WITHDRAWAL WITHOUT RECEIPT', then in the next step we must enter the amount and press the 'OK' button (see Fig. 4.2./2). Then the cash dispenser delivers the money and books the withdrawal on the debit side of the withdrawer's account and the credit side of the bank's cash account (grossly simplified representation).

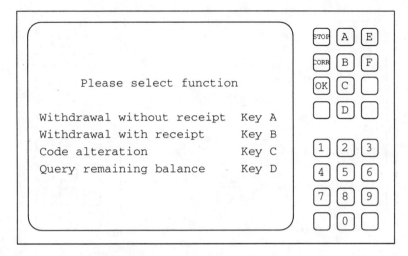

Fig. 4.2./1: The services of a cash dispenser machine

It is not possible to withdraw cash without booking the withdrawal, or to undertake the booking without making a withdrawal. If an error arises cash will not be dispensed and no booking will be made. In other words, the service 'WITHDRAWAL WITHOUT RECEIPT' is executed either in its entirety or not at all. This ensures that the cash dispenser is always in a consistent state. Data inconsistencies are not possible: for example, if the cash dispenser contains 50,000 CHF and we withdraw 1,000 CHF then the cash balance becomes 49,000 CHF and our account balance is reduced by 1,000 CHF. If an error arises the service is not permitted, and the cash balance in the machine and the balance in our account remain unchanged.

Each 'WITHDRAWAL WITHOUT RECEIPT' has the same effect: 'cash is paid out', 'withdrawal is booked' and the cash balance and the balance in the accounts affected are adjusted. This means that the flow can be described exactly (it can be formalized) and the effects are predictable ('cash is paid out' and 'withdrawal is booked' or neither of the two). 'WITHDRAWAL WITHOUT RECEIPT' is a *transaction*. Other transactions are 'WITHDRAWAL WITH RECEIPT', 'CODE ALTERATION' and 'QUERY REMAINING BALANCE'.

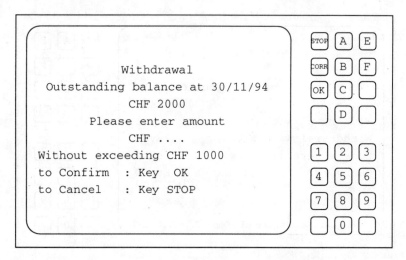

Fig. 4.2./2: Call up of the function 'WITHDRAWAL WITHOUT RECEIPT'

A *transaction* is a procedure on a computer, which is either performed in its entirety or not at all.

The most important characteristics of a transaction are:

- *Indivisibility*
  A transaction is either carried out in its entirety or - if errors arise - not at all.

- *Standardization*
  The operation performed by a transaction is always identical: it can be described precisely, and always generates the same result. The transaction 'WITHDRAWAL WITHOUT RECEIPT' pays out cash and books the withdrawal. 'CODE ALTERATION' always changes the identification code. The ability to formalize operations is a prerequisite for designing the transaction. This is also referred to as structurability or standardizability.

- *Consistency*
  On completion of 'WITHDRAWAL WITHOUT RECEIPT' in the above cash dispenser example, the sum of bookings on the debit and credit sides must be the same and must correspond to the total paid out. If the transaction is interrupted, cash is not paid out and bookings are not made. As a general rule the database is in a consistent state before and after the

transaction is performed. If the transaction is interrupted the database will remain in the same state as before the transaction was started. The database must be in a consistent state before and after any given transaction.

- *Formatted data*
When using 'WITHDRAWAL WITHOUT RECEIPT' the customer must enter the amount. The format for this is precisely defined: the transaction accepts only the numbers from 100 to 1,000, i.e. positive whole numbers in increments of a hundred. Swiss cash dispensers assume payment in Swiss Francs. They do not accept 'soft' information, such as 'more than 100' or 'a lot' or 'the usual amount'. Formatted (coded) data describe the real world in accordance with unambiguous rules (see Chapter 3.).

Transactions alter the entities stored in the database on the basis of the data entered. They read and/or write attribute values (see Sections 4.3. and 4.4.). Each attribute possesses a certain data type (format). Consequently, most transactions require the user to enter data in a format that is compatible with that used in the database.

The data and function design in this book deal exclusively with formatted information processing, or transaction systems.

A *specification* is a rule, and adherence to this rule must be verified.

How is a transaction specified? Let us examine the transaction 'WITHDRAWAL WITHOUT RECEIPT': the transaction accepts the entry 'amount entered' and processes the data. The desired amount of cash is dispensed and the withdrawal is booked. The operation of the cash dispensing mechanism, and the way in which the booking is undertaken, are of no interest to the customer. He is interested only in the functions offered by the cash dispenser, or in this case the transaction. As far as he is concerned, the transaction is a blackbox. How the output is created within the blackbox is primarily of relevance to the manufacturers of the cash dispensers and to the bank.

Each transaction takes entry data (input), processes them and generates the result (output) (see Fig. 4.2./3). The user-oriented rule 'input -> blackbox (output creation) -> output' is referred to as a *transaction specification*. This perspective generally relates to the content. Once a transaction is specified, we determine the method by which the transaction generates the output from the input. This is the subject of Section 4.9.

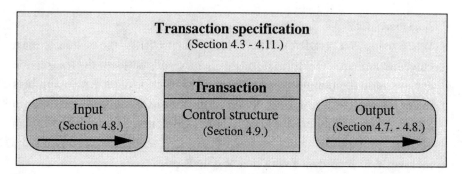

Fig. 4.2./3: Transaction specification

The differentiation between the content and the method is imprecise, but pragmatic. The content can only be defined once the output creation method has been defined. A specification is only as exact as the terms it uses, which are often based on intuitive understanding.

The specification of the transaction 'WITHDRAWAL WITHOUT RECEIPT' in terms of input, processing and output is perfectly adequate in practice, although it is restricted to the essentials. Thus it is scarcely obvious to the customer under what conditions the bank calculates certain charges, or what happens if the cash is not removed within ten seconds.

4.3.   Derivation of Transactions

Function design determines the transactions that support the user department employees in performing their activities. It proceeds from the following starting points [see Gutzwiller 1994, p. 202 ff.]:

Organizational Demands on Computer Support

Let us return to UNTEL's Sales IS. What computer support is needed by the 'order acquisition' sub-process? Organization design has broken down the 'order acquisition' (UNTEL) and 'order merchandise' (customer) sub-processes into activities in line with Fig. 4.3./1 and has formulated rough requirements for the applications and transactions in the activity catalogue (see also Section 2.5.).

Sub-process Activity	Applications / Transactions
UNTEL: Order acquisition	
Advise customer on procurement	
Receive order via sales representative	Order recording (laptop)
Order recording	Order recording
Order confirmation	Print confirmation (paper/EDIFACT - batch)
Customer: Order merchandise	
Specify requirements	
Select suppliers	
Select articles using catalogue	Electronic product catalogue
...	
Online order placement	Order recording (Online terminal)
EDIFACT order placement from catalogue	Electronic product catalogue
Make note of order	

Fig. 4.3./1: Breakdown of the 'order acquisition' sub-process (segment)

From the very vague notions of computer support identified by the organization design, function design derives the transactions needed.

In the Sales IS, these include the transaction 'online order recording by the sales representative' for the activity 'receive order via sales representative', the transaction 'central online order recording' for the activity 'order recording' and the transactions 'print order/modification confirmation', 'accept EDIFACT purchase order message' and 'reject EDIFACT purchase order message' for the activity 'order confirmation' (see Fig. 4.3./2). The electronic product catalogue is an independent application, to be developed within its own project, and will not be considered in the following discussion.

Activity	Transaction
Receive order via sales representative	Online order recording by sales rep.
Order recording	Central online order recording
Order confirmation	Print order/modification confirmation
	Accept EDIFACT purchase order message
	Reject EDIFACT purchase order message

Fig. 4.3./2: Deriving transactions from activities

The names given to the activities should differ from those of the transactions that support them, since a transaction usually supports only part of the activity's functionality.

The customer 'Meier AG' moves his business location to Basel from July 1st, 1995. The change of address is handled by the activity 'maintain customer documentation' in the 'account management' sub-process. The transactions 'modify customer data' and 'update customer data' are defined to support the activity (see also Section 3.8). The change of business location also results in alterations to the regional and sales representative assignment. Can the modification to account management be integrated with the transaction 'modifiy customer data'?

The transaction must be specified such that the operation performed is always the same and always produces the same result. Not every modification of customer data involves modification to account management. Consequently, we need two separate transactions, 'modify customer data' (changing the entities in 'customer data not in effect') and 'modify customer management' (changing the entities in 'customer management') . If we were to combine both operations in a single transaction, the result of the transaction would not always be the same.

We can identify the operations that transactions perform on the data:

- Append: Adding an entity.

- Read: Reading an entity.

- Modify: Modifying an entity.

- Delete: Deleting an entity.

The impact of an operation on a certain entity type is called the *effect*. A transaction always has the same effects, since its always performs the same operations on the same entity types.

If business relations with a customer are broken off, the customer data need to be deleted. We need another transaction 'delete customer'. Fig. 4.3./3 indicates the effects of the transactions 'modify customer data', 'modify customer management' and 'delete customer'. These three transactions support the performance of the activity 'maintain customer documentation'. Transactions are defined as elementary operations on the computer, and are not broken down any further. It is often the case that several transactions support the performance of a single activity (see Figs. 4.3./2 and 4).

Operational Tools

If a retailer opens a new outlet in Winterthur in addition to his existing outlet in Basel, UNTEL initially treats this business as a new customer. The sales representative does not need to enter existing customer data again. A large portion of this data can be reusedwhen recording the information regarding the customer's new outlet. Since this kind of data transfer is undertaken frequently, we can derive the transaction 'copy customer master data' which takes data from existing customers when creating a new customer entity. This reduces recording costs and is referred to accordingly as an 'operational tool'. In certain cases it provides a short cut to an existing transaction. Applications typically contain a multiplicity of such operational tools.

Transaction	Dialogue step	Effect	Entity type
Modify customer data	Entry of customer number by user		
	Display customer address, business type and contractual conditions on the screen	Read	Partner, customer, town
	Alteration to customer data by the user on the screen		
	Providing data history (see Section 3.8.): Changes to customer address and contractual conditions	Append	Customer data not in effect
Modify customer management	Entry of customer number by user		
	Display customer data, data for sales representative responsible, and the representatives rate of commission on the screen	Read	Partner, customer, town, sales representative, customer management
	Alteration to customer management by the user on the screen		
	Alteration to customer management: by providing data history a new entity is created of the customer management type	Append	Customer management
Delete customer	Entry of customer number by the user		
	Display current customer data on the screen	Read	Partner, customer, town, sales representative, customer management
	Confirmation of delete option by the user		
	Deletion of all customer data	Delete	Partner, customer, town, customer management, customer data not in effect

Fig. 4.3./3: Effects of transactions (simplified representation)

Retrieval

Each order must be assigned to precisely one customer. Customers often forget to give their customer number on their orders. If such an order is to be recorded, it is first necessary to find the relevant customer. We therefore define a transaction 'search/display customer address'. This transaction searches UNTEL's customer data for all customers fulfilling a specific search criterion (e.g. customer name = Maier) and displays them on the screen. The relevant customer can be identified and assigned to the order he has placed. The transaction 'search/display customer address' helps to search for, or retrieve, information (see also Section 4.4.2.).

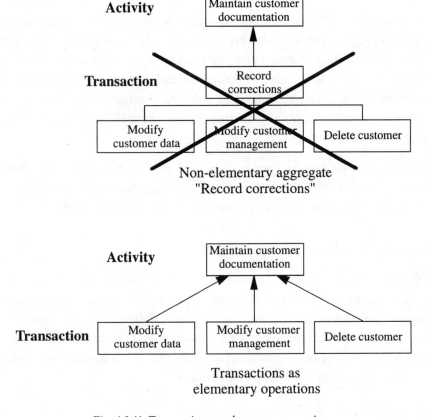

Fig. 4.3./4: Transactions as elementary operations

Examples of other retrieval transactions are 'display orders by customer' or 'display order'. A more complex example is the retrieval transaction 'check availability'. If an UNTEL customer plans a sales campaign, he wants to be sure that the articles are available at the right time. Consequently he needs to be able to check availability without having to place an order. To do this we define the transaction 'check availability', which has no direct relationship to a specific activity. The transaction 'check availability' assesses, on the basis of existing order and purchasing data, whether an article will be available at the desired date (Section 4.9. considers this transaction in greater detail)

Retrieval transactions are used to search for information. They are not assigned to a specific activity, but are generally available.

Evaluations

To manage the sale process UNTEL needs a wide variety of evaluations and reports (e.g. turnover by sales representative and region, or order rate by sales channel). Independent transactions are needed for evaluations (lists, see Section 4.7.). Consequently, we define the transactions 'determine regional turnover for the period', 'determine sales representative turnover for the period', 'determine number of orders per sales channel, and its proportion to total orders' etc.

The suggestions for deriving transactions thus far have been based on a business/organizational perspective. There are, however, more computer-technical approaches to deriving transactions, as discussed below.

Navigation Within an Application

Transactions do not run 'by themselves'. They must be activated. This usually happens by means of menus (see Section 4.8.2.). Menu control requires a new transaction. The transaction is performed at the start of the application, and is always activated if another transaction is completed and no follow-on transaction is automatically initiated. Each application needs a transaction for navigation within the application.

Archiving

UNTEL receives approximately 15,000 orders a year. With the help of the Sales IS, the data is recorded in the entity types 'order header' and 'order position'. After three years the entity set 'order header' contains about 45,000 entries and the entity set 'order position' about 150,000, which are mostly no longer needed for current business. Storage space is being absorbed unnecessarily. For legal and operational reasons the data can not simply be deleted. It would seem appropriate to store old orders on an external storage medium (e.g. magnetic tape) and delete them from the entity sets 'order header' and 'order position'. This is called data archiving. If necessary (e.g. for special evaluations), the old data must be transferred to the Sales IS. For this reason we need the transactions 'selectively archive orders' and 'selectively transfer archived orders'.

Nearly every application needs transactions for archiving and transferring data.

Data Exchange

Section 3.9. on data integration explained that an application needs transactions to exchange data with other applications. For example, the transaction 'receive and check EDIFACT purchase order message' for UNTEL's Sales IS electronically accepts orders in EDIFACT format from the customer's dealer system. Other transactions send order confirmations, etc. electronically. Similarly, the Sales IS needs transactions for internal exchanges, e.g. the transfer of outstanding debts from the Finance IS.

Applications need transactions for the electronic exchange of data with other applications, both within and beyond organizational boundaries.

Initial Data Transfer and Recording

UNTEL's new Sales IS replaces the existing, but outdated, information system 'Sales 80'. The database for this information system already contains certain data (e.g. parts of the customer data) which can be included in the Sales IS. This requires data transfer transactions. Some parts of the customer data do not yet exist, however, and must be newly recorded. This necessitates data-recording transactions. Since both these transactions are only needed during the transition phase between the old and new information systems, we refer to them as initial data transfer and initial data recording transactions. They are only required during the transition phase on introduction of the new information system and are usually grouped together as a special application.

Management of Code Tables

We have already discussed code tables in Section 3.7. Code tables define an attribute's domain as numbers. Operative activities are not allowed to alter their contents. Code tables require their own transactions for recording amending, archiving, transferring and deleting entities. These are usually combined into independent applications (e.g. ' code table management').

Summary

The following starting points are used to derive transactions:

- Organizational demands for computerization

- Operative tools

- Retrieval

- Evaluations

- Navigation within an application

- Archiving

- Data exchange

- Initial data recording and transfer

- Management of code tables

All transactions derived from these sources must represent elementary operations.

4.4. Checking for Completeness

Section 4.3. provided suggestions for deriving transactions. Effect modelling and the entity life history help check whether the transactions identified are complete.

4.4.1. Effect Modelling

This simples version of UNTEL's Sales IS consists of over 40 transactions and 30 entity types. For each transaction, we record the effects on the entity types. We describe the effects of the transactions presented in Fig. 4.3./3 in a matrix (see Fig. 4.4.1./1). The rows contain the names of the entity types, the columns the names of the transactions. The effects of the transactions are indicated at the intersections of the rows and columns. The resulting matrix is called an *effect model*.

Transaction Entity type	Modify customer data	Modify customer management	Delete customer	
Partner	R	R	RD	
Town	R	R	RD	
Customer	R	R	RD	Legend:
Customer data not in effect	A		D	A Append
Sales representative		R	R	R Read
Customer management		AR	RD	M Modify
Business type	R			D Delete

Fig. 4.4.1./1: Effect model

An *effect model* presents a descriptive overview of the effects (append, read, modify, delete) of transactions on entity types.

To determine the completeness of the derived transactions, the effect modelling poses the following questions:

• Does the function model contain all the transactions needed?

• Does the data model contain only entity types that are actually used by the transactions?

The effect modelling deduces the answers to these questions from the effects of the transactions on the entity types. Entities do not exist per se. They are recorded with the help of transactions. The recording of entities only makes sense, however, if the information they contain is actually needed, i.e. if it is read by transactions. The entities are usually only of interest for a limited period (e.g. for as long as a company is an UNTEL customer); hence we must be able to delete entities. For each entity type in the Sales IS, at least one transaction is needed to create, use (read) and delete the entities. In Fig. 4.4.1./1 this condition is only fulfilled for the entity type 'customer management'.

For the other entity types we need to check whether transactions in other information systems generate the missing effects. Sales representative data (the entity types 'partner' and 'sales representative') are administered by the Personnel IS, which records, modifies and deletes these data.

If transactions in other information systems do not generate the missing effects, the corresponding entity type is either unnecessary, or additional transactions with the missing effects must be derived. For example, the transaction 'add customer' is needed to record customer data (the entity types 'partner' and 'customer').

The effect model checks whether at least one transaction exists to create, read and delete entities for each entity type.

4.4.2.   Entity Life History

UNTEL's Sales staff use the transaction 'search/display customer address' to identify customers (see Section 4.3.). The transaction is used only to display already recorded customer data and provides read-only access to the data ('read' effect). This kind of transaction is called a *retrieval transaction*.

Retrieval transactions are used to search for entities. They do not record or modify entities.

This is not the case for the transactions 'add customer', 'update customer data' and 'delete customer': The first transaction records new customers and includes them in the customer records (entity types 'partner' and 'customer'). 'Update customer data' transfers the data stored in 'customer data not in effect' as soon as they become valid, the customer data have previously been recorded by the transaction 'modify customer data' in the entity type 'customer data not in effect' (see Section 3.8.). The transaction 'delete customer' deletes a customer from the customer records. These three transactions have the effects 'append', 'modify' and 'delete'. They are referred to as *update transactions* .

Update transactions are used to record, modify and delete entities.

We can only modify the data relating to customer Meier if he has already been recorded but not yet deleted. The customer Meier can only be deleted if he is present in the data records. The data can be modified any number of times before deletion. The initiation of transactions for administering a customer only makes sense in a particular sequence.

The entity Meier (entity type 'customer') finds itself at any point in one of three states: 'appended', 'modified' or 'deleted': the transaction 'add customer' creates the entity (status 'appended'), the transaction 'update customer data' alters it (status 'modified'), and 'delete customer' deletes the entity (status 'deleted').

An update transaction transforms an entity from its original state to its target state. However, the original state and target state can be identical. If we examine these states in their entirety, and the transfers between states, (caused by transactions) we obtain the life history of the entity. This is called the *Entity Life History*. It extends from birth (appended) to death (deleted) of the entity. Retrieval transactions do not alter the status of an entity. Thus they are not taken into account in the Entity Life History.

For the Entity Life History we use a graphic notation developed by [Gutzwiller 1994, p. 254] (see Fig. 4.4.2./1). All update transactions for an entity type are shown on the left-side of the diagram, while the states that these transactions have generated are shown on the right-side. Since there are several transactions that can append, modify and delete an entity the states are numbered continuously. Arrows represent the changes of state, i.e. which transactions transform an entity from one state to another. Arrows that have the same starting point are drawn next to each other and combined within ellipses.

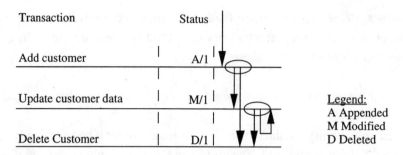

Fig. 4.4.2./1: Entity Life History of the entity type 'customer' (simplified)

Fig. 4.4.2./1 shows that the transaction 'add customer' appends entities in the entity type 'customer'. Entities can now be deleted or modified repeatedly.

The *Entity Life History* describes the permitted sequence of update transactions from the perspective of the entity type.

Analysis of the permitted sequence of update transactions for each entity type can provide indications of missing transactions. This is the case if the existing transactions cannot describe the entire life history of the entity type, i.e. when append, modify or delete transactions are absent.

The Entity Life History involves a substantial analytic effort and is only economical for the most important entity types. In the example from the Sales IS, these are principally the entity types 'customer' and 'order header'.

Not every Entity Life History is as simple as that of the entity type 'customer'. So let us examine the Entity Life History for the entity type 'order header' (see Fig. 4.4.2./2).

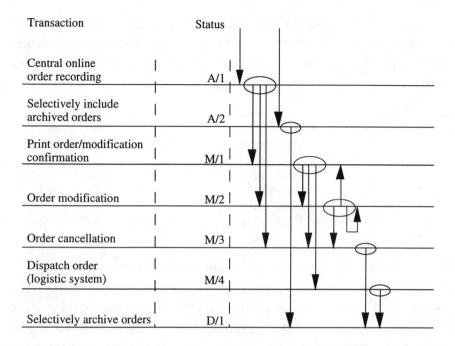

Fig. 4.4.2./2: Entity Life History of the entity type 'order header' (simplified)

UNTEL's Sales staff record the orders arriving by mail using the transaction 'central online order recording'. The transaction 'print order/modification confirmation' prints an order confirmation. The Logistics information system dispatches the orders on the delivery date. In the meantime, however, customers can modify the orders (transaction 'order modification') or even cancel them (transaction 'order cancellation'). UNTEL prints a modification confirmation for the modified orders (transaction 'print order/modification confirmation'). Since the order data are used for diverse evaluations (e.g. to determine cancellations per customer) none of the above transactions delete data. However, orders that have been delivered or cancelled are no longer needed in the data records, and hence are transferred to external storage media once a year (transaction 'selectively archive orders'). If needed (e.g. for special evaluations) the orders must be transferred (transaction 'selectively include archived orders').

In the Entity Life History of the entity type 'order header' we can recognize two different 'appended' states and four different 'modified' states. These states each constitute the starting point for different transactions. For instance, only cancelled (M/3) or delivered (M/4) orders can be selectively archived (transition to the state 'D/1' by the transaction 'selectively archive orders'). For this purpose we introduce an additional attribute 'order status' in the entity type 'order header' (see Fig. 4.4.2./3).

> **Order header**
> Order number
> Customer number
> Ordered by
> Order date
> Delivery date
> Discount rate
> Order status

Fig. 4.4.2./3: Entity type 'order header' with attribute 'order status'

The attribute 'order status' can assume the following values: recorded (A/1), confirmed (M/1), modified (M/2), cancelled (M/3 or A/2) and completed (M/4 or A/2). No attribute value is needed for the state D/1, since the entity has been deleted. The domain of the attribute 'order status' is determined by a list. Hence we define the code table 'order status' (see Section 3.7. and Fig. 4.4.2./4).

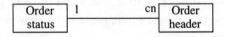

Fig. 4.4.2./4: ER diagram with order status code table

In the Entity Life History we write the appropriate order status in brackets after the status. The transactions 'selectively include archived orders' generate orders with the status 'cancelled' and 'completed'. The Entity Life History thus distinguishes between the states 'A/2 (cancelled)' and 'A/3 (completed)' (see Fig. 4.4.2./5).

Update transactions append, modify and delete entities. An entity's life cycle can assume the states of the type 'appended', of the type 'modified' and of the type 'deleted'.

Analysis of the permitted sequence of transaction performance allows us to check whether all the transactions needed are available, and what states an entity can assume in its life cycle. This may result in additional transactions, or in an additional code table for the entity status.

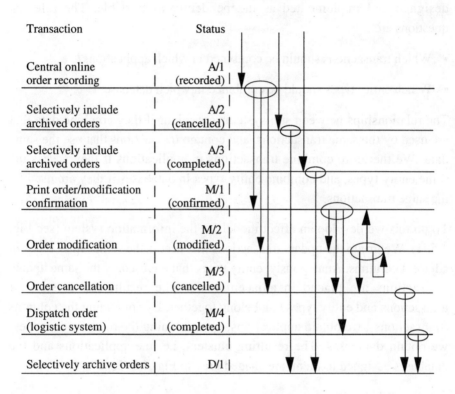

Transaction	Status
Central online order recording	A/1 (recorded)
Selectively include archived orders	A/2 (cancelled)
Selectively include archived orders	A/3 (completed)
Print order/modification confirmation	M/1 (confirmed)
Order modification	M/2 (modified)
Order cancellation	M/3 (cancelled)
Dispatch order (logistic system)	M/4 (completed)
Selectively archive orders	D/1

Fig. 4.4.2./5: Extended Entity Life History for the entity type 'order header' (simplified)

4.5. Derivation of Applications and Databases

UNTEL's Sales IS consists - as we have already stated - of more than 40 transactions and over 30 entity types. The transactions are implemented on the computer using programming languages, and the entity types using Data Definition Languages (see Section 3.10.1.). The large number of transactions and entity types as well as relationships between them, has led to unmanageability and loss of transparency. To reduce the complexity we create sub-systems which link transactions to applications and entity types to databases.

An information system should be structured so that the links within sub-systems are as great as possible, but there are few relationships between sub-systems (small interfaces). The sub-systems should also be capable of being designed and implemented as independently as possible. The relevant questions are:

- Which transactions should be combined in which applications?

- Which entity types should be combined in which databases?

The relationships between sub-systems are minor if they combine data that are used by the same transactions, and contain transactions that use the same data. We therefore combine transactions in applications if they access the same entity types, and combine entity types in databases if they are used by the same transactions.

To do this we develop an effect model for the information system (see Fig. 4.5./1). We group the update transactions that access the same entity types in adjacent columns. Analogously, entity types that are used by the same update transactions are placed in adjacent rows. The results are clusters of transactions and entity types that belong together. By combining the columns (transactions), we obtain applications; by combining the rows (entity types) we obtain databases. The resulting clusters, i.e. the applications and the databases assigned to them, are shaded grey in Fig. 4.5./2.

Entity type	Modify customer data	Update customer data	Modify customer management	Central online order recording	Order modification	Delete customer	⋮
Partner	R	M	R	R		RD	
Town	R	ARMD	R	R		RD	
Customer	R	M	R	R		RD	
Customer data not in effect	A	AD		R		D	
Sales representative			R			R	
Article				RM	RM		
Article group							
Structural element							
Customer management			AR			RD	
Order header				A	RM		
Order position				A	ARMD		
Business type	R						
...							

Fig. 4.5./1: Effect model

If we examine the effect model in Fig. 4.5./1, it becomes apparent that many transactions, or the activities on which they are based, access the same entity types. The transactions used to support customer acquisition primarily affect the partner data (including the entity types 'partner', 'customer', 'customer data not in effect' and 'customer management'). Order acquisition makes principal use of the entity types 'order header' and 'order position'. In the case of the Sales IS, this generates applications for customer management (including the transactions 'modify customer data', 'update customer data', 'modify customer management' and 'delete customer') and order management (including the transactions 'central online order recording' and 'order modification').

Entity type	Modify customer data	Update customer data	Modify customer management	Delete customer	:	Central online order recording	Order modification	:	:	Database
Partner	R	M	R	RD						
Town	R	ARMD	R	RD						
Customer	R	M	R	RD						Partner
Customer data not in effect	A	AD		D						database
Sales representative			R	R						
Customer management			AR	RD						
Business type	R									
...										
Order header						A	RM			Order
Order position						A	ARMD			database
...										
Article						RM	RM			Article
Article group										database
Structural element										
...										
...										...
Application	Customer management				Order management			...		

Fig. 4.5./2: Application and database formation

An *application* combines transactions which essentially access the same entity types.

Analogously to application formation, we combine entity types that are used by the same transactions into databases. In the Sales IS example entity types such as 'partner,' 'town', 'customer', 'customer data not in effect', 'customer management', and 'business types' form the partner database, 'order header' and 'order position' form the order database. The entity types 'article group', 'structural element' and 'article' are part of the article database, which is, however, not part of the Sales IS.

A *database* consists of a group of entity types which are essentially used by the same transactions.

The criterion of access to the same entity types is only a 'soft' rule. If many transactions access the same entity types and we still want to achieve transparent applications and databases, we must allow for deviations:

- We refrain from including retrieval transactions within applications. Clusters are formed primarily from update transactions (see Fig. 4.5./2.). Since only one application appends, modifies and deletes entities in an entity type, it is easy to ensure data consistency.

- If many transactions are closely linked in terms of their data, then the above restriction may not give rise to transparent applications. Then we would combine those transactions that append these entities into a single application. Given the limited scope of the didactic example this is unnecessary here.

Formation of applications and databases breaks down an information system into sub-systems which can largely be designed and implemented independently. To do this, it uses effect model clusterings ('entity type/transaction' matrix), as shown in Fig. 4.5./2. It is intuitively obvious that transactions which access the same entity types will also have a high degree of cohesion from the business perspective. The same is true of databases that are used by the same transactions.

A *(computerized) information system* is the sum of applications and databases within a corporate area or the entire company.

The effect model is the basis for forming applications and databases. Clustering assumes that transactions that use, and particularly modify, the same entity types have a high degree of substantive cohesion. It creates applications that make little access to each other's data.

4.6.   Transaction Network

The Entity Life History determines what states an entity can assume during its existence, and what transactions are permitted in the various states. The intervals at which transactions are performed may be very long - in some cases several years.

Whereas the Entity Life History views the sequence of transactions from the perspective of an entity (e.g. an order), the transaction network describes possible sequences of transactions during a dialogue session from the user's perspective. For example, an UNTEL Sales Support employee could display all orders from a given customer, select one order for examination and then modify it, once he has found the order he was looking for. The transaction network helps the designer to view an application flow from the user's perspective.

The transaction network distinguishes between online and batch transactions:

Online Transactions

Example 1: Availability check
UNTEL must be able to answer queries about the availability of a certain article at a certain delivery date. To do this, the Sales employee starts up the transaction 'check availability' from the menu (see Section 4.8.2.) and enters the article number, the quantity required and the delivery date requested. The transaction checks whether that quantity of the article will be available at that date. The transaction 'check availability' runs interactively in the form of questions and answers between the user and the computer system (dialogue processing). It is carried out simultaneously with the employee's activity - the answering of a query.

Example 2: Order recording
The Sales employee records a new order using the transaction 'central online order recording'. He must enter the customer number and the articles ordered, including order quantity and delivery date. If a customer attempts mistakenly to order an article not sold by UNTEL the error must be corrected immediately. This means that the transaction 'central online order recording' must check the existence of the article while performing the 'order recording' activity. This gives the customer and the UNTEL employee the opportunity to correct the article details immediately and place the order without any substantial delay or subsequent processing.

In both these examples the execution of the transaction coincides closely with the performance of the activity being supported. The transaction must be started when the performance of the activity is initiated and must be available throughout the entire duration of the performance (online availability). Manual and machine operations alternate. In this case we speak of *online* or *dialogue transactions*.

Online (dialogue) transactions are executed in an alternating sequence of manual and machine operations coinciding with the performance of an activity.

Batch Transactions

Despite all the advances in information technology, the power of computer systems remains limited. If many users initiate transactions simultaneously response times become greater, i.e. the individual transactions run more slowly from the user's perspective. However, the customer placing an order is not willing to accept long waiting times between recording of the individual order positions.

For this reason it is worth trying to carry out substantial transactions, i.e. transactions that require lots of processing capacity, at times when few other transactions are being used. This is only possible, of course, if the performance of the activity does not need to coincide with the execution of the transaction. For example, the month-end statistics for turnover per article could also run at night. The transaction 'determine turnover per article (group) for the period' is precisely defined before it is executed, i.e. the article(s) and period for which the turnover is to be calculated are specified. Once the transaction is started no further user interaction is required. The transaction 'determine turnover per article (group) for the period' is a *batch transaction*.

Batch transactions perform an operation without user interaction.

Since transactions ought to support activities at the time they are performed, online transactions are fundamentally to be preferred. For efficiency reasons, however, it is still necessary to execute some substantial transactions in batch mode. Transactions are only suitable if their time of execution is not required to coincide with the performance of the activity, and if they can be executed without user interaction.

Transaction Network

The customer 'Meier AG' telephones UNTEL head office. The previous day he placed an order with UNTEL, but now wants to bring the delivery date forward by one week. He has not yet received the order confirmation by mail, which means that he cannot give the Sales staff the order number.

The Sales employee initiates the transaction 'display orders by customer'. All orders placed by Meier AG together with the date of recording are presented on the screen. The employee then selects the order recorded the previous day and initiates the 'order modification' transaction. This causes the transaction 'display orders by customer' to be terminated and the 'order modification' transaction to be started. The desired order is displayed on the screen without having to enter the order number to initiate the 'order modification' transaction. The jump from the transaction 'display orders by customer' to the 'order modification' transaction means that the order number is automatically adopted.

The Sales employee can only initiate the 'order modification' transaction from within the transaction 'display orders by customer', if he has found the required customer order, i.e. if the transactions 'display orders by customer' has been successfully completed.

Meier AG now wishes to modify a further order, namely that with the order number 2300. The Sales employee initiates the 'order modification' transaction and enters the number 2300 in the field 'order to be modified'. However, no order with the number 2300 exists, so the 'order modification' transaction cannot be successfully completed. The Sales employee again views the orders from 'Meier AG' on the screen, by initiating the transaction 'display orders by customer'. Again he has initiated one transaction from within another. Here, successful completion of the first transaction is not necessary, since no data need to be transferred to the subsequent transaction. He can initiate the transaction 'display orders by customer' whether or not the 'order modification' transaction was successful.

Thus it is necessary to specify which transactions can be initiated by the user from within a given transaction, and whether successful completion of the transaction is a prerequisite for the initiation. Such decisions are recorded in a special precedence matrix, the so-called *transaction network*. Fig. 4.6./1 presents a segment from the (online) transaction network for the order management application. It contains ten examples of transactions, which may not all be explicitly described, but whose functions can largely be inferred from their names. The 'order management start transaction' is responsible for navigation through the order management function using menus (see Section 4.3.).

A precedence matrix describes general antecedent/subsequent relationships between functions. The transaction network contains the names of transactions in both the rows and the columns. The cells indicate whether it is possible to initiate one transaction (matrix column) from another transaction (matrix row):

- The transaction network only specifies whether we can initiate one transaction from *another*. Consequently we must fill the cells in the main diagonal with '-'.

- No entry indicates that we can never initiate transaction B from transaction A (e.g. we cannot initiate 'check availability' from 'display orders by customer').

- 'S' (for successful) means that we can only initiate transaction B from transaction A if transaction A has been successfully completed (e.g. initiating 'order modification' from 'display orders by customer). In this case, transaction A passes on data to transaction B (e.g. the order number of the order selected is passed from 'display orders by customer' to the 'order modification' transaction). The data transferred from transaction A to transaction B are called *interaction parameters*.

- 'C' (for conditional) means that we can initiate transaction B if A has been successfully completed or terminated (e.g. initiating 'display orders by customer' from the 'order modification' transaction). Whereas for 'S' a condition must be fulfilled before transaction B can be initiated, this is not necessary for 'C' . Furthermore, data are not usually transferred to the initiated transaction.

- 'A' (for automatic) means that transaction A initiates transaction B automatically without user interaction (i.e. without the user having to initiate transaction B). 'A' is only used to link batch transactions (see Fig. 4.6./2).

A transaction network is created for each application. But it also contains those transactions from outside the application that are accessible from within it. In Fig. 4.6./1, for example, the 'order management start transaction' can initiate the 'customer management start transaction' in the customer management application.

The transaction network constitutes an important starting point for structuring the dialogue flow (see Section 4.8.3.) and for dialogue prototyping (see Section 4.8.4.), and also helps to specify menus (see Section 4.8.2.) within a transaction.

Online and Batch Transaction Network

All transactions that can be initiated *by the user* from another transaction appear in the so-called *online transaction network* (the transactions are initiated online). The user decides whether he will make use of the possibility of initiating another transaction. Online transaction networks may only contain the cell entries ' ', '-', 'S' and 'C'.

Online transaction network for order management application / from transaction \ to transaction	Start order management transaction	Display orders to customer	Display order	Check availability	Central online order recording	Online recording of sales representative order	Order cancellation	Order modification	Determine turnover per article (group) in period	...	Customer management application	Start customer management transaction	Search /display customer address
Start order management transaction	-	C	C	C	C	C	C	C	C			C	
Display orders to customer		-	S		S	S	S	S					C
Display order		S	-		S	S	S	S					C
Check availability				-	S	S							
Central online order recording					-								C
Online recording of sales representative order						-							C
Order cancellation		C					-						C
Order modification		C						-					C
Determine turnover per article (group) in period									-				C
...													

Fig. 4.6./1: Online transaction network for the order management application (segment)

Fig. 4.6./1 is an online transactions network, whereas Fig. 4.6./2 describes a segment from a *batch transaction network*. A brief description of the latter follows: UNTEL customers can also place orders via EDIFACT (see Section 3.9.). EDIFACT refers to the order as a 'purchase order message'. The transaction 'receive and check EDIFACT purchase order message' receives EDIFACT orders and checks whether the order has been placed by an UNTEL customer. It also checks that the articles ordered are indeed UNTEL articles, that they are available at the desired delivery date, and that the customer has not exceeded his credit limit. If this is the case, the transaction 'accept EDIFACT purchase order message' is initiated, if not the case, the transaction 'reject EDIFACT purchase order message' takes place. The transaction 'accept EDIFACT purchase order message' places the EDIFACT order in the stock of orders. If the order is accepted, the EDIFACT message 'purchase order response message' is created by the transaction 'accept EDIFACT purchase order message', if it is rejected this is accomplished by the transaction 'reject EDIFACT purchase order message'. The computer system automatically initiates one of these transactions without human intervention ('A', automatic). The batch transaction network contains all transactions on whose completion the computer system automatically initiates subsequent transactions. The cells may only contain the entries ' ', '–' and 'A' .

Batch transaction network for order management application	to transaction	Receive and check EDIFACT purchase order message	Accept EDIFACT purchase order message	Reject EDIFACT purchase order message
from transaction				
Receive and check EDIFACT purchase order message		–	A	A
Accept EDIFACT purchase order message			–	
Reject EDIFACT purchase order message				–

Fig. 4.6./2: Transaction network for batch transactions (segment)

We describe *transaction networks* in a special precedence matrix. This indicates,

• which transactions can be initiated from which other transactions,

- under what circumstances (S, C or A) this initiation is possible, and
- which transactions can be initiated from outside the application.

We distinguish between *online* and *batch transaction networks*: Online transaction networks contain all transactions that the user ('S' or 'C') can initiate from other transactions, whereas the transactions in batch transaction networks are automatically ('A') initiated by the computer system.

Fig. 4.6./1 shows that it is perfectly possible for online transaction networks to contain batch transactions (e.g. 'determine turnover per article (group) for the period'). In this case the batch transactions are initiated from within an online transaction (in this case the transaction 'order management start transaction', i.e. in a menu).

4.7.   Lists and Messages

UNTEL sends its customers order confirmations (see Fig. 4.7./1). These are printed using the transaction 'print order/modification confirmation'.

An order confirmation consists of certain data elements (e.g. customer address), which are presented in a specific structure (e.g. in a table of order positions) and a specific format (font, text attributes, graphics, etc.). Even the electronic equivalent of this order confirmation (see Section 3.9.4.), the 'purchase order response message', has a precisely defined structure (laid down by EDIFACT).

Messages are communications in electronic form, while *lists* are printed on paper. Messages and lists are created by transactions. Their contents and structure are determined.

```
┌─────────────────────────────────────────────────────────────────┐
│ UNTEL                                                             │
│ Guisanstr. 40                                                     │
│ 8003 Zürich                                                       │
│                                                                   │
│                                                                   │
│                                     Meier AG                      │
│                                     Bahnhofstr. 2                 │
│                                     8001 Zürich                   │
│                                                                   │
│                                                                   │
│                                     Zürich, 13 May 1995           │
│                                                                   │
│ Order confiramtion: Order number 1300                            │
│                                                                   │
│ Our thanks for you order of 13 March 1995:                       │
│                                                                   │
│ Order position   Article number  Article description  Quantity Price   Amount │
│ 1                4711            DT 386 SX 210/4   10     1'500.--  15'000.--  │
│                                                                   │
│ Total                                                    15'000.-- │
│                                                         ═════════  │
│                                                                   │
│ The articles ordered will be delivered to you on 30 April 1995.  │
│                                                                   │
│ Yours faithfully                                                  │
└─────────────────────────────────────────────────────────────────┘
```

Fig. 4.7./1: Order confirmation created by the transaction 'print order/modification confirmation'

Since information systems create many different lists and messages, we have to characterize them with individual names (e.g. 'order/modification confirmation', 'purchase order response message', 'sales representative turnover per period' and 'number, turnover and proportion of orders in the total number of orders per sales channel').

The data contained in the order confirmation are largely available in the Sales IS: the customer address in the entity type 'partner', the order data in the entity types 'order header' and 'order position', and the article data in the entity type 'article'. Consequently, transactions for creating lists and messages access the attributes from the relevant entity types.

In designing lists we describe (see Fig. 4.7./2),

- which transaction(s) create(s) the list.

- which list elements appear in the list

- which attributes in which entity types correspond to the list elements

- which list elements have no corresponding entity type attributes (this is indicated by '-' in the entity type and attribute columns)

- how often the list element appears in the list

- how the data elements are calculated

For EDIFACT messages (e.g. purchase order response message), we must adhere to the EDIFACT standards (see Section 3.9.4.).

List: Order/modification confirmation				
Generating transaction(s) Print order/modification transaction				
List elements				*Frequency of appearance*
Name	*Entity type*	*Attribute*		*Calculation formula*
Name	Partner	Name	1	
Street	Partner	Street	1	
...				
Quantity	Order position	Sales quantity	n	
Price	Article	Selling price	n	
Amount	-	-	n	Price * quantity
Total	-	-	1	Σ Amount

Fig. 4.7./2: Description of list elements for the list 'order/modification confirmation'

4.8.   Designing the User Interface

With the help of the Sales IS the Sales employee records orders, modifies customer data, displays article data on the screen, etc. He expects the Sales IS transactions to support him effectively in performing his activities (functionality) and to be able to operate the Sales IS with ease (user friendliness).

How does he initiate and terminate transactions? How does he enter data? How is information presented on the screen? The design of the user interface, i.e. the screen masks, menus and dialogue flows, has a decisive influence on an application's acceptance by the user.

The *user interface* comprises the tools for communication between application and user.

The following sections deal with a few fundamental tools for communication between man and machine in transaction systems.

4.8.1.   Screen Masks

In the transaction 'central online order recording', the Sales employee enters the customer number, the name of the person placing the order and the desired delivery date (see Fig. 4.8.1./1).

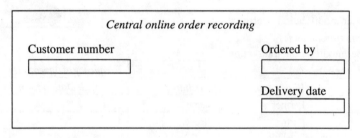

Fig. 4.8.1./1: Screen mask 'central online order recording'

The transaction then automatically assigns the order number and the order position number (P. No.), identifies the customer name from the customer number entry and asks for entry of the article number and the associated order quantity (see Fig. 4.8.1./2). If orders with more than four order positions are recorded the screen mask in Fig. 4.8.1./2 is presented. If all the articles ordered are available at the desired delivery date, the transaction 'central online order recording' stores the order in the order database. However, if an article is not available, a window containing an error message appears (see Fig. 4.8.1./3). The relevant order position must be altered before the order can be stored in the order records.

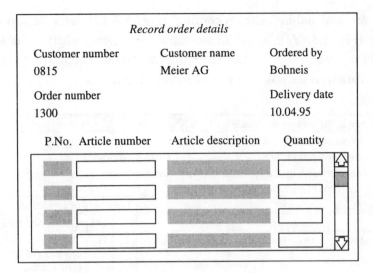

Fig. 4.8.1./2: Screen mask 'record order details'

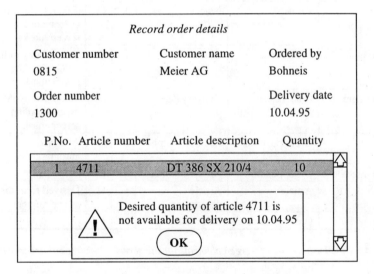

Fig. 4.8.1./3: Screen mask 'display error message'

A *screen mask* is used to record and display data and to produce messages. It specifies which data should appear where and how on the screen.

As with lists (see Section 4.7.) we specify the contents and structure of screen masks (see Fig. 4.8.1./4). In the previous case we name the screen masks 'central online order recording' (Fig. 4.8.1./1) and 'record order details' (Fig. 4.8.1./2). In the 'I/O' column we indicate whether the screen element is used to input data ('I'), to display data on the screen ('O') or to display data with the possibility of alteration ('I/O').

Screen mask: Record order details					
Used by transaction(s)):					
Central online order recording		Order modification			
Online order recording by the customer		Display order			
Online order recording by the sales representative					
Screen mask element				Frequency of appearance	
Name	*Entity type*	*Attribute*		I/O	*Calculation formula*
Order number	Order header	Order number	1	O	Taken from 'online order recording' screen mask
Customer number	Order header	Customer number	1	O	Taken from 'online order recording' screen mask
Name	Partner	Name	1	O	Taken from 'online order recording' screen mask
Ordered by	Order header	Ordered by	1	O	Taken from 'online order recording' screen mask
Delivery date	Order header	Delivery date	1	O	Taken from 'online order recording' screen mask
P. No.	Order position	Position number	n	O	Assigned automatically
Article number	Order position	Article number	n	I	
Article description	Article	Article description	n	O	Derived from the article number
Quantity	Order position	Sales quantity	n	I	

Fig. 4.8.1./4: Description of screen elements for the screen mask 'record order details'

4.8.2.   Menus

An application consists of a set of transactions from which the user can choose.

Possibilities for Selecting Transactions

Fig. 4.2./1 showed the call up of transactions using function keys for the example of the cash dispenser. Fig. 4.8.2./1 presents the selection of transactions using menu and mouse.

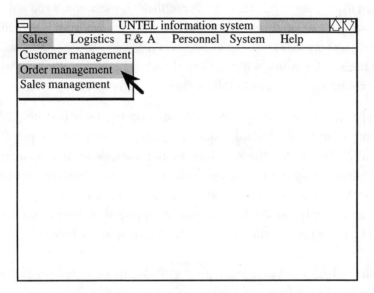

Fig. 4.8.2./1: Selection of transactions using menu and mouse

Some variants for the initiation of functions are:

- *Menu and mouse*
  The application presents the user with a menu (toolbar, command list etc.) from which he can select a function by mouse click. This function can itself be another menu or a processing function (e.g. a transaction). In place of the mouse, pens (e.g. Personal Digital Assistants, PDAs) or the finger (with Touch Screens) may be used.

- *Menu and keyboard*
  Some applications offer the user the same functionality as in the previous menu variant, but use the keyboard for entry - either alphanumeric (numbers and letters), using key combinations, or function keys (as in the cash dispenser). In some applications the keyboard is partly replaced by speech entry.

- *Command language*

  Older operating systems (e.g. MS-DOS) and applications often require that commands be typed in. In applications this is an abbreviated transaction name, the so-called transaction code. Whereas the user can see the options available in a menu, he must know the code by heart, or read it from a list, when using command language. Nevertheless, users who need only a few transactions to perform their activities often prefer using commands for calling up transactions to the alternatives listed above, simply because they are faster. This is frequently observed with experienced PC users who use key combinations instead of the mouse in word processing systems.

The type of transaction selection depends on the technical possibilities, frequency of use and standards. Many applications allow several possibilities in parallel and leave the decision to the user. Within informatics an independent discipline is dealing with such issues (software ergonomics, man-machine interface, user modelling, etc.). The user interface is not an application-specific issue, but a technical application design problem that should be solved and standardized for the company as a whole.

A *menu* is a list of transactions, that are available to a user at a particular point in an information system, an application or a transaction.

Menu Grouping

In contrast, an application-specific issue concerns which transactions are available at all, and how these should be combined into menus (groups) so that the user is presented with an overview of the transactions that are relevant to his activity from the large number of transactions available in any real application. The central criterion for combining transactions into menus is provided by the activities that an employee has to perform, as specified by the organization design. Within the order management application (which was called up in Fig. 4.8.2./1) we thus differentiate menus for order recording, inventory management and maintenance (see Fig. 4.8.2./2). The order recording menu, for instance, is aimed at the 'order acquisition' sub-process and the inventory control menu at the 'order adjustment' sub-process.

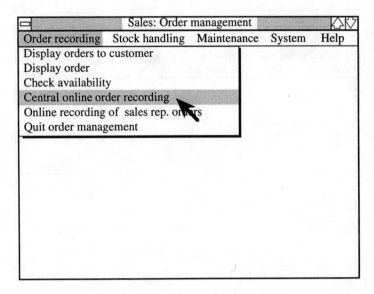

Fig. 4.8.2./2: Order management menu

The online transaction network from Section 4.6. allows the jump from the transaction 'central online order recording' to the transaction 'search/display customer address' (entry 'C'). The screen mask 'central online order recording' in Fig. 4.8.1./1 thus needs to be extended with a menu containing the transaction 'search/display customer address' (see Fig. 4.8.2./3). The dialogue flow (see Section 4.8.3.) summarizes the sequence of masks from the user perspective.

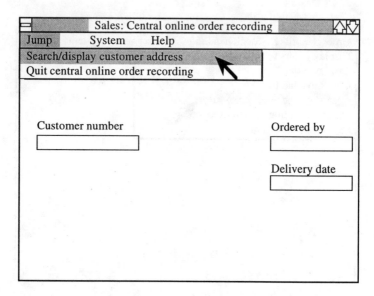

Fig. 4.8.2./3: Screen mask 'central online order recording' with menu

Information systems contain menus at diverse levels. In our example, we have menus for the information system, application and transaction levels. Fig. 4.8.2./4 presents a small extract from the Sales IS menu structure. Sub-menus and transactions can appear in several menus. An independent transaction is responsible for menu control (see Section 4.3.). This is always activated when an application is started or a transaction is terminated without calling up a subsequent transaction.

Since diverse employees in diverse processes can use the same transactions, it is common to design different menus for different users or user groups, or to leave the combining of transactions into menus to the user.

The *menu structure* distributes transactions to menus on a process-specific basis.

4.8.3.   Dialogue Flow

Design of the user interface concerns itself next with the dialogue flow, this involves the sequence of screen masks with which the user is confronted in the course of a transaction.

To record new orders the Sales employee initiates the transactions 'central online order recording'. To do this he selects the transaction 'central online order recording' from the order management sub-menu (see Fig. 4.8.2./2). The screen masks are presented, as in Fig. 4.8.1./1, for 'central online order recording' and then 'record order details' (see Fig. 4.8.1./2) for recording the order positions.

Sales menu
    Customer management menu
       ...
    Order management menu
       Order recording menu
          Transaction 'display orders by customer'
          Transaction 'display order'
          Transaction 'check availability'
          Transaction 'central online order recording'
          Transaction 'online order recording by sales representative'
       Inventory management menu (orders)
          Transaction 'cancel order'
          Transaction 'modify order'
       Maintenance order
          Transaction 'selectively archive orders'
          Transaction 'selectively transfer archived orders'
    Sales management menu
       ...

Fig. 4.8.2./4: Menu structure of the Sales IS (segment)

The transaction 'central online order recording' can also be initiated from other transactions: 'display orders by customer', 'display order' or 'check availability' (see Fig. 4.6./1).

The *dialogue flow* describes the sequence in which the screen masks for a transaction appear. It indicates the screen masks, menus and transactions from which you can get to these screen masks, and the screen masks and transactions to which it is possible to jump from them.

Dialogue Flow Diagram

For reasons of transparency, we describe the dialogue flow graphically (see Fig. 4.8.3./1).

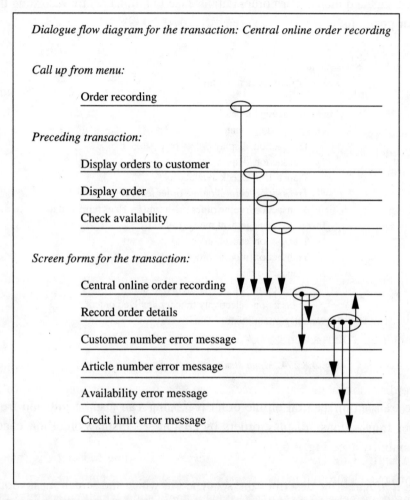

Fig. 4.8.3./1: Dialogue flow diagram for the transaction 'central online order recording'
(first draft)

The upper part of the diagram indicates in which menu and transaction we can initiate the transaction 'central online order recording'. The lower part lists the screen masks for the transaction 'central online order recording'. An arrow indicates one route from a menu, transaction or screen mask to another screen mask. Arrows with the same starting point are located adjacent to each other. Their starting points are combined in an ellipse. If the screen mask 'availability error message' appears on the screen (see Fig. 4.8.1./3), by clicking on the OK button we automatically jump to the 'record order details' mask. In the dialogue flow diagram we represent this feature by marking the arrow (dialogue flow) from 'record order details' to 'availability error message' with a point ('•').

When recording an order the Sales employee often does not know the customer number and the exact customer name. He must search the customer records to find the name and number. To do this he terminates the transaction 'central on line order recording', initiates the transaction 'search/display customer address', identifies the relevant customer, selects him and restarts the transaction 'online order recording'. The customer number of the person placing the order is then automatically transferred (see 'S' in the transaction network in Section 4.6.). We extend the dialogue flow diagram from Fig. 4.8.3./1 to include this option (see Fig. 4.8.3./2).

In the dialogue flow described the Sales employee must know the customer number to successfully complete the transaction 'central online order recording'. The Sales employee thus needs to enter the transaction with a key value (the customer number; attribute partner number/customer). This method of entering a transaction is referred to as 'out of the blue'.

We can also design the dialogue flow for the transaction 'central online order recording' so that the Sales employee can search for the customer from within the transaction. The user then receives continuous queries and directions until he has attained the desired result. This type of entry is called 'homing in'.

The Entity Life History analysis observes the update transactions that an entity passes through in the course of its existence; the entity is central. The transaction network examines for each application which antecedents and successors each transaction can have; here the application is central. The dialogue flow analyses for each transaction which antecedents and successors its screen masks can have; the transaction is central.

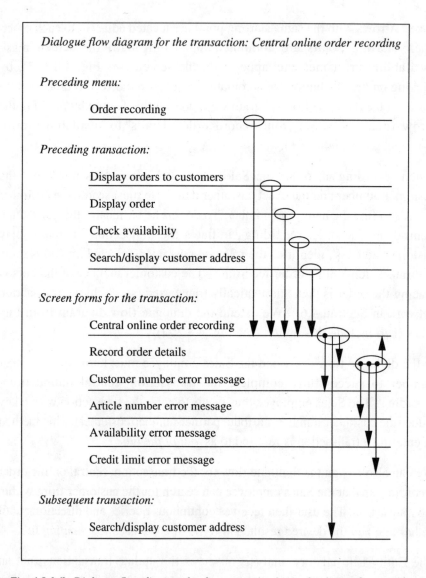

Fig. 4.8.3./2: Dialogue flow diagram for the transaction 'central online order recording'

Whereas the smallest unit of consideration (level of detail) in the Entity Life History and the transaction network is the transaction, the dialogue flow analysis goes to the more detailed level of the screen mask. However, it makes no statements about the conditions for initiating transactions (no distinction between 'S' and 'C').

The *dialogue flow diagram* describes the menus and transactions from which it is possible to reach the screen masks, which screen masks it is possible to jump to from within the transaction, and which transactions can be initiated.

4.8.4. Dialogue Prototyping

One fundamental problem with organization design, but even more with data and function design, is conceptualization. The results of the design techniques are static, abstract specifications of the target state. Furthermore, it is difficult for even experienced organization and systems analysts to imagine the process and the information system in practical use; it is much more difficult for the user who has no experience with these techniques and has seldom thought about information processing at this abstract level.

For everyone involved, it is much easier to go through and understand a process using a concrete business example. This can be done by creating a prototype which can be used to examine the essential features of the future information system before it is implemented at high cost.

A *dialogue prototype* is a simplified model of an information system from the user's perspective. It explains the information system to the user by means of the user interface.

Dialogue prototypes allow the user to try out the menus, screen masks and dialogue flow using examples. They comprise only the functionality for screen mask display, data entry, and dialogue navigation. Prototypes usually dispense with checking, processing and storing the data entered. Of course, they completely disregard functions for authorization, providing data history, managing code tables, data exchange, etc. and as a result constitute only a small portion of the cost of systems development.

The designer of UNTEL's Sales IS decides to use a prototyping tool. Together with potential users, he first sketches the screen masks, for the 'order acquisition' sub-process, for example. Then he determines the most important transactions, formulates the menus and dialogue flows using the prototyping tool, and returns to the user with this rudimentary model of the sub-system. Together with the designer, the users 'elaborate' several practical examples. The dialogue prototype gives the user the opportunity to get to know the sub-process at the micro-level together with its supporting transactions. He can change screen masks, supplement his functionality requirements or change the dialogue flow. In other words, he can check the functionality and handling, and so improve and fine-tune the design of the process and the information system.

Modern development tools allow the prototype to be developed step by step into a productive system, without losing the working results. The functionality of the prototype is extended until the application is implemented in its entirety (productive system). The prototyping procedure depends largely on the development tools used. Hence we cannot provide a detailed description here.

Dialogue prototyping is no substitute for the design techniques described above, but rather an extension to them. No amount of experimentation, however thorough, can generate a systematic data model design, or deal with issues such as data history, data integration, or ensure the complete derivation of all transactions required.

Dialogue prototyping offers an excellent opportunity to present an abstract and static concept of a process and an information system to the user in terms of its dynamic behaviour. Expensive development errors arising from a misunderstood specification can be avoided.

4.9. Control Structure

Function design has the objective of specifying an information system's functions so that software development receives clear guidelines and can check its results against the specification (see Sections 4.1. and 4.2.). It derives the functionality needed within an application from a process's activities (see Section 4.3.); thus the transactions are observed from the 'outside' (see Fig. 4.2./3).

If the software developer has some business understanding of the application area, then specification of the transactions, as they have been elaborated in the preceding sections, will suffice as a guideline. However, if the software developer cannot derive the substance of the solution from transaction specifications in this form, then the designer must also specify the processing rules for a transaction, as the following example illustrates.

On May 16, 1995 a customer inquires by telephone with UNTEL whether 10 units of article 'DT 386 SX 210/4', article number 4711, will be available on May 30, 1995. What does the transaction 'check availability' (see Section 4.3.) have to do in order to answer this query?

- First the article number, quantity and desired delivery date must be recorded.

- Articles that UNTEL can obtain from its suppliers by the delivery date are certainly available for delivery. The transaction first checks whether the desired delivery date is later than the date of entry plus the reorder time for the article. If this is the case then the article is regarded as available at that delivery date.

- If this is not the case checks are made to see if inventory levels for the desired article are sufficiently large: the transaction subtracts all orders for the desired article with delivery dates from today up to and including the desired delivery date from the current inventory level, furthermore, it adds all purchase orders for the article that will be delivered to UNTEL before the desired delivery date. If the result is less than the desired quantity, then the article is not available at that delivery date.

- If the article is available according to the above analysis it is still necessary to check whether this will impair fulfilment of already recorded orders. The transaction must therefore check whether understocking will result between the desired delivery date and the earliest reorder date (= entry date + reorder time): it checks whether the inventory level reduced by orders to be delivered and increased by incoming deliveries of the relevant article for each day in the period between the desired delivery date and the earliest reorder date is greater than, or equal to, zero. If this is always the case, the article is available at the desired delivery date.

These rules for checking availability do not arise automatically from the components of the transaction specification as elaborated above; alternative rules would also be conceivable. The rules are part of the business solution and need to be established by the designer in the specification.

We have just given a verbal description of the transaction 'check availability' in natural language. Even for this simple transaction this verbal description lacks transparency, is not always unambiguous, and is difficult to comprehend. To achieve a transparent and uniform specification of transaction logic we therefore use a formalized description tool such as pseudocode, decision trees and decision tables

Pseudocode

Pseudocode is a type of simplified programming language. It simply standardizes the key words of the control structure (flow control) and leaves the processing instructions to be formulated in natural language.

The transaction 'check availability' first requires that the article number, desired quantity and desired delivery date be entered. Then the availability of the article is checked and a corresponding message appears on the screen. We represent these five processing steps in the form of *instructions* (see Fig. 4.9./1), that are performed one after the other (sequentially).

```
Enter article number
Enter desired quantity
Enter delivery date
Check availability of article at delivery date
Display availability
```

Fig. 4.9./1: Sequence in the transaction 'check availability'

The pseudocode expresses a sequence in terms of a series of instructions (Fig. 4.9./2).

```
Instruction 1
Instruction 2
...
Instruction n
```

Fig. 4.9./2: Representing a sequence in pseudocode

The *sequence* indicates that the instructions contained are to be carried out sequentially.

Let us now elaborate the instruction 'check availability of the article at the desired delivery date': A check is made as to whether the desired delivery date is before the entry date, increased by the reorder time for the article. If this is not the case the article is available at the desired delivery date. Otherwise we must check the inventory level at the desired delivery date (see pseudocode in Fig. 4.9./3).

Enter article number
Enter desired quantity
Enter delivery date

```
IF delivery date < (date of entry + average reorder time)
THEN
    check inventory level at delivery date
ELSE
    availability = TRUE
ENDIF
```

Display availability

Fig. 4.9./3: Selection in the transaction 'check availability'

The choice between two alternative processing routes is called *selection*. The pseudocode control constructs are 'IF ... THEN ... ELSE ... ENDIF'.

The result of the check is stored in the variable availability (availability = TRUE). However, we only know the result for the case where the delivery date is beyond the reorder date (ELSE route); in the other case (THEN route), it depends on checking the inventory level. At the end of the transaction, the availability of the article is displayed on the screen (instruction 'display availability ').

Selection chooses between alternative processing routes on the basis of a condition.

Pseudocode offers two kinds of selection:

- *Simple selection* chooses between precisely two alternatives (see Figs. 4.9./3 and 4). The THEN and ELSE routes contain an instruction or the symbol for 'no instruction' ('-'). An instruction is a processing instruction or a control construct (sequence, selection, etc.).

```
IF Condition
THEN
        Instruction 1
ELSE
        Instruction 2
ENDIF
```

Fig. 4.9./4: Representing a simple selection in pseudocode

- *Multiple selection* chooses between more than two alternatives. One example of this is the choice of a menu option by mouse. Clicking the option 'display order' in Fig. 4.8.2./2, for example, initiates the transaction 'display order'. However, if the click is made on part of the screen that does not belong to the (menu) selection, the menu is closed. The multiple selection in this example is thus: 'if the mouse click is on the option 'display orders by customer' then the transaction 'display orders by customer' is initiated. If the click is not on a menu option then close the pull-down' (see Fig. 4.9./5).

```
CASE mouseclick OF
    Menu option 'display orders by customer':     Initiates transaction 'display orders
                                                  by customer'
    Menu option 'display order':                  Initiates transaction 'display order'
    ...
    OTHERWISE:                                    Close pull-down menu
ENDCASE
```

Fig. 4.9./5: Menu selection in pseudocode

Pseudocode expresses multiple selection with 'CASE ... OF' (see Fig. 4.9./6). The instruction 'OTHERWISE' consists of all other cases (usually the exceptional situations).

```
CASE expression OF
      Value-1:        Instruction 1
      Value-2:        Instruction 2
      ...
      OTHERWISE:  Instruction for other cases (this instruction is optional)
ENDCASE
```

Fig. 4.9./6: Representing multiple selection in pseudocode

Let us return to the transaction 'check availability' and elaborate the instruction 'check inventory level at delivery date' from Fig. 4.9./3 (see Fig. 4.9./7).

```
Enter article number
Enter desired quantity
Enter delivery date
IF delivery date < (Entry date + Average reorder time)
THEN
      Daily inventory level = Inventory level at entry date
      Shipment date = Entry date
```
```
      WHILE Shipment date <= Order delivery date
            Daily inventory level = Daily inventory level - Order positions for the
                  desired article with delivery date equal to shipment date + Purchase order
                  positions for the desired article with delivery date equal to shipment date
            Shipment date = Shipment date + 1
      ENDWHILE
```
```
      IF Daily inventory level < Desired quantity
      THEN
            Availability = FALSE
      ELSE
            Check impairment of recorded orders
      ENDIF
ELSE
      Availability = TRUE
ENDIF
Display availability
```

Fig. 4.9./7: Iteration of the transaction 'check availability'

All orders for the article concerned due before the desired delivery date are subtracted from the current inventory level. Then incoming deliveries, up to that date, are added. For every day between the entry date and the desired delivery date, we must search the data records for incoming deliveries and outgoing shipments of the article, adding or subtracting them, i.e. calculation of the inventory level is performed repeatedly for every day up to the desired delivery date (*iteration*).

Iteration is the repeated performance of an instruction. The repetition continues as long as the repeat condition is fulfilled.

Pseudocode offers two kinds of iteration:

- The repeat condition is checked at the beginning of the loop (see Fig. 4.9./8). The instruction in the iteration is only carried out if the condition is fulfilled.

> WHILE Repeat condition
>   Instruction
> ENDWHILE

Fig. 4.9./8: Iteration using WHILE repeat condition ... ENDWHILE

- The repeat condition is checked at the end of the loop (see Fig. 4.9./9). The instruction in the iteration is performed at least once before the repeat condition is checked.

> DO
>   Instruction
> WHILE Repeat condition

Fig. 4.9./9: Iteration using DO ... WHILE repeat condition

The control constructs sequence, iteration and selection establish the sequence in which the instructions in a transaction are performed. They constitute the *control structure*.

Let us now elaborate the instruction 'check impairment of recorded orders' and indicate the start of the transaction with 'PROGRAM transaction name' and the end with 'ENDPROGRAM' (see Fig. 4.9./10).

PROGRAM Check availability
Enter article number
Enter desired quantity
Enter delivery date
IF Delivery date < (Entry date + Average reorder time)
THEN
    Daily inventory level = Inventory level at entry date
    Shipment date = Entry date
    WHILE Shipment date <= Order delivery date
        Daily inventory level = Daily inventory level - Order positions for the
            desired article with delivery date equal to shipment date + Purchase order
            positions for the desired article with delivery date equal to shipment date
        Shipment date = Shipment date + 1
    ENDWHILE
    IF Daily inventory level < Desired quantity
    THEN
        Availability = FALSE
    ELSE
        Availability = TRUE
        Daily inventory level = Daily inventory level - Desired quantity
        WHILE (Shipment date < (Entry date + Average reorder time)) AND
        (Availability = TRUE)
            Daily inventory level = Daily inventory level - Order positions for the
            desired article with delivery date equal to shipment date + Purchase
            order positions for the desired article with delivery date equal to
            shipment date
            IF Daily inventory level < 0
            THEN
                Availability = FALSE
            ELSE
                Shipment date = Shipment date + 1
            ENDIF
        ENDWHILE
    ENDIF
ELSE
    Availability = TRUE
ENDIF
Display availability
ENDPROGRAM

Fig. 4.9./10: Pseudocode for the transaction 'check availability' (segment)

Decision Tree and Decision Table

Operational reality often has to deal with complex decision situations in which several conditions are applied together. The small example of UNTEL's 'customer acquisition' should serve to illustrate this.

UNTEL only accepts potential customers (applicants) into its stock of customers if they fulfil the following conditions:

1. The credit investigation must be positive.

2. The potential customer must have an annual turnover in UNTEL articles of over 40,000 CHF.

3. If conditions 1 and 2 are fulfilled and the potential customer is a mail order company he is accepted as a customer.

4. If conditions 1 and 2 are fulfilled and the potential customer is not a mail order company he is only accepted if the population in the catchment area of his business location is larger than 5,000 or the distance from the nearest UNTEL customer with the same type of business is greater than 0.5 km.

In representing this kind of decision situation, the decision tree is more suitable than pseudo code (see Fig. 4.9./11). From the starting point (root) of a decision tree, branches spread out at whose ends a decision criterion (e.g. 'credit investigation OK' and 'credit investigation not OK') is found. Further branches can spread out from the individual decision criteria. The actions to be carried out if the preceding decision criteria are fulfilled are at the ends of the tree (leaves). The decision tree gives an overview of all decision and action variants.

The general structure of a decision tree is presented in Fig. 4.9./12.

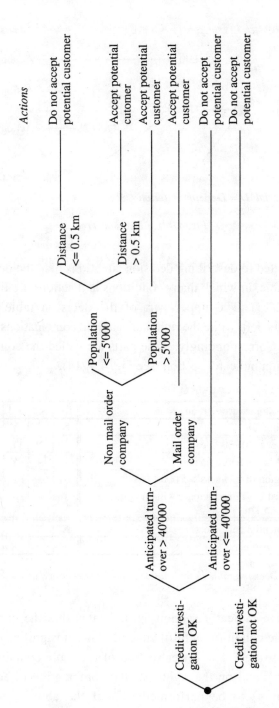

Fig. 4.9./11: Decision tree in the context of the 'customer acquisition' sub-process

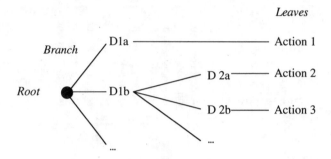

Legend: D = Decision criterion

Fig. 4.9./12: Decision Tree

Even better suited to describing decision situations than the decision tree, is the decision table, in which many conditions and actions are linked together (see Fig. 4.9./13). The upper part of the decision table contains the conditions on the left, while the right indicates the combinations for fulfilment of conditions. Correspondingly, these parts are called the condition section and the condition indicator section (see Fig. 4.9./14).

Decision table 'customer acquisition'	R1	R2	R3	R4	R5	R6
Credit investigation OK	N	-	Y	Y	Y	Y
Estimated turnover > 40'000 / year	-	N	Y	Y	Y	Y
Business type = Mail order company	-	-	Y	N	N	N
Population in region of business > 5'000	-	-	-	Y	N	N
Distance to nearest UNTEL customer with the same business type > 0.5 km	-	-	-	-	Y	N
Do not accept potential customers	X	X				X
Accept potential customer			X	X	X	

Fig. 4.9./13: Decision table in the context of the 'customer acquisition' sub-process

In the condition indicator section 'N' indicates that the condition is not fulfilled, 'Y' the condition is fulfilled, and '-' it is insignificant whether the condition is fulfilled. The lower section of the table contains the actions (action section), and on the right-side the combination of actions (action indicator section) to be performed ('X') if the above combination of conditions apply.

Name of the decision table	Rules
Condition section	**Condition-indicator section**
Action section	**Action-indicator section**

Fig. 4.9./14: Decision table

In creating the decision table, we first establish the conditions and the actions. Then we formulate the rules. A rule indicates what actions should be performed if the individual conditions are fulfilled or not. We enter an 'N', 'Y' or '-' for each condition on the condition indicator section. Then we determine what actions are to be performed if the corresponding conditions apply. The actions to be performed are indicated by an 'X'. Each column generates a rule.

Decision trees and *decision tables* are suited to representing wide-ranging decision problems.

4.10. Authorization

Authorization is the machine support for assigning and controlling authority. It gives an employee the right to perform certain transactions and access certain data. Function design is primarily concerned with transaction authorization. However, to avoid repetition, we will deal with this issue now as it also relates to data.

In UNTEL, for example, a sales representative is given the right to record orders and check the availability of goods in store. He is also given the right to access customer documentation. In contrast, UNTEL's personnel data are not accessible to him, since he does not need them to perform his duties. This prevents him from examining his colleagues' rates of commission, and from altering his own rate of commission.

Transaction Authorization

Transaction authorization confers an organizational position with access to certain transactions. In an authorization matrix (see Fig. 4.10./1), an 'X' indicates that a given position can perform the transactions assigned to it.

Transaction	Position				
	CS	RS	SS	SR	O
Order management start transaction	X	X	X	X	X
Display orders by customer	X	X	X	X	
Display order	X	X	X	X	
Check availability	X	X	X	X	
Central online order recording	X	X	X		
Online order recording by sales representative	X	X	X	X	
Order modification	X	X	X		
Delete order	X	X	X		
Selectively archive orders					X
Selectively transfer archived orders					X

CS   Central sales and consultancy management
RS   Regional sales and consultancy management
SS   Sales support
SR   Sales representative
O   Operator

Fig. 4.10./1: Authorization matrix for transactions (segment)

Transaction authorization specifies which positions can initiate which transactions.

Data Authorization

The right to use certain transactions includes the right to access the data that are associated with it. If a sales representative has the right to use the transaction 'online order recording by sales representative', this implicitly states that he may record order data (include them in the database), but only using this transaction. It does not mean that he may modify data that has already been recorded.

Thus, function authorization involves a certain level of data authorization. This is inadequate, however, since there are other computer functions, in addition to transactions, that are not restricted to specific data. Examples are word processing programs, spreadsheet systems, or database query languages (see Section 3.10.2.).

In these cases we use a data authorization matrix (see Fig. 4.10./3). An entry in a cell of the matrix indicates what effects a position is allowed to have on certain data. We distinguish between the effects append (A), read (R), modify (M) and delete (D) in the senses used in Section 4.3. The SQL commands GRANT and REVOKE are used to administer authorization in a relational database. GRANT confers authorization and REVOKE cancels it:

'GRANT <access type> ON <entity type> TO <user name>'
'REVOKE <access type> ON <entity type> FROM <user name>'

A relational DBMS such as ORACLE 7.0 differentiates the following types of access (see Fig. 4.10./2):

Effect	Access type
Append	INSERT
Read	SELECT
Modify	UPDATE
Delete	DELETE

Fig. 4.10./2: Types of access in a relational DBMS

In the case of data, we distinguish between databases and document bases (see Section 2.2.2.5.). Database authorization relates to entity types (and attributes), document base authorization to directories (e.g. collections of documents held in a document base for reference when using an operating system).

Since all the entity types in our example contain critical operative data, only read access is allowed outside the transactions; otherwise the consistency of the database could scarcely be guaranteed. In the case of directories a distinction is drawn between personally produced documents and those of other employees. The operator has the widest power to delete since he must be able to remove old documents in the course of data archiving.

Data authorization using a matrix like that in Fig. 4.10./3 is only a very crude instrument. Specific database, network, groupwork and operating systems offer considerably greater possibilities for degrees of authorization in data access.

Data authorization establishes the rights of given positions to access data.

Entity type	Position				
	CS	RS	SS	SR	O
Customer	R	R	R	R	
Order	R	R	R	R	
Order position	R	R	R	R	
Article	R	R	R	R	
Sales representative	R	R			
Directory	CS	RS	SS	SR	O
Own consultancy reports	ARMD	ARMD		ARMD	
All consultancy reports	R	R	R	R	D
Article descriptions	R	R	ARMD	R	D
Own article problem reports		ARMD	ARMD	ARM	
All article problem reports	R	R	R	R	D
Order cost estimation	R	RM		ARM	D

CS	Central sales and consultancy management	A	Append
RS	Regional sales and consultancy management	R	Read
SS	Sales support	M	Modify
SR	Sales representative	D	Delete
O	Operator		

Fig. 4.10./3: Data authorization matrix (segment)

Summary

A position uses transactions to perform its activities. Authorization gives an employee the right to access those transactions that he needs in accordance with the organization design.

An employee can also be given the right to access certain data using a database query language circumventing the transaction. In such cases the access right must be assigned to the employee on a data-specific basis.

In addition, rights to documents that are available within a network in the office application context (word processing, spreadsheets, graphics, etc.) must be specified.

4.11. Workflow Design

The transaction network determines permitted sequences of transactions. The dialogue flow elaborates the flow analysis of transactions down to a transaction's menus and screen masks. Dialogue prototyping tries out the flows prior to implementing the transactions using business examples. But none of these techniques incorporate the functionality to control flows, as was postulated by workflow planning in Section 2.6.

In the past, large companies have developed their own transactions for flow control - to control the processing of insurance claims, for instance. Nowadays, Workflow Management Systems (WFMS), which are available on the market as standard software, are taking over the control of microprocesses. They perform functions that up to now have either been built into the applications, or solved organizationally without computer support. They aim to plan, initiate and monitor administrative activities analogously to industrial manufacture.

4.11.1. Functionality of WFMS

Section 2.6.2. outlined the way a WFMS operates using the example of the microprocess 'accept EDIFACT order'. From the microprocess in workflow planning workflow design derives a technical workflow specification. WFMS offer their own workflow specification components for this task. These contain graphic editors for activity chain diagrams, screen mask editors, etc.

In general the following flow control functions can be recognized in modern WFMS:

- *Operation control*
  An event (e.g. arrival of EDIFACT purchase order) initiates an operation (the processing of the EDIFACT purchase order). The WFMS recognizes the type of event, generates an operation from it, and passes the operation to an employee (or computer application) for each activity to be performed.

It treats the operation like a production order that must undergo processing at production stations in accordance with a work schedule. The WFMS controls the operation until a concluding event arises (e.g. accept EDIFACT purchase order).

- *Provision of applications and transactions*
  An employee often needs more than one application to undertake an activity. To 'check conditions' the sales representative uses the transaction 'search/display customer address' from the customer management application, the 'order modification' transaction from order management, and the spreadsheet system with a template for estimating the cost of deviation from conditions. The WFMS takes on as much of the handling as possible, so that the sales representative can concentrate on the subject matter of his activities. It handles the call-up of applications and transactions, as well as the transfer of data between applications, etc.

- *Assignment of tasks*
  The WFMS assigns an operation to an employee for performance of a particular activity. Thus it transfers an EDIFACT purchase order for which a deviation from conditions has been identified, to the sales representative responsible for the customer concerned. The WFMS can also take the capacity situation into account, however, or assign the activity to a group of employees. If the sales representative responsible is on holiday, the WFMS can pass the operation on to another representative.

- *Managing the stock of tasks*
  An employee typically has several operations awaiting processing. Conventionally, this is signalled by a stack of files that are processed on a 'first come - first served' basis. A WFMS gives an employee the option of examining an overview of his set of tasks, assigning priorities or setting provisional deadlines for their completion.

- *Deadline control*
  The WFMS monitors intermediate and final deadlines for operations. At any point the WFMS can provide information about the status of an operation, activities already undertaken, activities still outstanding, expected time of completion, etc.

- *Resubmission*
  If an employee cannot complete an activity (e.g. because he must obtain additional information) he can specify a time for resubmission, at which point the WFMS will remind him of the postponed operation.

- *Electronic signature*
  The WFMS offers a procedure for electronic signatures, so that it is not necessary to produce files in paper form simply for the sake of a signature.

- *Interruption of an operation*
  If an operation is interrupted, the WFMS removes the file from the stack and informs the employees concerned. This could arise, for instance, if a customer withdraws an EDIFACT purchase order before processing is complete.

- *Documenting the operation*
  The WFMS can document the entire processing of an operation. This provides process or organization management with an extremely powerful tool for the analysis of the organization as it actually works (see Section 2.13.).

A WFMS generalizes administrative tasks that are needed to control flows of all kinds in the same way.

4.11.2. Separation of Transactions and Workflow

Up to now many application have contained flow control functions. The mixture of transactions for processing activities (e.g. order management) and transactions for flow control results in substantial costs, since many flow control functions are developed anew for each application, and subsequently need to be maintained. In addition, they appear to the user in a wide variety of contexts.

A WFMS separates the flow control from the applications for performance of activities.

Fig. 4.11.2./1 presents an ideal concept of the interaction between WFMS and applications. The microprocess is the result of organization design, taking into account existing, purchased, or newly developed applications and their transactions. The microprocess 'accept EDIFACT order' uses transactions from the customer management and order management applications, as well as spreadsheet and word processing applications. Flow control for the microprocess is handled by a WFMS, which offers its own transactions for this task, e.g. 'assign an operation to an employee' (not indicated in the figure).

The customer and order management applications do not only enter into the microprocess 'accept EDIFACT order', but also into any number of other microprocesses. Examples might be the microprocesses 'record sales representative order', 'order correction' and 'place order via merchandise management system'. The transactions in the applications must be designed so that they can be used in diverse contexts.

The WFMS avoids the application-specific development of flow control transactions, and facilitates the reusability of transactions, since a transaction without flow control is more independent of a specific activity in a specific microprocess.

In the ideal concept presented, the employee involved in the process learns to execute a microprocess, and not how to operate an application, as at present. He scarcely notices that the WFMS is accessing different applications.

We will remain a long way from this ideal for some time to come

- since existing applications contain their own flow logic, but cannot be replaced at short notice,

- since existing applications employ different kinds of user support,

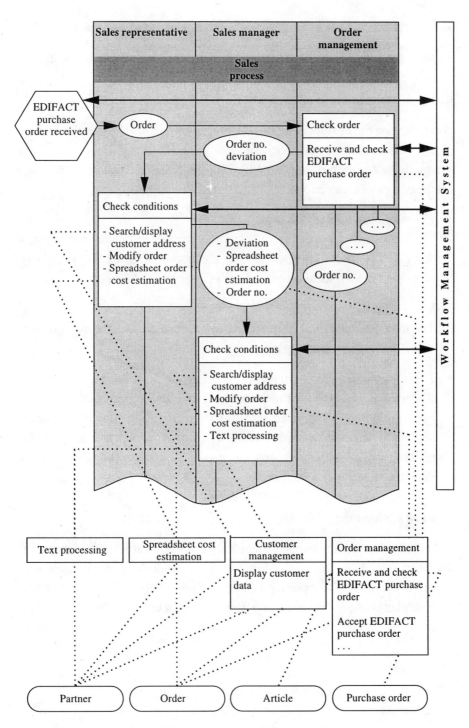

Fig. 4.11.2./1: Interaction of WFMS and applications

- since purchased package software exists in a world of its own, and

- since the WFMSs available are still far from meeting all requirements.

4.11.3. Implications for Function Design

Nevertheless, the development of new processes and new applications should already be aiming at the vision of flow control, so that flow control can gradually be transferred to a WFMS. This generates the following demands on the design of transactions:

- *Transactions without flow logic*
  The transactions for performing activities should contain no flow logic, so that they can be used in any activities and microprocesses. Thus they must be limited to their local activity, the manipulation of a database.

- *Standardized user interface*
  The user interface must be standardized. At present this means company-specific standards in many areas.

- *Tools for workflow specification*
  If a company has decided in favour of a specific WFMS, function design can employ the associated workflow specification tool to derive the technical workflow specification from the workflow planning microprocess. Such tools contain graphical editors for activity chain diagram, screen mask editors, etc.

4.11.4. Summary

A WFMS should plan, instigate and monitor administrative activities just like the work cycles in industrial manufacture. It should separate the flow logic from the transactions supporting activities. This means that transactions must be specified without flow logic and with a uniform user interface.

4.12. Further Reading

Literaturstelle	Punkt	4.1. Ziele des Funktionsentwurfs	4.2. Funktionsmodell	4.3. Ableitung von Transaktionen	4.4. Prüfung auf Vollständigkeit	4.5. Ableitung von Applikationen und Datenbanken	4.6. Transaktionsnetzwerk	4.7. Listen und Messages	4.8. Gestaltung der Benutzerschnittstelle	4.9. Kontrollstruktur	4.10. Autorisierung	4.11. Workflowkonstruktion
[Balzert 1982]										X		
[BIFOA 1993]												X
[Bodendorf 1992]									X			
[Böhm et al. 1993]			X		X	X	X	X	X	X	X	X	
[Gutzwiller 1994]		X	X	X	X	X	X	X	X		X	
[Hansen 1992]			X						X		X	
[Heilmann 1994]												X
[Heinrich/Burgholzer 1989]									X	X		
[Martin/McClure 1988]										X		
[Pomberger/Blaschek 1993]									X			
[Scheer 1994]			X							X		
[Schönthaler/Németh 1990]									X	X		
[Spitta 1989]									X			
[Thimbleby 1990]									X			
[Thoma 1993]					X							
[Vogler 1993]												X
[White/Fischer 1994]												X
[Zehnder 1989]											X	

5. Foundations of a Business Engineering Method

Business Engineering designs the organization, data, and function dimensions at the strategy, process, and information system levels (see Section 1.3.3.).

This book presents techniques for designing the organization, function, and data, and is thus organized in terms of the Business Engineering dimensions. However, the techniques used in the execution of a Business Engineering project are not applied in the order that they are presented in the chapters of this book.

A *Business Engineering level* refers to a certain level of detail and certain contents of the design.

A project typically works at a certain level (see Section 1.3.2.) and concentrates only on a few dimensions. In a project at the strategy level, for example, UNTEL planning has included the organization, function, data, personnel, technology, finance and markets. In the project 'Reorganization of UNTEL's Sales' it is designing the process level, where the organization, function and data dimensions are of greatest importance. This does not mean that the other dimensions are irrelevant. A qualification program for sales representatives or financial planning of the reorganization must be included. But the project focus lies on the three dimensions: organization, function and data. The 'Sales IS' project is limited to the information system level. In addition to the organization, function and data, it must also devote attention to the information technology, but it delegates the planning and creation of the information technology infrastructure to a special (sub-) project.

5.1. Business Engineering Levels

Fig. 5.1./1 isolates a few design statements from the wide-ranging UNTEL example. Using examples it illustrates the subject matter of the levels and dimensions. It also highlights the relationships between statements at the same level (thin black lines) and relationships between levels (thick grey lines). Relationships at the same level indicate, for example, that the 'regional sales and consultancy management' is responsible for the activity 'order approval', that it uses the transaction 'search/display customer address' and that this transaction accesses the entity type 'customer'. An example of relationships between the levels is the indication that the order management application contains the 'order modification' transaction, and that an inventory management (orders)' menu exists to call up this transaction.

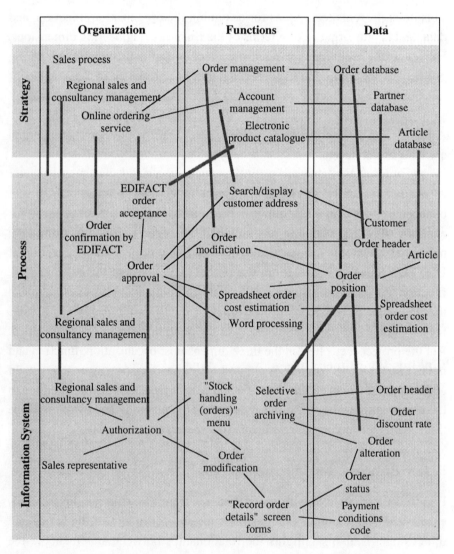

Fig. 5.1./1: Examples of design statements by level and dimension

5.1.1.   Strategy

The *strategy level* documents the company's position in the market, and the key decisions for the company and its business segments.

Organization

In its new strategy, UNTEL decisions include the creation of the sales process and regionalization using the 'regional sales and consultancy management' positions. A further strategic decision is to offer the customer an online ordering service. These three decisions affect the organization's processes, structures, and process flows (or the associated process outputs).

Function

The strategic planning of the information system establishes that applications for an order management, customer management and electronic product catalogue are to be developed or purchased. The order and customer management applications are needed to implement an online ordering service. The electronic product catalogue was included in the IS Strategy to improve customer service.

Data

The two applications require databases for orders, partners, and articles.

Linking the Dimensions of the Strategic Design

Organization, function and data are only three of many dimensions within a business strategy (see Fig. 2.3.5./1.). In Figs. 5.1./1 and 5.2./1 the function and data dimensions occupy a lot of space. This emphasizes the universality of the three levels (to present the organization, function and data at the three levels: strategy, process and information system) and reflects Business Engineering's focus on these levels.

In contrast to this approach, the theory and practice of strategic development neglect the function and data dimensions. They fail to exploit the potential of information technology, thereby reducing the chances of successfully implementing the strategy.

Business Engineering exploits the potential of information technology for the strategy by concentrating on the organization, data and function dimensions.

5.1.2. Process

The *process level* details the organizational structure and derives the outputs, flows, computer support and management tools from the strategy. The emphasis is on the organizational view (process).

Organization

While the strategic level defines the process, the process level provides the detailed design. From the process output 'online ordering service', process development derives the sub-process 'accept EDIFACT order', the 'order approval' activity it includes, and the sub-process output 'EDIFACT order confirmation'. In some cases the activity 'order approval' lies within the competence of the organizational unit 'regional sales and consultancy management'. The process level thus refines and extends the organizational decisions from the strategy level.

Function

The activity 'order approval' needs the transactions 'search/display customer address', 'order modification', the spreadsheet system with the order cost estimation template, and the word processing application (see Fig. 2.6.2./1).

Data

At the process level, the entity types for articles, etc. are defined for these transactions.

Linking the Process Design Dimensions

In order to implement the transaction 'accept EDIFACT order' in the form specified in Fig. 2.6.2./1, UNTEL needs the transactions and applications named, and these in turn require the associated data. If these information system components are not attainable - for cost reasons for example - then the process flow cannot be implemented. In contrast, new information technology developments, such as a purchased expert system for checking customers' credit worthiness or a Workflow Management System, can give new impulses for the flows.

Process development designs the organizational solution and the information technology tools (computer functions) that are required. At the process level the organization is basically central, but the organization, function and data dimensions are so closely intertwined that they need to be designed collectively.

Thus far we have assumed that the information system is being newly developed. If the company is using existing or purchased (package) software instead then the transactions and their data are already predefined. This alters the process development procedure:

If process development is based upon new software development it is used to define the tasks and flows and to derive the transactions and data from them. If process development is based on existing software the organization is based on the existing transactions and data [see IMG 1994b]. This applies whether the existing software has been purchased (e.g. package software) or developed individually.

5.1.3. Information System

The *information system level* gives concrete form to the process design; it delivers guidelines for the organizational and information technical implementation. The emphasis is on the function and data dimensions (information system).

Organization

Authorization for the necessary transactions is given to the sales representatives and 'regional sales and consultancy management' (for reasons of space, only partially indicated in Fig. 5.1./1).

Function

The transactions from the process level can be elaborated and supplemented, by 'selectively archive orders'. In addition, screen masks such as 'record order details' are added.

Data

Similarly, the information system level elaborates and supplements the data side. It specifies attributes such as order discount rate, order status and the code table 'payment conditions', etc.

Linking the IS Design Dimensions

At the information system level the design details are so closely interconnected that the results can scarcely be assigned to the individual dimensions. Authorization links organizational units with transactions and data, and the user interfaces links data (in screen masks), combines transactions into menus, and develops special variants for special organizational units.

5.1.4.   Linking the Business Engineering Levels

Fig. 5.1./1 uses thick grey lines to establish the links between design statements from different levels. The decision to create a sales process results in the development of the process. Regionalization results in layered flows for the approval of deviations from conditions in customer orders. Once UNTEL has decided in favour of an online ordering service, a sub-process for the receipt of EDIFACT orders must be created. The 'electronic product catalogue' is a prerequisite for this, or at least greatly facilitates it.

We have indicated only a few examples of the interconnections between the levels. Many others would have been possible even for this small segment of the documentation. Certain design details (e.g. order modification) have been extracted from the lower levels to demonstrate their relationship to other details.

There is a tendency to give the lines arrow heads directed from top to bottom. We have avoided this to underline the reciprocal interconnections between the levels. Let us assume, for example, that the costs of developing the transactions needed by the sub-process 'accept EDIFACT order' are so high that the company management agree to dispense with them in the first instance for reasons of economy. As a result UNTEL's online ordering service would also be eliminated.

Intensive relationships exist in both directions between the Business Engineering levels. They relate to refinements, extensions and adjustments.

The relationships between the levels illustrate the implementation of strategic decisions down to the operative levels, as explained in Section 1.3.1. They can also represent innovations that arise in the operative business and have effects on the strategy.

5.2.   Business Engineering Meta-Model

The example in Fig. 5.1./1 shows only a minute sample of the design statements and the relationships between them. This gives some idea of how many design statements are needed in actual projects, and how many relationships exist between them [see also Picot/Maier 1993].

Fig. 5.2./1 generalizes the contents of the levels and dimensions. It names the objects that are the result of the techniques, and describes them in the simplified form of an ER diagram. The loops by the objects 'organizational unit' and 'activity' symbolize a hierarchy (direct recursion, see Fig. 3.3./17) of these objects. The thick grey lines in Fig. 5.2./1 create the relationships between equivalent objects at different levels.

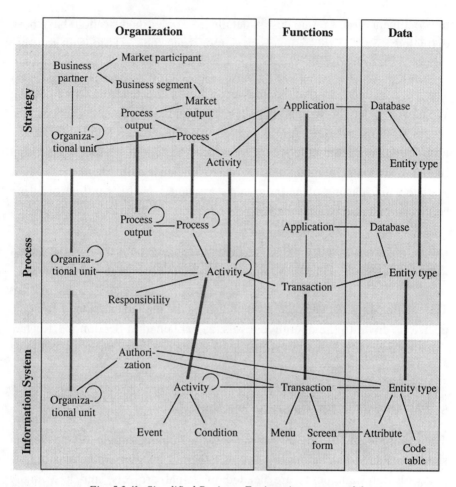

Fig. 5.2./1: Simplified Business Engineering meta-model

The ER diagram in Fig. 5.2./1 is a rudimentary Business Engineering data model. Business Engineering is the process that develops other processes (including the strategy and the information system). This is referred to as a meta-process, and the Business Engineering data model as a meta-(data) model.

A *meta-model* describes the components (data) of the design techniques and the relationships between these components.

The meta-model in Fig. 5.2./1 describes the Business Engineering objects at the strategy, process and information levels in the organization, function and data dimensions. At each level it repeats the objects that have been adopted and elaborated from the previous level. For didactic reasons it is restricted to the most important objects and ignores process management. For a complete description of the meta-model see [IMG 1994a].

5.3. Business Engineering Method

A method prescribes a sequence in which the design results of the meta-model are to be developed. For example, it specifies,

- that at the start of a process development project, an activity 'create first version of the process vision' should be performed,

- that the result of this activity generates the business network document and the directory of ideas,

- that the documents are to be created using the process vision technique,

- that this activity employs the IT map generated by the activity 'document IT map', and hence must be subsequent to that activity

- that this activity is concerned with the objects: market participant, process, activity, process output, etc,

- that the performance indicators for the process are determined by the line managers involved (role of project participants),

- that a one-day meta-plan workshop should take place (sub-activity) and that spreadsheet, word processing and graphic systems will be used to document the results.

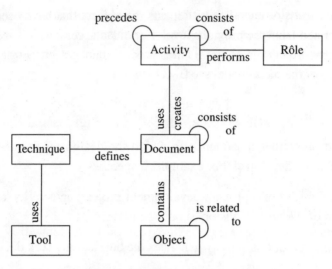

Fig. 5.3./1: Method meta-model

A method, in the sense of Method Engineering, consists of the following components (see Fig. 5.3./1) [see Gutzwiller 1994, p. 11 ff.]:

- Activities (corresponding to the activities in the process model)
  Examples: 'create first version of process vision', 'extend the data model to provide data history'

- Procedures (flows) a succession of activities
  Examples: The activity 'document IT map' precedes the activity 'create first version of process vision', which precedes the activity 'record existing outputs'. The activity 'record existing outputs' runs parallel to the activity 'record customer views in questionnaire'.

- Documents (in the process model forms and screen masks) as the results of activities, created in accordance with the rules of the technique
  Examples: business network, ER diagram

- Techniques for developing solutions, and thus creating documents
  Examples: process vision, providing data history

- Meta-model (data model) with the objects and the relationships between the objects
  Examples: activities, entity types, 'activity modifies entity type'

- Roles (responsibilities within an organizational unit) that employees fulfil
  in the process development
  Examples: process manager, IT specialist, user representative (e.g. sales
  representative)

- Tools (applications and transactions) for supporting techniques
  Examples: meta-plan workshop, graphic editor for manipulating activity
  chains

Business Engineering projects are extremely complex. A method is reponsible for breaking a project down into manageable activities. A Business Engineering method first differentiates projects the levels (strategy, process and information system) concentrates these on the organization, data and function dimensions, and breaks the project down into activities and steps (in accordance with the techniques). A method also divides projects into sub-projects for sub-processes. It is not only concerned with the breakdown into tiny steps, but with the interactions between the parts, or the links between the activities. A method thus regulates the project management.

A *method* breaks a project down into activities, specifies techniques, tools and roles, and defines the results.

A Business Engineering method provides the operative details for practical process design projects (and for continuous improvement). Such methods are not the subject of textbooks, but of handbooks and development tools [see IMG 1994a].

Bibliography

[Balzert 1982]
Balzer, H., Die Entwicklung von Software-Systemen: Prinzipien, Methoden, Sprachen, Werkzeuge, Bibliographisches Institut, Mannheim/Wien/Zürich 1982

[Berkley/Nohria 1991]
Berkley, J. D., Nohria, N., Lithonia Lighting (A), Harvard Business School (Hrsg.), Lecturers Note No. 9-492-003, Boston 1991

[BIFOA 1993]
BIFOA (Hrsg.), BIFOA-Marktübersicht Vorgangsmanagementsysteme, Köln 1993

[Bleicher 1992]
Bleicher, K., Das Konzept Integriertes Management, 2. Aufl., Campus, Frankfurt/New York 1992

[Bodendorf 1992]
Bodendorf, F., Benutzermodelle - ein konzeptioneller Überblick, in: Wirtschaftsinformatik, Jg. 34 , 1992, Heft 2, S. 233-245

[Böhm et al. 1993]
Böhm, R., Fuchs, E., Pacher, G., System-Entwicklung in der Wirtschaftsinformatik, 2. Aufl., Verlag der Fachvereine, Zürich 1993

[Booch 1994]
Booch, G., Object-Oriented Analysis and Design, 2. Aufl., Benjamin/Cummings, Menlo Park 1994

[Bossert 1991]
Bossert, J. L., Quality Function Deployment: A Practitioner's Approach, ASQC Quality Press, Milwaukee 1991

[Brenner/Kolbe 1994]
Brenner, W., Kolbe, L., Die computerunterstützte Informationsverarbeitung der privaten Haushalte als Herausforderung für Wissenschaft und Wirtschaft, in: Wirtschaftsinformatik, Jg. 36, 1994, Heft 4, S. 369-378.

[Carmichael 1994]
Carmichael, A. (Hrsg.), Object Development Methods, SIGS Books, New York 1994

[Chen 1976]
Chen, P. P.-S., The Entity-Relationship Model - Toward a Unified View of Data, in: ACM Transactions on Database Systems, Jg. 1, 1976, Heft 1, S. 9-36

[Codd 1970]
    Codd, E. F., A Relational Model for Large Shared Data Banks, in:
    Communications of the ACM, Jg. 13, 1970, Heft 6, S. 377-387

[Cooper 1990]
    Cooper, R., Activity-Based Costing: Wann brauche ich ein Activity-
    Based Cost-System und welche Kostentreiber sind notwendig?, in: Ko-
    stenrechnungspraxis, 1990, Heft 5, S. 271-279

[Copeland/McKenny 1988]
    Copeland, D. G., McKenny, J. L., Airline Reservations Systems:
    Lessons From History, in: MIS Quarterly, Jg. 12, September 1988,
    Heft 3, S. 353-370

[Corsten 1989]
    Corsten, H. (Hrsg.), Die Gestaltung von Innovationsprozessen: Hinder-
    nisse und Erfolgsfaktoren im Organisations-, Finanz- und Informations-
    bereich, Erich Schmidt, Berlin 1989

[CW 1993a]
    o.V., IT-Markt in Europa soll 1993 um insgesamt vier Prozent wachsen,
    in: Computerwoche, 12.3.1993, S. 1-2

[CW 1993b]
    o.V., Software und Services bestimmen den Herzschlag der IT-Industrie,
    in: Computerwoche, 16.7.1993, S. 39

[Date 1986]
    Date, C. J., An introduction to database systems, Vol. 1, 4. Aufl.,
    Addison-Wesley, Massachusetts, 1986

[Davenport 1993]
    Davenport, Th. H., Process Innovation - Reengineering Work through
    Information Technology, Harvard Business School Press,
    Boston/Massachusetts 1993

[Davenport/Short 1990]
    Davenport, Th. H., Short, J. E., The New Industrial Engineering: Infor-
    mation Technology and Business Process Redesign, in: Sloan Manage-
    ment Review, Jg. 31, 1990, Heft 4, S. 11-27

[Deming 1982]
    Deming, W. E., Quality, Productivity and Competitive Position,
    Massachusetts Institute of Technology, Cambridge 1982

[DIN 1990]
    DIN (Hrsg.), DIN ISO 9000: Qualitätsmanagement- und Qualitätssiche-
    rungsnormen - Leitfaden zur Auswahl und Anwendung, Berlin 1990

[Earl 1989]
    Earl, M., Management Strategies for Information Technology, Prentice
    Hall, New York 1989

[Eiff 1991]
Eiff, W. v., Prozeßkettenanalyse durch TOP-Mapping, in: Eiff, W. v. (Hrsg.), Organisation - Erfolgsfaktor der Unternehmensführung, Moderne Industrie, Landsberg am Lech 1991, S. 333-346

[Eversheim et al. 1992]
Eversheim, W., Müller, S., Heuser, Th., "Schlanke" Informationsflüsse schaffen: Integration der Produktion in Unternehmen des Sondermaschinen- und Anlagebaus, Teil 2, in: VDI-Zeitung, Jg. 134, 1992, Heft 11, S. 66-69

[Ferstl/Sinz 1990]
Ferstl, O. K., Sinz, E. J., Objektmodellierung betrieblicher Informationssysteme im Semantischen Objektmodell (SOM), in: Wirtschaftsinformatik, Jg. 32, 1990, Heft 6, S. 566-581

[Ferstl/Sinz 1991]
Ferstl, O. K., Sinz, E. J., Ein Vorgehensmodell zur Objektmodellierung betrieblicher Informationssysteme im Semantischen Objektmodell (SOM), in: Wirtschaftsinformatik, Jg. 33, 1991, Heft 6, S. 477-491

[Ferstl/Sinz 1993]
Ferstl, O. K., Sinz, E. J., Grundlagen der Wirtschaftsinformatik, Band 1, R. Oldenbourg, München/Wien 1993

[Ferstl/Sinz 1994]
Ferstl, O. K., Sinz, E. J., From Business Process Modeling to the Specification of Distributed Business Application Systems - An Object Oriented Approach, Bamberger Beiträge zur Wirtschaftsinformatik, Heft 20, Bamberg 1994

[Frank 1991]
Frank, U., Anwendungsnahe Standards der Datenverarbeitung: Anforderungen und Potentiale - Illustriert am Beispiel von ODA/ODIF und EDIFACT, in: Wirtschaftsinformatik, Jg. 33, 1991, Heft 2, S. 100-111

[Frey 1990]
Frey, M., Elektronische Datenverarbeitung: Nur wenig Überlebende, in: Afheldt, H., Wirtschaftswoche Handbuch 1991, Gesellschaft für Wirtschaftspublizistik, November 1990, S. 84-86

[Gabriel/Röhrs 1994]
Gabriel, R., Röhrs, H.-P., Datenbanksysteme. Konzeptionelle Datenmodellierung und Datenbankarchitekturen, Springer, Berlin 1994

[Gaitanides 1983]
Gaitanides, M., Prozeßorganisation: Entwicklung, Ansätze und Programme prozeßorientierter Organisationsgestaltung, Vahlen, München 1983

[Gale 1994]
Gale Research (Hrsg.), Gale Directory of Online Databases - Volume 1: Online Databases, Gale Research, Detroit 1994

[Garvin 1993]
Garvin, D., Building a Learning Organization, in: Harvard Business Review, Jg. 71, 1993, Heft Juli/August, S. 78-91

[Gerybadze 1988]
Gerybadze, A., Innovationswettbewerb: Der Hase und der Igel in den Märkten von morgen, in: Arthur D. Little (Hrsg.), Management des geordneten Wandels, Gabler, Wiesbaden 1988, S. 107-122

[Gerybadze 1995]
Gerybadze, A., Technologie, Strategie und Organisation, Gabler, Wiesbaden 1995 (in Vorbereitung)

[Gomez 1993]
Gomez, P., Wertmanagement. Vernetzte Strategien für Unternehmen im Wandel, Econ, Düsseldorf 1993

[Gomez/Probst 1987]
Gomez, P., Probst, G., Vernetztes Denken im Management, in: Die Orientierung, Heft 89, Schweizerische Volksbank, Bern 1987

[Gomez/Zimmermann 1993]
Gomez, P., Zimmermann, T., Unternehmensorganisation: Profile, Dynamik, Methodik, 2. Aufl., Campus, Frankfurt/New York 1993

[Grill 1987]
Grill, E., Relationale Datenbanken: Vom logischen Konzept zur physischen Realisierung, 3. Aufl., Angewandte Informationstechnik, Hallbergmoos 1987

[Grobe 1992]
Grobe, H.-J., Informatik-Branche. Gespaltene Konjunktur, in: Diebold Management Report, 1992, Heft 3, S. 3-7

[Grund/Jähnig 1994]
Grund, K., Jähnig, F., Modell zur Analyse und Simulation von Geschäftsprozessen, in: Management & Computer, Jg. 2, 1994, Heft 1, S. 49-56

[Gutzwiller 1994]
Gutzwiller, Th., Das CC RIM-Referenzmodell für den Entwurf von betrieblichen transaktionsorientierten Informationssystemen, Physica, Heidelberg 1994

[Hackstein/Köhl 1991]
Hackstein, R., Köhl, E., Datenintegration: Wunsch oder Wirklichkeit?, in: CIM Management, 1991, Heft 1, S. 30-34

[Haist/Fromm 1991]
Haist, F., Fromm, H., Qualität im Unternehmen: Prinzipien-Methoden-Techniken, 2. Aufl., Hanser, München 1991

[Hamel/Prahalad 1994]
Hamel, G., Prahalad, C. K., Competing for the Future: Breakthrough Strategies for Seizing Control of your Industry and Creating the Markets of Tomorrow, Havard Business School Press, Boston 1994

[Hammer 1990]
Hammer, M., Reengineering Work: Don't Automate-Obliterate, in: Harvard Business Review, Jg. 68, 1990, Heft Juli/August, S. 104-111

[Hammer/Champy 1993]
Hammer, M., Champy, J., Reengineering the Corporation, Harper Business, New York 1993

[Hansen 1992]
Hansen, H. R., Wirtschaftsinformatik I: Einführung in die betriebliche Datenverarbeitung, 6. Aufl., Gustav Fischer, Stuttgart 1992

[Hax/Majluf 1984]
Hax, A. C., Majluf, N. S., Strategic Management: an Integrative Perspective, Prentice-Hall Englwood Cliffs, NJ, 1984

[Harrington 1991]
Harrington, H. J., Business Process Improvement, McGraw-Hill, New York 1991

[Heilmann 1994]
Heilmann, H., Workflow Management: Integration von Organisation und Informationsverarbeitung, in: HMD, Jg. 31, 1994, Heft 176, S. 8-21

[Heinrich 1992]
Heinrich; L. J., Informationsmanagement. Planung, Überwachung und Steuerung der Informationsinfrastruktur, 4. Aufl., R. Oldenbourg, München/Wien 1992

[Heinrich/Burgholzer 1989]
Heinrich, L. J., Burgholzer, P., Systemplanung I, 4. Aufl., R. Oldenbourg, München/Wien 1989

[Heinrich/Burgholzer 1990]
Heinrich, L. J., Burgholzer, P., Systemplanung II, 4. Aufl., R. Oldenbourg, München/Wien 1990

[Heym 1995]
Heym, M., Software-Entwicklung für Informationssysteme, Springer, Heidelberg 1995 (in Vorbereitung)

[Hinterhuber 1992]
Hinterhuber, H. H., Strategische Unternehmensführung, Band 1 und 2, 5. Aufl., de Gruyter, Berlin/New York 1992

[Hofman/Rockart 1989]
Hofman, J. D., Rockart, J. F., Lithonia Lighting Case Study, CISR WP No. 20, Massachusetts Institute of Technology, Dezember 1989

[Horváth 1990]
Horváth, P., Controlling, 3. Aufl., Vahlen, München 1990

[Horváth et al. 1993]
Horváth, P., Kieninger, M., Mayer, R., Schimank, C., Prozeßkosten-rechnung - oder wie die Praxis die Theorie überholt, in: Die Betriebswirt-schaft, Jg. 53, 1993, Heft 5, S. 609-628

[Horváth/Herter 1992]
Horváth, P., Herter, R. N., Benchmarking - Vergleich mit den Besten der Besten, in: Controlling, Jg. 4, 1992, Heft 1, S. 4-11

[Horváth/Mayer 1989]
Horváth, P., Mayer, R., Prozeßkostenrechnung, in: Controlling, Jg. 1, 1989, Heft 4, S. 214-219

[Hübner 1993]
Hübner, T., "Electronic Commerce" - Konzepte der elektronischen Kommunikation mit Lieferanten in der Automobilindustrie, in: Manage-ment & Computer, Jg. 1, 1993, Heft 1, S. 19-24

[Hughes 1991]
Hughes, J. G., Object-Oriented Databases, Prentice-Hall, Englewood Cliffs 1991

[Hull/King 1987]
Hull, R., King, R., Semantic Database Modeling: Survey, Applications and Research Issues, in: ACM Computing Surveys, Jg. 19, 1987, Heft 3, S. 201-260

[IIS 1993]
Institute for Information Studies (Hrsg.), The Knowledge Economy, Eigenverlag, Nashville/Queenstown 1993

[IMG 1994a]
Information Management Gesellschaft, PROMET BPR - Methodenhand-buch für den Entwurf von Geschäftsprozessen, Version 1.0, St. Gallen/München 1994

[IMG 1994b]
Information Management Gesellschaft, PROMET SSW - Projekt-Methode zur Einführung von Standardsoftware, Version 2.0, St. Gallen/München 1994

[Ishikawa 1985]
Ishikawa, K., What Is Total Quality Control? The Japanese Way, Prentice-Hall, Englewood Cliffs 1985

[Ives/Learmonth 1984]
Ives, B., Learmonth, G. P., The information system as a competitive weapon, in: Communications of the ACM, Jg. 27, 1984, Heft 12, S. 1193-1201

[Jacobson et al. 1993]
Jacobson, I., Christerson, M., Jonsson, P., Övergaard, G., Object-Oriented Software Engineering, Addison-Wesley, Wokingham 1993

[Kaplan/Murdock 1991]
Kaplan, R. B., Murdock, L., Core Process Redesign, in: The McKinsey Quarterly, Jg. 27, 1991, Heft 2, S. 27-43

[Kargl 1990]
Kargl, H., Fachentwurf für DV-Anwendungssysteme, R. Oldenbourg, München/Wien 1990

[Krüger 1993]
Krüger, W., Organisation der Unternehmung, 2. Aufl., Kohlhammer, Stuttgart/Berlin/Köln 1993

[Landmark 1988]
Landmark Systems Corporation (Hrsg.), The Monitor for CICS: General Information Manual, o. O. 1988

[Liebelt/Sulzberger 1992]
Liebelt, W., Sulzerberger, M., Grundlagen der Ablauforganisation, Dr. Götz Schmidt, Gießen 1992

[Lindtner 1990]
Lindtner, P., Domänenwissen in Methoden zur Analyse betrieblicher Informationssysteme, Hochschule St. Gallen, Diss., St. Gallen 1990

[Malik 1991]
Malik, F., Management-Systeme, in: Die Orientierung, 4. Aufl., Schweizerische Volksbank, Bern 1991

[Malone et al. 1993]
Malone, Th. W., Crowston, K., Lee, J., Pentland, B., Tools for inventing organizations: Toward a handbook of organizational processes, Working Paper, Center for Coordination Science, Massachusetts Institute of Technology, Cambridge MA, Januar 1993

[Martin/McClure 1988]
Martin, J., McClure, C., Structured Techniques - the basis for CASE, Prentice-Hall, Englewood Cliffs 1988

[Medina-Mora et al. 1992]
Medina-Mora, R., Winograd, T., Flores, R., Flores, F., The Action Workflow Approach to Workflow Management Technology, in: Proceedings, ACM 1992 Conference on Computing-Supported Cooperative Work. Sharing Perspectives, 31. Oktober - 4. November 1992, Toronto 1992

[Meier 1992]
Meier, A., Relationale Datenbanken - eine Einführung für die Praxis, Springer, Berlin 1992

[Mende 1994]
Mende, M., Ein Führungssystem für Geschäftsprozesse, Hochschule St. Gallen, Diss., St. Gallen 1994

[Mertens/Griese 1993]
Mertens, P., Griese, J., Integrierte Informationsverarbeitung 2 - Planungs- und Kontrollsysteme in der Industrie, 7. Aufl., Gabler, Wiesbaden 1993

[Mertens/Plattfaut 1986]
Mertens, P., Plattfaut, E., Informationstechnik als strategische Waffe, in: Information Management, Jg. 2, 1986, Heft 1, S. 6-17

[Nefiodow 1990]
Nefiodow, L. A., Der fünfte Kondratieff. Strategien zum Strukturwandel in Wirtschaft und Gesellschaft, Frankfurter Allg., Frankfurt, und Gabler, Wiesbaden 1990

[Ortner/Söllner 1989]
Ortner, E., Söllner, B., Semantische Datenmodellierung nach der Objekttypenmethode, in: Informatik-Spektrum, 1989, Heft 12, S. 31-42

[Österle 1991]
Österle, H., Innovation durch Informationstechnik - Ein Beitrag zur informationsbewußten Unternehmensführung, in: Proceedings zur 6. Internationalen Fachkonferenz des Komitees für Wirtschaftlichkeit in Information und Dokumentation der Deutschen Gesellschaft für Dokumentation e.V: in Zusammenarbeit mit der Gesellschaft für Informatik e.V., Garmisch-Partenkirchen 1991

[Österle et al. 1994]
Österle, H., Saxer, R., Hüttenhain, T., Business Process Monitoring, in: Proceedings of the Second Conference on Information Systems, Nijenrode University, Nijenrode University Press 1994, S. 553-567

[Österle/Brecht 1994]
Österle, H., Brecht, L., Die Informationstechnik im Wandel. Konsequenzen für die Schweiz, in: Die Volkswirtschaft, Jg. 67, 1994, Heft 4, S. 29-39

[Österle/Steinbock 1994a]
Österle, H., Steinbock, H.-J., Das informationstechnische Potential
- Stand und Perspektiven (Teil I), in: Information Management, Jg. 9,
1994, Heft 2, S. 26-31

[Österle/Steinbock 1994b]
Österle, H., Steinbock, H.-J., Das informationstechnische Potential
- Stand und Perspektiven (Teil II), in: Information Management, Jg. 9,
1994, Heft 3, S. 52-59

[Osterloh/Frost 1994]
Osterloh, M., Frost, J., Business Reengineering. Modeerscheinung oder
"Business Revolution"?, in: Zeitschrift Führung und Organisation, Jg.
63, 1994 (in Vorbereitung)

[Pálffy 1989]
Pálffy, T., Denormalisierung beim Datenentwurf, in: Scheibl, H.-J.
(Hrsg.), Software-Entwicklungs-Systeme und -Werkzeuge, 3. Kollo-
quium, Technische Akademie Esslingen, 5. - 7. September 1989, S. 7.1-
1 - 7.1-11

[Picot 1993]
Picot, A., Organisationsstrukturen der Wirtschaft und ihre Anforderun-
gen an die Informations- und Kommunikationstechnik, in: Scheer, A.-W.
(Hrsg.), Handbuch Informationsmanagement: Aufgaben - Konzepte -
Praxislösungen, Gabler, Wiesbaden 1993, S. 49-68

[Picot/Maier 1993]
Picot, A., Maier, M., Interdependenzen zwischen betriebswirtschaftli-
chen Organisationsmodellen und Informationsmodellen, in: Information
Management, Jg. 8, 1993, Heft 3, S. 6-15

[Pieske 1992]
Pieske, R., Am Klassenbesten orientieren. Quellen für Wettbewerbsvor-
teile, in: Absatzwirtschaft, Sondernummer Oktober 1992, S. 149-152

[Plattner et al. 1990]
Plattner, B., Lanz, G., Lubich, H., Müller, M., Walter, T., Datenkom-
munikation und elektronische Post, Addison-Wesley, Bonn 1990

[Pomberger/Blaschek 1993]
Pomberger, G., Blaschek, G., Grundlagen des Software Engineering,
Hanser, München/Wien 1993

[Porter 1985]
Porter, M. E., Competive Advantage: Creating and Substaining Superior
Performance, Macmillan New York/Free Press New York, 1985

[Porter 1988]
Porter, M. E., Wettbewerbsstrategien: Methoden zur Analyse von Bran-
chen und Konkurrenten, 5. Aufl., Campus, Frankfurt 1988

[Porter/Millar 1985]
Porter, M., Millar V. E., How information gives you competitive advantage, in: Harvard Business Review, Jg. 63, 1985, Heft 4, S. 149-160

[Prahalad/Hamel 1990]
Prahalad, C. K., Hamel, G., The Core Competence of the Corporation, in: Harvard Business Review, Jg. 68, 1990, Heft Mai/Juni, S. 257-269

[Pümpin 1986]
Pümpin, C., Erfolgspositionen: Management strategischer Erfolgspositionen, 3. Aufl., Haupt, Bern/Stuttgart 1986

[Raasch 1991]
Raasch, J., Systementwicklung mit Strukturierten Methoden - ein Leitfaden für Praxis und Studium, Hanser, München 1991

[Reiner 1993]
Reiner, Th., Analyse der Kundenbedürfnisse und der Kundenzufriedenheit als Voraussetzung einer konsequenten Kundenorientierung, Hochschule St. Gallen, Diss., St. Gallen 1993

[Rockart 1979]
Rockart, J. F., Chief Executives Define Their Own Data Needs, in: Harvard Business Review, Jg. 57, 1979, Heft März/April, S. 81-93

[Rowe et al. 1989]
Rowe, A. J., et al., Strategic Management: A Methodological Approach, 3. Edition, Addison-Wesley, Reading et al. 1989

[Sabisch 1994]
Sabisch, H., Ständige Verbesserung von Marketingprozessen durch Benchmarking, in: Belz, C., Schipel, M., Kramer, M., Lean Management & Lean Marketing, St. Gallen 1994

[SAP 1994]
SAP, Geschäftsprozeßoptimierung mit dem SAP-System R/3, in: SAPinfo, März 1994, S. 4-7

[Saxer 1993]
Saxer, R., Monitoring des Informationssystems - ein Instrument zur Organisationsanalyse, Hochschule St. Gallen, Diss., St. Gallen 1993

[Scheer 1994]
Scheer, A.-W., Wirtschaftsinformatik: Referenzmodelle für industrielle Geschäftsprozesse, 4. Aufl., Springer, Berlin 1994

[Scherr 1993]
Scherr, L., A new approach to business processes, in: IBM systems journal, Jg. 32, 1993, Heft 1, S. 80-98

[Schildknecht 1992]
Schildknecht, R., Total Quality Management, Campus, Frankfurt 1992

[Schlageter/Stucky 1989]
Schlageter, G., Stucky, W., Datenbanksysteme: Konzepte und Modelle, 3. Aufl., Teubner, Stuttgart 1989

[Schmid 1993]
Schmid, B., Elektronische Märkte, in: Wirtschaftsinformatik, Jg. 35, 1993, Heft 5, S. 465-480

[Schmidt 1991]
Schmidt, G., Methode und Techniken der Organisation, 9. Aufl., Dr. Götz Schmidt, Gießen 1991

[Schönthaler/Németh 1990]
Schönthaler, F., Németh, T., Software-Entwicklungswerkzeuge - methodische Grundlagen, Teubner, Stuttgart 1990

[Schumann 1992]
Schumann, M., Betriebliche Nutzeffekte und Strategiebeiträge der groß-integrierten Informationsverarbeitung, Springer, Berlin 1992

[Schwarze 1994]
Schwarze, J., Einführung in die Wirtschaftsinformatik, 3. Aufl., Neue Wirtschafts-Briefe, Herne/Berlin 1994

[Scott Morton 1991]
Scott Morton, M., The Corporation of the 1990s: information technology and organizational transformation, Oxford University Press, New York/Oxford 1991

[SEGA 1994]
Was bringt SECOM den SEGA- und INTERSETTLE-Teilnehmern?, in: SEGA ANTENNE, September 1994, S. 1-9

[SEGA o. J.]
SEGA - Ein aussergewöhnliches Unternehmen, SEGA, Zürich o. J.

[Seghezzi 1994]
Seghezzi, H. D., Qualitätsmanagement - Ansatz eines St. Galler Konzepts - Integriertes Qualitätsmanagement, Schäffer-Poeschel, Stuttgart, und Neue Zürcher Zeitung, Zürich 1994

[Short/Venkatraman 1992]
Short, J. E., Venkatraman, N., Beyond Business Process Redesign: Redefining Baxter's Business Network, in: Sloan Management Review, Jg. 33, 1992, Heft 1, S. 7-21

[Sommerlatte/Wedekind 1989]
Sommerlatte, T., Wedekind, E., Leistungsprozesse und Organisationsstrukturen, in: Arthur D. Little (Hrsg.), Management der Hochleistungs-
organisation, Wiesbaden 1989, S. 25-40

[Spitta 1989]
Spitta, T., Software Engineering und Prototyping: Eine Konstruktions-
lehre für administrative Softwaresysteme, Springer, Berlin 1989

[Stalk/Haut 1990]
Stalk, G., Haut T., Zeitwettbewerb - Schnelligkeit entscheidet auf den
Märkten der Zukunft, Campus, Frankfurt/New York 1990

[Steinbock 1994]
Steinbock, H.-J., Potentiale der Informationstechnik, Teubner, Stuttgart
1994

[Steppan/Mertens 1990]
Steppan, G., Mertens, P., Computer-Aided Selling - Neuere Entwicklun-
gen bei der DV-Unterstützung des industriellen Vertriebs, in: Informatik-
Spektrum, Jg. 13, 1990, S. 137-150

[Striening 1992]
Striening, H.-D., Qualität im indirekten Bereich durch Prozeßmanage-
ment, in: Zink, K. J. (Hrsg.), Qualität als Managementaufgabe, 2. Aufl.,
Moderne Industrie, Landsberg/Lech 1992, S. 153-183

[The Economist 1994]
o.V., Feeling for the future, in: The Economist, A Survey of Television,
12.2.1994, S. 3-18

[Thimbleby 1990]
Thimbleby, H., User interface design, Addison-Wesley, Wokingham
1990

[Thoma 1993]
Thoma, H., Integration von Applikationen und Datenbanken mit Hilfe
einer Applikations-Architektur, in: Müller-Ettrich, G. (Hrsg.), Fachliche
Modellierung von Informationssystemen: Methoden, Vorgehen, Werkzeuge, Addison-Wesley, Paris 1993, S. 217-259

[VDI 1977]
VDI (Hrsg.), VDI-Richtlinie 2222, Konstruktionsmethodik 1977, Blatt
1, Konstruktionsmethodik: Konzipieren technischer Produkte, Düsseldorf 1977

[Vetter 1991]
Vetter, M., Aufbau betrieblicher Informationssysteme mittels objektorien-
tierter, konzeptioneller Datenmodellierung, 7. Aufl., Teubner, Stuttgart
1991

[Vogler 1993]
Vogler, P., Konzeption und Realisierung eines Unterstützungssystems zur Vorgangsabwicklung und Informationslogistik in verteilten Büroumgebungen, Universität Erlangen-Nürnberg, Diss., Nürnberg 1993

[Ward et al. 1990]
Ward, J., Griffiths, P., Whitmore, P., Strategic Planning for Information Systems, Wiley, Chichester 1990

[White/Fischer 1994]
White, T. E., Fischer, L., The Workflow Paradigma: The Impact of Information Technology on Business Process Reengineering. Future Strategies, Almaden 1994

[Wiseman 1988]
Wiseman, C., Strategic Information Systems, Irwin, Homewood 1988

[Wunderer 1993]
Wunderer, R., Führung und Zusammenarbeit, Schäffer-Poeschel, Stuttgart 1993

[Zehnder 1989]
Zehnder, C. A., Informationssysteme und Datenbanken, Verlag der Fachvereine, Zürich 1989

[Zeithamel et al. 1992]
Zeithamel, V., Parasuraman, A., Berry, L., Qualitätsservice, Campus, Frankfurt 1992

Index

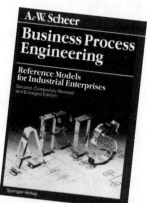